MW01006859

DOUBLE TALKIN' JIVE

DOUBLE TALKIN' JIVE

MATT SORUM

WITH **LEIF ERIKSSON** AND **MARTIN SVENSSON**
FOREWORD BY **BILLY F GIBBONS**

RARE BIRD
Los Angeles, Calif.

THIS IS A GENUINE RARE BIRD BOOK

Rare Bird Books
453 South Spring Street, Suite 302
Los Angeles, CA 90013
rarebirdlit.com

Copyright © 2021 by Matt Sorum, Leif Eriksson, and Martin Svensson
Foreword copyright © 2021 by Billy F Gibbons

All rights reserved, including the right to reproduce this book or portions
thereof in any form whatsoever, including but not limited to print, audio, and
electronic. For more information, address:
Rare Bird Books Subsidiary Rights Department
453 South Spring Street, Suite 302
Los Angeles, CA 90013.

Set in Dante
Printed in the United States

10 9 8 7 6 5 4 3 2 1

Library of Congress Cataloging-in-Publication Data
Names: Sorum, Matt, 1960- author. | Eriksson, Leif, 1957- author. |
Svensson, Martin, 1978- author. | Gibbons, Billy F., 1949- writer of foreword.
Title: Double talkin' jive: true rock 'n' roll stories from the drummer of
Guns n' Roses, the Cult, and Velvet Revolver / Matt Sorum, with Leif
Eriksson and Martin Svensson ; foreword by Billy F Gibbons.
Description: Los Angeles, Calif.: Rare Bird, 2021.
Identifiers: LCCN 2021020049 | ISBN 9781644282212 (hardback)
Subjects: LCSH: Sorum, Matt, 1960- | Drummers (Musicians)—United
States—Biography. | Rock musicians—United States—Biography. | LCGFT:
Autobiographies.
Classification: LCC ML419.S668 A3 2021 | DDC 782.42166092 [B]—dc23
LC record available at https://lccn.loc.gov/2021020049

"A fun read...all the essentials about Matt's rock 'n' roll success story are here. I found it particularly illuminating about his time in and relationships with Guns N' Roses and negotiating all the personalities involved!"

—**Billy Idol**

"Matt lights up rooms, corridors, clubs, theaters, arenas, and stadiums with the kind of infectious rock 'n' roll energy that is increasingly becoming obsolete. His dedication to his craft remains virtually peerless, and when the sticks are resting, you'll have to go a long way to find someone cooler in rock 'n' roll. Dive into these shenanigan-saturated pages immediately and find out for yourself!"

—**Lars Ulrich**, Metallica

"A colorfully dark look into the f***ed-up psyche of a legendary and badass drummer. I want to read it over and over."

—**Jonas Åkerlund**, director of *Lords of Chaos* and *Spun*

"Matt is a true journeyman drummer who's got the chops and the showmanship to have a great career with all the ups, downs, and sideways that you would expect from a cat like him, though with his share of surprises he really needed to get his story told. *Double Talkin' Jive* is his version of what it's like to have 'the best seat in the house' with some of the wildest, hardest rockin' bands to come down the pike."

—**Joe Perry**, Aerosmith

"Still alive and playing like hell... This is the stuff from which rock documentaries are made."

—**Robin Zander**, Cheap Trick

"I have witnessed the sheer power, drive, and determination of Matt from the outside for a long time now, as the drummer for the likes of The Cult, Guns N' Roses, and Velvet Revolver, but I have also seen him from the inside when we have shared the stage as the Kings of Chaos. Always smiling, always ready, and as solid as Mt. Rushmore, you could say he's one of the last of a dying breed, a big hitter who can also show restraint, the real deal."

—**Joe Elliott**, Def Leppard

FOREWORD

by *Billy F Gibbons*

MATT SORUM AND HIS journey of decadent decades through his personal rock 'n' roll "did this, done that" is all here for the taking. Unselfishly, Matt takes us on a terrific and sometimes terrifying tack, tripping through his almost never-ending touring trail.

These are the kinds of trials and tribulations, through and through, that tall tales are made of. Yet, in this case, at each corner, Matt's unflagging adventure down his rock 'n' roll avenue is quite matter-of-fact—that unnerving thing that leaves you on the edge of your seat. And then some.

And at the heart of all this wildness is Matt's insatiable appetite for the backbeat. ving these episodes page by page is the unrelenting ferociousness of the Sorum style of drumming. Loud, crisp, and clear, the beat is always at the fore. It's inescapable. Whether it's Guns N' Roses, The Cult, Velvet Revolver, or the "Big Bad Blues" tour, the unmistakable force from the drum riser hits ya like a ton o' bricks. And that's Matt. And you ask, "What drives a man to the depths of this kind of obsession?" It's all inside. Read it and freak!

There's a house afire in here, and just when you thought you knew about rockin' the sonically insane path through it all... Well... just wait. You haven't dreamed this up even in your wildest!

Dig on, Matt. Matt. Matt is where it's at. *Bueno*!

NOTE TO READERS

SOME NAMES OF INDIVIDUALS mentioned in this book have been fictionalized. All fictional names are indicated by the use of SMALL CAPS on first mention. Any similarity between the fictionalized names and the names of real people is strictly coincidental.

PREFACE

I'M AT THE AFTER-PARTY for John Stamos and Rebecca Romijn's wedding in Beverly Hills. People are everywhere, and I'm looking for my girlfriend. Whenever I bump into friends, acquaintances, and people I vaguely recognize, I ask if they've seen her. No one seems to know where she is.

For some reason, I get the feeling they're not telling me the whole truth.

The air is hot and sticky. I undo the top button on my shirt and knock back the drink I'm clutching. I know that I'm far too drunk. I can't feel it, but I can see it on people's faces when I talk to them. And they all take a slight step back.

Suddenly, I spot her in the Jacuzzi out back—naked with three random dudes. My stomach turns; my legs become weak and heavy. Everything happens very quickly after that. I grab a flowerpot and throw it toward the pool, hurling a chair in the same direction a second or two later. People scatter; they're probably shouting too, but in my mind everything is silent. The host of the party comes over and tries to calm me down, but it's like my entire being has been reduced to a mix of anger and despair—the guy doesn't even have time to put his hand on my shoulder before I've knocked him out.

Next thing I know, a whole gang is holding me back, dragging me into a car, driving off with me.

My memories after that are pretty fragmented. Two guys hold me down in the backseat as I'm lashing out and trying to break free. They eventually throw me out on some street in Westwood, and I struggle to my feet and start running.

I alternate between sweating and freezing, and at some point it dawns on me that I'm naked. I hail a cab and give the driver my girlfriend's address. He drives me over there, and I climb the fence to get into the house. I pull on a jacket and a pair of pants and get some money for him. Then I go back inside and break everything I can find. My girlfriend has come home by this point. Somewhere in the distance, I can hear her shouting.

I must've passed out after that, because when I wake up two cops are standing on either side of me, their guns in my face.

My next memory is being locked up in a drunk tank, slumped on the floor. A homeless, disheveled-looking man is sitting in one corner. He's drooling, doesn't have any teeth. When he spots me, he hisses rather than speaks: "Hey, rock star…how's it feel to be down here in the gutter with us crackheads?"

1

Long Beach, 1965

I stab my brother with a weed-picker, and Lee Harris moves in.

I WAS FIVE WHEN I realized I wanted to be a drummer. I was on the couch with Mom, Dad, and my older brothers, Mark and Mike, eating popcorn in front of *The Ed Sullivan Show*. It was something we did every Sunday.

"Okay, it's cozy popcorn time!" Dad would shout from the living room, and my brothers and I would immediately come running.

This particular Sunday, the Beatles were on the show. Ed had just introduced Ringo Starr. He'd introduced the rest of the band too, of course, but there was something about Ringo that had me spellbound—and once they started playing "I Feel Fine," I turned to my mom, pointed at Ringo, and said, "I want to be like him."

A few days later, my brother Mark gave me a 45 of "A Hard Day's Night." It was my first record, and I played it on Mark's Crosley turntable (the kind that looks like a briefcase, with built-in speakers) until the vinyl was so scratched it didn't work anymore.

We lived in a corner house at the time, in Long Beach. The vibe at home was tough, irritated. My parents fought constantly—until one day, when Dad was just gone. I know I asked my mom what had happened, but all she said was "me and your dad are gonna separate for a while."

He came back to pick up his things a few weeks later, and I never saw him after that—not for a long time, anyway. Another guy started showing up at the house instead. His name was Lee Harris, and he was the principal at the school where both my parents worked as teachers. In the beginning, he only came over some afternoons, but before long he was in Dad's old seat on the couch watching TV with us. Not long after that, he started sleeping with Mom in her and Dad's bedroom. The whole thing made me so confused and insecure, and I remember missing my dad so much that it hurt. The fact that my brothers started picking on me didn't make things any easier. They said Mom had wanted a girl rather than a third boy, stuff like that.

Around this time, Mom bought a new refrigerator and freezer. My brothers used the cardboard boxes they came in to build a fort in the backyard. They had pillows and blankets inside, and Mark had made a periscope he could wind up and look through. I wanted to join in, of course, and one day when I was creeping about outside, I saw that Mark had scrawled KEEP OUT, MATT! in huge letters on the door.

Since I already had a vague feeling of abandonment, it really hurt me—and I headed straight into the garage to get the weed-picker, which was a long metal stick with a forked end. I went back to Mark's fort and repeatedly jammed it straight through the wall. Mark yelled. I cut him pretty good.

That Christmas, I got a Sears drum kit from my mom. Maybe she had a guilty conscience—what do I know? In any case, the drums were known as Tigger Tigers, and they were kid-sized. They didn't have proper skins, as the material was more like paper. But I thought they were fantastic all the same and banged away on them several hours a day. It drove my brothers crazy, and they would yell at me to be quiet. Sometimes, they would come in while I was playing and give me a noogie (an irritating, fast rubbing motion with their knuckles on the side of your head that created a horrible burning sensation). I kept playing anyway, or I did until the day I got home from kindergarten and saw that they'd slashed the whole drum kit with a knife.

At about this time, Mom told me we were going to move, but before I get into that I should probably rewind to when I was born—November 19, 1960. There was a huge scandal at Long Beach Community Hospital at the time, because the hospital mixed up a bunch of babies. Considering everything that came later, and how my parents behaved in particular, I often wondered whether I was really their kid. Anyway, I was only nine months old when I almost died for the first time. The family had checked in to a hotel on the California coast for the weekend, and for some reason I have a few clear memories from that day. Maybe they're from the photographs I've seen in Mom's albums. Maybe they really are my own memories. In any case, I can clearly picture exactly how my parents looked in the minutes before it happened. Mom's hair was up, in a bouffant style. It was frosted, meaning she'd sprayed silver color over the whole thing. Dad wore a suit and a slim tie. My brothers Mike and Mark, who were four and two years older than me, were also smartly dressed. Maybe we'd been to church beforehand—I actually have no idea. What I do know is that my mom was a pretty avid smoker, and she was having a cigarette and bickering with my dad while my brothers chased one another. That's when I crawled over to the pool and fell in.

Even though I was just a baby, I can still picture it—the way I sank to the bottom and watched my parents, who were peering over the edge of the pool, gesturing wildly. After what felt like an eternity, Dad jumped in and rescued me, bringing me back to life via mouth-to-mouth.

The majority of people in California had pools out the back of their houses at the time, and there was a real problem of kids drowning in them. These drowning accidents were like an epidemic, so when it nearly happened to me, my parents decided to enroll me in swim school.

2

Los Alamitos

I discover that my mom might be a swinger,
play doctor with the girl next door, and start a fire with Mark.

IN 1966, MY BROTHERS, Mom, and I moved into a condo in Los Alamitos—a small city about nine miles from Long Beach. Even though Lee was in the picture now, I think my mom was struggling both practically and financially, and that's the main reason she sold the house. The condo was split over two floors, and we had a garage. I had to share a room with Mark, which meant the place felt tiny.

Since Mom worked every day, she found us a babysitter: a spooky old lady that my brothers and I called Hatchet Head. She had huge veined hands and eyes full of hatred for kids. People often tell me that I've got really long earlobes, and I always say that it's because of Hatchet Head—she used to pull my ears so hard that my eyes started to water. She was violent in other ways, too. Sometimes she just smacked me on the back of the head, for example. I was always on guard whenever Hatchet Head was at our place, always ready for anything to happen.

My kid-sized drum kit was ruined, but that didn't stop me from drumming—I used my hands on my legs, the table, the couch. I lined up cans, pots, and pans and drummed on them using spoons. I used whatever I could get my hands on.

By that time, Mike had already started to become increasingly introverted, and he often shut himself in his room to study. But Mark and I started finding stuff to do together.

I remember one time in particular, when we somehow managed to get hold of a surfboard. There was no wax on it, so we hauled it into the garage, lit a candle, and dripped wax onto the board. We thought that was how people did it. While we were busy with that, we managed to set fire to a cardboard box on the floor of the garage. Even now, I can remember how I froze when I realized what we'd done. I stomped on the box with both feet, but the fire spread and soon there were flames everywhere. The black smoke made our eyes sting, and Mark grabbed my arm and dragged me out onto the driveway. Luckily, one of the neighbors had called the police, and next thing we knew a fire truck had arrived and they managed to put out the blaze. They called Mom, and she came straight home from work to give us the world's biggest reprimand.

The next day, Hatchet Head also punished us by locking Mark and me in a room together. It felt horrible to be shut in like that, but it was still better than a beating.

That evening, I woke from a nightmare. My pajamas were soaked with sweat, and my heart was still racing when I left the room Mark and I shared to look for Mom. I spotted her pretty quickly, in the living room with a man I didn't recognize. She was straddling him, a cigarette in one hand and a drink in the other. To one side, Lee was kissing a woman I didn't know, and I realized then that there were a whole bunch of other people there. It was all so confusing that I froze, not knowing what to do or say.

"Mommy?" I eventually managed.

She looked up then, caught sight of me, and shouted, "You go to bed!"

I ran back to our room, but I couldn't get to sleep.

In Mom's defense, it was the early sixties. Both she and Lee were smoking and drinking all the time, and these swingers' parties weren't just something that happened at our place. Free love was starting to blossom everywhere. I guess the real problem was that— ironically enough—our home was anything but loving.

When Mom and Lee got home in the evening, they would sit down at our dinner table, always in the same seats, to drink gin and tonic and smoke. Mom smoked True Blues (a kind of menthol cigarette), and Lee smoked King Edward cigars that cost eight cents a piece and smelled like ass.

We kids knew we weren't allowed to disturb them there. We weren't even allowed to talk to them until they'd each had a drink. I remember one occasion when I had to ask something. I went in, waited until they stopped speaking, and shared what was on my chest. My stepfather turned to me then, gave me an indifferent look, and mumbled something like, "This is our quiet time. It's happy hour for us. Go away!"

I looked at my mom, but she just sighed, "Don't talk to us right now."

With all this going on, I started to experiment with sex. I remember going over to the place next door and playing doctor with the girl who lived there. We were only seven, but she was pretty developed for her age. Looking back now, I guess she must have gone through something bad. I mean, she knew exactly what she was doing and told me how to please her while she played with my dick. For my part, I think it was just a way for me to express my feelings. My brothers and I tried to adapt to our new situation. Mike switched off and withdrew. Mark became rebellious, and I became obsessed with sex.

3

Mission Viejo

I fall in love and experience racism for the first time.

BETWEEN 1965 AND 1968, I barely saw my dad at all. It's one of the reasons I started to idolize him. Another is that he went traveling around Europe in 1969, to places like Germany and Czechoslovakia, occasionally sending me postcards saying things like, "Son! I'm in Sweden, and there are nine women to every man!" or, "Son, I just got out of jail, they arrested me for taking a picture of two women fighting over a chicken." My dad became a counterweight to all the strict dullness at home. I used to fantasize about what his travels were like and created a romanticized vision of him and his Great Adventure.

Mom and Lee got married, but I don't remember a wedding. Maybe they just went to the courthouse. In any case, suddenly they were married, and not long after that they bought a house in Mission Viejo, which is what was known at the time as a planned community. Everything was so homogeneous; every third house was the same. The area had been built by the cigarette manufacturer Philip Morris, and the city's pride and joy was a swim team called Mission Viejo Nadadores.

Long Beach had felt more like a city, and Los Alamitos had been close to Long Beach. Suddenly, we were moving deep into Orange County.

Our house was on a street called Arcada Drive, on a hillside, and it was a cul-de-sac—a dead-end street with a circle to turn around. We had the fourth house from the turning space, and the neighborhood was deserted for summer when we moved in.

It didn't take me long to realize that my stepfather was an asshole. If we were eating together, he might suddenly look at my plate and say, "I see you've left a lot of your peas. No dessert for you."

Even now, I have trouble eating peas because of it. Other than the huge amount of peas we were always served, the portions weren't very big. I don't remember ever being full or opening the refrigerator and seeing a lot of food inside. Lee had placed a padlock on the refrigerator in the garage, and that's where they kept the most expensive food—as well as things like ice cream, Twinkies, and Ding Dongs.

While we ate, we were never allowed to have our elbows on the table. Lee sat at one end, and I was always closest to him, and if I happened to put my elbows on the table, he would say, "Elbows off the table, Mabel!" I'll never forget what happened one time when I made the mistake of putting both elbows on the table. Lee said his usual phrase, but rather than obeying him I just gave him a look. He stabbed me in the arm with a fork. It cut so deep that it hung there for a few seconds before dropping to the floor, and when I looked up at him his eyes were completely black.

My stepfather could be a violent man in general. He had a paddle and used to hit us with it, for example. He was a junior high school principal, and since this was the 1960s, he used it on kids at school. So naturally he did the same at home. The minute we did anything wrong, even if it was just forgetting to turn out a light or put the cap back on the toothpaste, he'd hit us. My brothers and I were really knocked around.

I remember him taking me into the garage and telling me to drop my pants. He would hit me several times after that, as hard as he could, until my ass stung. Sometimes, he'd grab me for no reason while we were at the kitchen table, dragging me over his knee and hitting me with the paddle. After a while, it almost became a ritual.

Looking back now, I'm convinced he got some kind of sadistic pleasure out of it.

I'd gone to kindergarten and first grade in Long Beach, but when I started second grade at my new school, Cordillera Elementary School, my teacher began the term by doing a roll call. He read out the names and pointed to the students. After saying "Matt Harris," he pointed at me.

I must've looked confused, because he said, "Aren't you Matt Harris?"

"No," I said. "I'm Matt Sorum."

The teacher continued, "It says here your name is Matt Harris."

When I got home from school that day, I told Mark everything: "Mark, Mom's trying to change my name to Matt Harris."

"What?!" he said. "That's the dumbest thing I ever heard... We're staying Sorum."

My biological father called not long after that; he was angry at Mom. I cried and said I didn't want a new last name. Mom had probably thought that since I was so young, she could change my name without me understanding or caring. But I wouldn't agree to it, and with my brothers' help—after lots of back and forth—I was allowed to keep my name.

That Christmas, Mom gave me a glittery blue St. George drum kit. Once the Christmas break was over, I took the snare drum and stand to school with me. I stood in the yard and played a song called "Wipe Out" and the theme to the TV show *Hogan's Heroes*. After a while, kids started crowding around me, and I remember I loved the attention.

Mission Viejo was a real white suburbia. There were no Latinos and no African Americans except for one family. The dad in that family was a judge at the courthouse, and I fell in love with his daughter that spring. Her name was TESSA, she had an Afro, and she was the only one who really stood out. The minute I saw her, I decided she would be my girlfriend, and I gave her a St. Christopher necklace. That was practically the same as saying, "Do you want to go steady with me?"

19

During summer break, when I traveled to Minnesota to visit Dad's side of the family, I sent her postcards. That was how you stayed in touch back then. But when my grandmother and aunt found out that Tessa was black, they got upset and more or less threatened to disown me unless I immediately broke up with her. I'd never experienced racism like that before, but I've since seen plenty of parents and older relatives trying to force their kids into making equally idiotic decisions.

The reason my brothers and I went to Minnesota that summer, staying with our grandmother Corolla and grandfather Kermit, was that Mom wanted to be alone with Lee. It made no difference to me; I actually thought it was great. It meant I got to play with my cousins. Our grandmother was also really loving and kind to me and always used to bake German chocolate cake whenever I went to stay—just because she knew I loved it. Her family was from Germany, and my grandfather's family was from Norway.

Grandpa worked as a stockbroker in Minneapolis at the time, so it was mostly Grandma who took care of us. That said, it was my grandfather who got me interested in fashion. He always wore nice suits, and in photos—even when I'm just ten or so—you can see me wearing wallabee or earth shoes, flared corduroy trousers, and Hang Ten T-shirts.

I didn't get any of it from Mom or Lee; I stole it all from shops.

It was cool staying with Grandma. That summer, she took us to their little summerhouse by Green Lake, which had been in the family since the 1920s, when it was built by her father, William. His three daughters later inherited the house, but it was Grandma who had it when I was a kid.

After we'd been at the house for a few weeks, my cousins came out too—my aunt's kids, Amy, Zibby, and Katie. The house had a huge loft full of kids' beds, and that's where I had my first wet dream.

I also had other "adventures" with different girls down by that lake, and when I got back to Mission Viejo, I gave my girlfriend Tessa oral sex for the first time.

4

Grandpa Dies

I smoke weed, learn to bet on horses, and get Montezuma's revenge.

THE YEAR I TURNED twelve, Dad reappeared in my life. He and Mom had been going through all kinds of legal stuff. I don't really know what it was all about, but it finally seemed to be over, and Dad started taking me and my brothers on weekend trips.

During the first few, we went out into the Mojave desert in Dad's dune buggy, exploring the ghost towns in Death Valley. These were small towns that had popped up near mines.

Around this time the Charlie Manson murders took place, and I remember we once camped in a valley where Manson had lived. Dad told us about how he and his so-called family of young girls had holed up on a ranch out there before they were found and arrested. I thought their demons might still be out there, haunting the area, and couldn't get a wink of sleep as I lay next to Dad and my brothers in a sleeping bag beneath the stars.

By this time, Dad had become a kind of hero to me, and since he was now back in my life, I constantly wished it was the weekend. When Easter came around that year, I got to spend a little more time with him than usual. I was ready with my bag packed long before he had said he would arrive.

Guadalajara, our destination for that trip, was over two thousand miles south of the Mexican border, and since this was the early 1970s, the road there was two lanes, and in pretty bad shape. I remember there were cattle on it sometimes, so we had to drive really slowly. In the evenings, especially, we had to just creep along, because the Mexicans seemed to drive without headlights—to save the batteries or something. All along the edge of the road were flowers and small statues of the Virgin Mary where people had crashed.

It was hot out—at least 100 degrees—and at some point, we were stopped by the *federates* (the police). I have no idea what Dad had done, or whether it was just a routine stop. In any case, they signaled for him to pull over at the side of the road, and Dad turned to me and said, "Okay, boys, don't say anything." The officers came over to the car and said something I couldn't understand. Dad peeled a couple of bills from the money clip he always kept in his pocket and handed them over. They let us go then. I remember thinking the whole thing was so cool.

By Sunday, we had reached Guadalajara, and Dad said, "Whatever you boys do, don't drink the water."

An hour or two later, we had checked into a hotel. Since the place looked so fancy to me, I thought that drinking water straight from the faucet couldn't be so dangerous. I got Montezuma's revenge, of course, with such bad diarrhea that I thought I was going to die. Other than that, the trip was great.

Dad always dropped off me and my brothers late, but it was mostly because we didn't want to go back. I even cried and said, "I don't wanna go home." It drove Mom crazy, and I remember that she often used to badmouth Dad. She would say things like "he's a drunk" or "he doesn't take responsibility for you." Yes, we smoked pot with Dad, and he sometimes bought us beer, even though we were just kids. He took us to see movies we shouldn't have seen—*The Exorcist*, for example, which genuinely scared the crap out of me. He also took us to the horse races, and it wasn't until much later that I realized he was a gambling addict—and that this was the main reason Mom had wanted a divorce. He'd gambled away practically all their money.

Despite that, I still thought it was much better to be with Dad than with Mom and Lee. More accurately, I loved every minute

I spent with Dad, and our days at the races could be really fun. We went to the track in Los Alamitos sometimes, to Hollywood Park other times, and it wasn't long before Mark and Mike also developed an interest in gambling. But I didn't really care about the horses or the betting, I just liked helping Dad. He might say to me, "Go follow that guy and see what he bets on."

And I would sneak after people. Sometimes they would spot me and tell me to scram. Normally, though, I would calmly make my way back to Dad and tell him what they'd bet on. Much later, I found out that the people Dad asked me to follow were the trainers and horse owners.

I saw Dad both win and lose at the track. I remember that he once cashed in winnings of $18,000 and then smiled and said, "Well, it's a good day today, boys!"

But like I said, he was an addict, which meant he *had* to bet on every race—not just the ones he knew about and could judge, and it meant that he lost more often than he won.

The next summer, in 1974, I was at Grandma's like usual. A few months earlier, Grandpa had found out that he had leukemia and had decided to quit his job in Minneapolis. I remember one day when Grandma told me to go with him to help clear out his office.

I did as she said, but his belongings had been packed up when we got there. There was just a load of boxes on the floor, so I carried them out for Grandpa one by one. After we loaded the final box into the car, he said, "We're just going to go in here for a minute, Matty," pointing to a stockbroker bar on the other side of the street.

When we got inside, he said to the bartender, "Hey, Bob, is it okay if my grandkid sits here?"

We sat down at the bar, and Grandpa knocked back a couple of drinks. I remember he was drinking Seagram's 7. I was always finding those bottles stashed all over the house—beneath the couch, behind the closet door, even in the basement.

Once he finished drinking and paid up, we went back to the car—a Buick Riviera—to drive home to Grandma. The car was drifting all over the road, and after he parked in the driveway we went straight into the mudroom. Grandma came in, took one look at Grandpa, and said, "I can smell on your breath that you've been drinking!" Then she shook her head. "I can't believe you'd drive your grandson home drunk!"

The summer after that, when I went out to stay with my grandparents, Grandpa was in the hospital in Minneapolis, and we went to visit him. Dad, my uncle Kerm, and my aunt Karen were there too.

Two days later, Grandpa was dead. I remember I was out on the lawn in front of the lake house, looking at the water and the boathouse when I heard the news. It was my uncle who came over to tell me. I couldn't make any sense of it—I'd *just* seen Grandpa.

In any case, his funeral took place, and Dad, who had been alone with Grandpa as he died, told me what he had said just before: "Son, can you get me a Seagram's 7?"

It was my first experience with death.

5

My Brothers

Mark beats the shit out of Lee, and I become a human oddity.

A LONG LINE OF events probably led to Mark being forced out of the house—but as far as I can remember, it all started with a frog.

It was Friday afternoon, and I was watching a cop show from the couch. Even now, I can just picture the room: the L-shaped couch, the RCA-brand TV, the wallpaper with the birds on it, the lime-green shag rug on the floor.

Since I was a couple years younger than Mark, he'd always thought it was fun to mess with me. As I was lying on the couch that day in my Fruit of the Loom underwear, he came running in and threw a frog at me. It landed on my chest and got such a fright that it pissed all over me.

I grabbed the frog and threw it back at Mark, then I leaped off the couch and chased him out into the hallway. Mark ran out through the front door, which was wooden at the bottom and glass at the top. "I'll kill you, motherfucker!" I yelled.

Mark shouted something back and slammed the door behind him. Unfortunately, I was moving so quickly that I didn't have time to stop. I went straight through the glass, my entire upper body hanging out of the door. When I tried to stand up, I realized I couldn't move. The shards of glass in the frame had cut into me, meaning I was stuck. In an almost a blacked-out blur I tried to free myself, but I broke out in a cold sweat and felt sick. When I tried again to get free, I heard Mark shout at the top of his voice, "Don't move!"

A large shard of glass had pierced my side. Mark could see it and realized that if I moved my upper body any further, it would slice me wide open.

He managed to get past me in the doorway, where I was standing in a twisted position, and gently freed me from the piece of glass. I'll never forget the squelching sound it made as he pulled it out of my body, nor the indescribable exhaustion that washed over me as I slumped to the floor.

There was still a large piece of glass in me, and when Mark pulled one shard out, I started spurting blood. Mark was leaning over me, shouting and completely distraught.

I was actually still relatively calm, thanks to the shock. Everything just felt weird, and I didn't feel pain either.

"Call an ambulance," I mumbled, turning my head and catching sight of my arm. Right then, I felt the panic wash over me. A large chunk of skin was missing, and the flesh was bare. I could see the entire muscle on my upper arm. That's when I passed out.

I later found out that Mark dragged me to the bathroom at the other end of the hall, leaving a long blood trail on the floor. He called an ambulance and then ran across the street to get our neighbor, who was a nurse. By the time she got to the bathroom, I'd regained consciousness, and I heard her shout to Mark, "Just keep pressure on everything!"

The ambulance arrived soon after, at roughly the same time as my mom got home from work. She was hysterical when she saw me, and then she screamed at my brother, "Have you killed him?!"

A reason why Mark later went off the rails the way he did is probably that Mom blamed him for what happened. If I'm perfectly honest, I have to admit that the accident was also my fault. I told Mom, "He slammed the door in my face." But that wasn't true, because when I looked at the door later, I realized it didn't open that way.

Mark later apologized to me for all this, and whenever I joke about it I say, "Dude, it all started with a fucking frog."

In any case, I was taken straight into surgery when I got to the hospital. It took six hours and 212 stitches to patch me up, and I still have a whole bunch of scars across my body. Much later, I got tattoos over the scars on my arms.

Despite everything, the accident did have some positives. There were rumors at school that Matt Sorum had been cut in half, so I got visits from a whole bunch of girls—cheerleaders who had never given a damn about me before, for example, but who now brought me candy. It was my first experience with people's morbid fascination, such as *wanting* to go to funerals or lingering at the scene of car accidents. Simply put, I'd become a human oddity, and when I got back to school after a few weeks, they welcomed me like some kind of hero.

During this time, nearly everything in Mission Viejo revolved around sports. In elementary school I had been on the football team, but I had dropped out after missing a pass during a game. I'd accidentally dropped the ball, and I heard the coach yell, "Come on, butterfingers!" That became my nickname, which was traumatic for me at a young age.

I had also been on the swim team in fifth grade, and took part in amateur competitions in freestyle, butterfly, and backstroke. I'll never forget when the time came to compete for the first time. I stood on the starting block, the buzzer went, and next thing I knew I was in the water, swimming as fast as I could. Before long, I was out of my lane and crashed into another kid, meaning we both got disqualified.

Something else that contributed to me deciding sports were lame was that I was a hairless wonder. I had no hair on my legs or my pubic area. Even now, I think it's almost unheard of to have no hair on your body. I genuinely have no hair anywhere apart from my head and face. In any case, it was the main reason I stopped getting changed for gym, and every time my coach saw me he would say, "Sorum, you haven't dressed down again today?" He gave me an F.

After that, I avoided sport of any kind. I started devoting more time to the drums instead and to listening to bands like Black Sabbath, Led Zeppelin, and Deep Purple. I spent my weekends delivering papers so I could save up for a new, better drum kit. One morning, while Mark and I were having breakfast, he said, "I saw an ad for a Ludwig kit in the paper. It's secondhand, and I think we can get it for three hundred and fifty bucks."

I looked up at him and shrugged. "Well," I said, "I have, like, seventy-five."

"No worries," said Mark. "I'll lend you the rest."

Mark was sixteen and had started working at McDonald's, and while he still liked to fuck with me, he was also my big brother and my protector. If any of the other kids did anything to me, I would shout, "My brother's gonna kick your ass!" At home, too, he protected me. I remember one particular occasion when I got sick of Lee hitting me and shouted, "Fuck you!" I tried to hit him back, but Mom grabbed my arms and held them behind my back. Lee then hit me as hard as he could. I remember he used to wear a ring, and he cut me with it.

Mark suddenly came home and saw me bleeding, and when he heard what had happened, he shouted, "You motherfucker!" and gave Lee a couple of serious punches.

Lee always wore a toupee, and as my brother hit him, it flew off. I couldn't stop myself from laughing; it really did look funny. It also became painfully obvious that our stepfather's bark was worse than his bite. He was a total pussy.

A week later, Mark and one of his friends stole a car from a car lot. Mark and his friend went off on a wild car chase that had the police after them. They tried to outrun them. Before long, Mark lost control of the car and drove into a ditch. Thankfully, he wasn't seriously injured, but he did end up in juvenile hall.

Mom had to go bail him out, and when they got home, I met them in the hallway. Mom turned to me. "You know where your dad is?"

The last time I spoke to Grandma, she said he was in Alaska, so that's what I told Mom.

Later that night, I heard her on the phone with him: "You've got to take care of your second son—he's incorrigible!"

Around roughly the same time that Mark moved to Alaska to live with Dad, Mike came home with a girl. He had never—as far as I knew—been with anyone before, but there he was, standing in the kitchen with a girl named Kendra. She was younger than him and not very attractive. He turned to Mom and said, "I got married."

Within the space of a few weeks, Mike had also left home. I soon found out that he had gotten Kendra pregnant, and by that time the next year, I had a niece.

In any case, I thought it was pretty crappy that both of my brothers were gone. Suddenly, I was all alone with Mom and Lee.

Lee was in the habit of coming into my room to shake me in the morning. I remember one occasion in particular when Lee stood by my bed with a cheap King Edward cigar in his mouth, blowing smoke in my face. "Fuck off," I mumbled.

"Get up!" he shouted, kicking my bed. Then he blew even more of his cheap cigar smoke in my face.

Everything about Lee was cheap, which had the effect of giving me habits as an adult that are the exact opposite. If I'm going to smoke a cigar, I'll smoke a Cohiba; they cost twenty-nine dollars apiece and actually taste and smell good. I don't smoke ordinary cigarettes, nor do my brothers. There's a simple explanation: Mom chain-smoked when we were kids. Whenever we were in the car with her, it always felt like we were about to suffocate. "Mom, open the window!" we used to shout at her.

"I can't," she would reply, indifferent. "It'll ruin my hair."

6

I Become Matt Sorum, Drummer

My stepsister Bonnie Lee moves in, I see Peter Criss's drum solo, and I talk about cocks in the Mission Viejo High School assembly.

NOT LONG AFTER MY brothers left home, my stepsister moved in. Her name was Bonnie Lee, but I used to call her Bonnie Pee. I didn't like her. She was cold, and not very friendly.

Bonnie had the room next to mine. She only lived with us for a few months, and once she moved back out, Mom had the wall knocked down to make my room bigger. She would try and do nice things for me like that sometimes but the only problem was she always reminded me of it when she got mad and would use it against me.

I remember doing what I could to make the room nice. I pinned up cool rock photos from Circus magazine and black-velvet posters that glowed in the dark. My Rachel Welch poster from One Million Years BC was my favorite. My friend Darryl Brooks and I (he was best man at my wedding and is still one of my closest friends) took the sliding doors out of the closet and put my stereo inside, backed by a really colorful tapestry and shelves for my vinyl records.

A few days later, I went to Radio Shack to look for speaker parts. For next to no money at all, you could buy all this stuff that usually cost a fortune, leftover parts no one else wanted. I grabbed a few sheets of particleboard and built my very first speakers. It was around this time that I started collecting records seriously. I quickly became interested in everyone who'd worked on the records—read all the sleeve notes about who the producer was, which musicians had been involved, and so on.

Much later, the famous TV presenter and VJ Matt Pinfield said to me, "You're like the encyclopedia of rock 'n' roll, right after me."

Once I had worked out how to build a speaker, I decided to build a PA system too. So I went back to Radio Shack.

When the PA system was finished, I spray-painted everything black and put the speakers in the corner of my room. The drum kit was facing the window, and I used to put on *Burn* by Deep Purple and play along with it—one side at a time—from start to finish.

I'd wanted to be a drummer ever since that time I saw Ringo on *The Ed Sullivan Show*, but only when I went to a Kiss show at the Long Beach Arena that spring did I realize I really *could* be.

It was in late May of 1975, and one of my best friends, Randy Daniels, tagged along with me. Or maybe it was more that I tagged along with him. I'd heard of Kiss before, but I wasn't really a fan. In any case, we drove to the arena in Randy's car. We didn't have tickets—in fact, we only had about six dollars each—and by the time we got to the arena, the crowd had already gone in. The people working the ticket booths had started packing up for the day. We rushed over to one of the windows and asked the woman if she had any tickets left. By this point, we were both pretty sure we'd have to drive straight back home again. But the woman's face lit up, and she said, "You know what, it's your lucky day, because I got two seats fifth row center for five dollars and fifty cents each."

The concert was due to start any moment. Randy and I ran into the arena, which held eighteen thousand people, and had just managed to find our seats in the crowd when a rumbling voice started booming from the loudspeakers: "You want the best, you got the best. The hottest band in the land...Kiss!"

And then they were onstage. Since I wasn't the biggest fan, I don't remember which song they opened with. *Dressed to Kill* had just come out, so I guess it was probably a track from that record.

A few minutes into the gig, Gene Simmons started his fire-eating trick, and it wasn't long before his hair caught fire. It looked like part of the show, but I later found out that it was an accident that could've ended really badly if one of the backline guys hadn't managed to put it out so quickly with a fire extinguisher.

Still, what I remember from that gig was the moment when the whole band but Peter Criss left the stage, and he played a drum solo. I thought, *He's not very good.* I shouted to Randy, "If he can do it, I can do it!"

Randy nodded and yelled back, "Yeah, man, you're way better than him!"

It might sound strange, but it was like I realized, right there and then, that I could actually be a drummer. If someone like Peter could play the Long Beach Arena, I could too. I thought, *I can play everything he plays and more.* That really was true. I was seriously into Deep Purple and Ian Paice, the group's insanely good drummer. Kiss was more the kind of band with songs any drummer could play— their music was what I called dumbed down, super simple. And they offset their talent with a massive show of pyro and production. Seeing through all of that, I truly believed that I could be on that stage someday. Years later I played with Gene Simmons in Kings of Chaos. I also saw Alice Cooper and Aerosmith that spring and went on to play with them too.

I've played with many of the artists I grew up listening to during that period.

That fall, I really started to neglect school. I was always late to band, which was the first class of the day. When teachers did a roll call of students, someone else always shouted "yeah" for me. Sadly, they got found out a few times too many, and I soon landed myself in trouble for smoking weed on a band field trip. Mom was head of the music board at school, so she was my music teacher's boss, and I'll never forget the day my teacher Terry Newman called the house to tell her what had happened.

Mom was completely floored. All she could manage was, "Oh…" Terry was actually pretty cool—one of the few teachers who, despite everything, seemed to like me and encouraged me to try to become a professional musician.

But even if I was skipping school, I was actually pretty popular among my school friends at the time. I was chosen to represent the class in our nomination for the student council election. I'll never forget that first meeting in the hall. Kids from each class were there, and the idea was we would go up onstage and give a quick speech about who we were going to nominate to the student council. The year before, Richard Nixon had been under threat of impeachment for the Watergate scandal, which ultimately led him to resign as president of the United States. His nickname was Tricky Dick. We all thought a boy in our class named Kelly Cox should be the council representative. So I got up onstage and said, "My class is thinking that if we can put a Dick in the White House, we can put Cox in the Mission Viejo High School assembly!"

The hall erupted in laughter, and as I went to sit down I suddenly found myself being pulled from my seat by a teacher, who said, in a firm voice, "Come here, Sorum." He dragged me off to the counselor's office. They gave me a reprimand, and when I excused myself by explaining that Cox was Kelly's surname, the counselor said, "You're suspended for three days."

Shortly after that, I found out that I wasn't allowed to return to Mission Viejo High School at all. Instead, I had to enroll at Silverado Continuation High School, which was where all the pregnant girls and weed-smoking, out-of-control boys were sent. To me, it made absolutely no difference because Randy was also kicked out at roughly the same time, and we started there together.

Randy was hyperactive and unafraid, and dreamed of being a stuntman. He would jump off buildings and bridges the minute he got the chance, and I remember that we used to make Super 8 films of him doing his stunt tricks.

It was Randy who taught me how to skateboard behind cars by grabbing the bumper. When the car stopped at a red light, you grabbed hold of the rear bumper as soon as it set off again. I always let go before Randy did.

There was a real steep slope near where we lived—at the intersection of Chrisanta Drive and Arcada Drive—and Randy always used to skate right from the very top. It's a miracle nothing serious ever happened, because we didn't wear any protection—no helmets, with crappy wheels on our boards. If we'd even run over a rock, it would've been "see ya!"

7

Prophecy

I play in Hollywood, get my first blow job, and drop out of school.

I'D STARTED MY FIRST band in the fifth grade—Liquid Earth. We wore Hawaiian shirts and took part, among other things, in a fifth-grade talent show, where we played "Our House" by Crosby, Stills, Nash & Young. Still, it was only once I turned fifteen and started playing in a band called Prophecy that I really felt like it was serious. One reason might be that the moment I joined the band I became the coolest motherfucker in the neighborhood—primarily because a guy named Jeff was our guitarist, and he was a badass. He was a few years older than me, and was the brother of Tessa, my first girlfriend. We had a cool bassist, too—Dave Pagan—but Jeff was the obvious front man, and also the reason we got a gig in Hollywood. The Starwood Club on Santa Monica Boulevard used to host something called Amateur Night on Sundays. Jeff sent in our demo tape and a picture, and a few weeks later the club gave us a slot.

During this time, Jeff had a station wagon big enough for both us and our equipment. I couldn't drive; after Mark stole that car and got caught by the cops, Mom had refused to let me get my driver's license. "You'll have to wait until you turn eighteen and apply yourself," she said.

In any case, Jeff drove us to the Starwood, and I lied to Mom and said I was staying over at a friend's place—she would never have let me go to LA. Since we were the youngest band, we always played early. Still, we were also a tight trio and had no problem with

35

that. We played covers, as well as some of our own stuff. Jeff was a Christian, and I specifically remember a song he wrote called "Let Go, Let God." He sang, "Let go, let go, let God!"

I always thought it was weird that he sang about Jesus in a rock 'n' roll band, but Jeff was very spiritual and said to Dave and me, "When I sing 'Let God,' you should point at the ceiling."

Before long, we were booked to play across the whole of Orange County—at clubs and parties. When we played a party near to Mission Viejo, the cops showed up. Everything was shut down. For some reason, I kept playing until a policeman came over and grabbed my arm. "Stop!" he said.

I stopped playing and glared at him. "You got a warrant?"

He pushed me against the wall, cuffed me, and arrested me for obstruction of justice, then drove me to juvenile detention. The whole way there, I shouted that I had rights and that the police couldn't do that.

After a while, they pulled over in a deserted parking lot. There was another police car already waiting there, and they seemed to want to transfer me into it. I'd been drinking and felt like a rebel, so I kept shouting at them.

One of the policemen grabbed my head and slammed it against the hood. He took off the cuffs so that the cops in the other car could put theirs on instead. Once that was done, they threw me into the back of the other car and drove off. Since I was pretty drunk, I vomited, which hardly made the cops hate me any less.

A little later, once I was at juvenile detention in Santa Ana, they let me make a call. I called Mom, who said, "You can stay there over the weekend. It'll do you good." Sadly, it didn't have the effect she was hoping for; when they released me on Sunday, I just felt experienced, cool.

By now, a guy named Jim Dowd and another named Mark Klink had also joined Prophecy. We recorded a few songs and had some T-shirts made. We really did go for it, and at some point during 1976 we got our first gig at Gazzarri's Crazy Horse West, a club on Sunset

Strip. The place was legendary; the Doors had played there before their big break. Later called Key Club, it was run by the infamous Bill Gazzarri, who always wore a white suit and a big white hat. People called him the Godfather.

On that particular evening, a girl from Mission Viejo had come to watch us play. She was really cute, really short, and a bit chunky, and her name was TRACY. When we came offstage, she was all over me, and whispered in my ear that she liked watching me play drums. People were running in and out of the little dressing room we were in, and I didn't know what to say. We toasted, and Tracy said she felt like doing a line of coke and giving me a blow job.

I hadn't tried coke or been sucked off before, but it really must have turned me on, because not long after I was sitting in the passenger seat of her car, totally high, with my pants around my ankles.

That fall, I took the GED test to finish with school early so I could spend more time playing music. I passed, and only a week or two later my mom came in my room. She said, "Your stepfather and I are going to sell the house so we can buy a boat and sail around the world."

I remember the thoughts swirling around my head. I was barely eighteen. Mom and Lee did usually spend their summers sailing, but not around the world.

"You can come with us if you want."

"How long are you gonna be gone?"

"Five years."

I remember staring at her as I said, "I can't do that. I'm in a band."

Mom just shook her head and sighed. "You've always been such a dreamer."

With those words, she left me. Lee came in shortly afterward.

"From now on, you'll have to look after yourself," he said. I didn't bother looking at him, but I could tell from his voice that he was smiling as he continued, "You're gonna see what it's like to live in the real world. Your mom and I won't give you a nickel—not a single nickel."

8

The Shoot-Out

*I start selling drugs, have sex with a coke addict for the first time,
and manage to cause a shoot-out.*

MY NEW CIRCUMSTANCES MEANT that the future felt uncertain, to say
the least. Mom and Lee were in full swing with selling the house,
and I had to find both somewhere to live and a way to bring in money.

A guy named NICK BEAL had recently moved into my
neighborhood, and he was a famous skateboarder—he'd been in
a lot of magazines. I was constantly hearing people say, "Did you
know Nick Beal moved into the area?"

Before Nick bought the house next door, a guy my own age
had lived there. He was a bit of an oddball, and he'd taught me how
to roll a joint. I used to buy weed from him, maybe an ounce at a
time, and sometimes sold the joints that I'd rolled. One day, the guy
suddenly hanged himself in his garage. He was a friend of a friend,
and it was the first time anyone around me had died by suicide.
I was sad, of course, but above all I was confused. I just couldn't
understand why he'd done it.

Not long after, Nick moved in. I bumped into him as I was walking
past the house one day, and we got to chatting. I guess we must have
clicked, because from then on we hung out almost every day, even
though he was a few years older. I was also able to buy weed from him,
and it didn't take long before we started dealing pot together.

I had also started taking cocaine by this point, and selling it too,
and it was definitely profitable. The cocaine also turned out to have

other benefits: I met a super hot girl named CANDIE around the same time, and she really loved the drug. I gave her as much as she wanted, and in exchange I could do anything I wanted with her. I guess you could say it was my first sexual experience with a coke addict, and she was also the first woman who dressed up for me. I thought she was unbelievably sexy, and before long, we had moved in together.

It was a pretty simple apartment with just one bedroom, but I liked it. I still had my rock 'n' roll dreams, but to tide myself over I sold weed and coke.

It was actually through my dealing that I met a guy named JOHN—a tall, powerful, red-haired dude. He dealt weed too, and after we had chatted for a while, he said, "We can work on a bigger scale. What do you think?"

Not far from Mission Viejo, where I grew up, there's a place called Dana Point. It's a small coastal city, but it's also a hub for smuggling and importing drugs. I had friends who were involved in that kind of thing.

I pulled a few strings, and a few days later I took John and his van down to the harbor. We met the guy I'd been in contact with there and bought a whole load of pot—bundled up in bales that weighed around fifty pounds apiece. Since Mexico was so close, most of the weed came from there. We loaded everything into the van and drove to John's house, where we spread the bales out on the living room floor. The weed was compressed, and we immediately got to work redistributing it into small plastic pouches. We had a few different types: Mexican Sensei, African Hash Plant, and Thai sticks, the last of which was really popular at the time.

The Mexican Sensei weed was sometimes a little too dry, and John and I realized that if we sprayed it with water we didn't just add moisture to it, we also increased the weight by half a pound or so.

Pretty soon, business was going so well that we agreed not to sell any less than a pound at a time.

People came over to John's place, and we gave them what they wanted in the doorway. In return, they gave us cash. I had been broke practically all of my life, but now I could suddenly afford a car. Instead I traded a guy forty dollars' worth of weed for a Rambler station wagon. It was kind of rusty and green, but it could fit all my drums. And after I installed a $500 stereo with an 8-track player and Powerplay speakers, I was rollin' down the highway like a king, cranking "War Pigs" at full volume.

During this time, I didn't have any contact with my mom. She had left family life behind her and was on a sailboat somewhere in the middle of the ocean with my stepfather. There weren't any cell phones at the time, so if you wanted to reach anyone you had to do it via pay phone, landline, postcard, or letter. I didn't hear from her for over a year.

Regardless, I was happy with Candie. We often spent entire nights at home, fucking and snorting coke. It was totally insane—in a terrifying but also incredible way. It continued that way right up until my cocaine consumption went into overdrive and I realized I would die if I didn't stop. I told her that one day, while we were in the kitchen. "I think we're doing too much coke, so I'm thinking about stopping."

Candie just stared at me like I'd told her I didn't love her anymore. Then she turned and left the apartment, and I didn't see her for three days. I asked people I knew whether they'd seen her, and on the fourth day I was given a tip that tied a knot in my stomach. "Check with Nick Beal," someone said.

I immediately jumped into my car and drove over to Nick's place. He opened the door in his underwear, and I could tell right away from the look on his face that Candie was there. Next thing I knew, I had spotted her behind him. But rather than pushing past Nick, I just turned and left without saying a word. Still, I couldn't think about anything else for the rest of the day.

That evening, I had a gig with Prophecy at a bowling alley in Orange County, and I nearly dropped my sticks when I spotted Nick and Candie in the crowd. "What the fuck?!" I shouted, so loudly that Jeff turned around and stared at me with a confused expression.

I could hardly explain the situation to him and had to pull myself together to finish the set as I frantically wondered what the hell they were doing there.

Once I was done playing, I went out into the parking lot in front of the club. I spotted them again and walked straight over to Nick and said, "Dude, what the fuck, that's my girl! You stole my girlfriend!"

I noticed that Nick's eyes had darkened, but he only had time to shove me before I launched at him and knocked him onto his back on the wet asphalt. Candie, in turn, threw herself onto me and pulled and kicked while shouting, "You fucking quitter!" I didn't really care about her; I was just sitting with my knees on Nick's shoulders so that he couldn't get up. All that was going through my head as I hit him was that he was my friend and he'd stabbed me in the back. Before long, I had knocked him unconscious and split his cheek wide open. It was like I went into this blackout rage and wanted to kill the fucker.

When I eventually came out of it, I was still beating him. I remember looking down and seeing his face all bloodied. Without a word, I got up and slowly walked away, with Candie shouting all kinds of nasty things at me.

It was only as I drove to John's place in the rain that I realized what I had just done, and I knew Nick would take revenge. Just a few nights later, he and three friends turned up outside John's. I was upstairs at the time, but in the glow of the streetlights I could see that they were armed.

John came in and stood next to me by the window. Then he said, "I'll sort this out," and went down to the front door.

John was a pretty big guy, whereas I was kind of skinny, weighing maybe 160 pounds at most. I saw John walk up to Nick and the others on the driveway, and through the open front door I heard his deep, powerful voice: "Get the hell out of here...now!"

What I saw—but which John was completely unaware of—was that one of the guys had moved to one side and snuck up behind him with a knife. The blade flashed in the light, and I guess only sheer intuition made John spin around just as the guy jabbed the knife toward him. John's huge hand wrapped around the blade, and I saw blood spurt across the asphalt. Next thing I knew, John grabbed the knife, threw it over the fence into the neighbor's yard, and rushed back into the house. For a second, I thought he was running away, but I heard him yell, "Fuck them! Get the guns!"

We did have weapons, after all—and not just any old junk. We had a .357 Magnum revolver, bought one night after watching Clint Eastwood as Dirty Harry. John grabbed the gun with his bloody hand and hissed at me, "You stay here. If you show your face out there they'll shoot you."

I wasn't especially afraid, but I also didn't want to die. John was in a different league; he was the toughest guy in that part of California, a really mean motherfucker. Everyone knew that you didn't fuck with John, but now someone had. As he rushed back outside, I thought that I wouldn't want to be one of those guys.

I hurried back to the window and got there in time to see him fire four shots into the ground right by their feet. Rather than trying to return fire, they just turned around and ran off as fast as they could. I felt the tension leave my body but knew, deep down, that I couldn't hope this was all over.

I was right. Just a few days later, the phone rang, and I heard Nick's voice on the other end: "You won't know where or when, but we're gonna get you."

9

Hollywood

Mario Maglieri supplies me with food,
and I manage to jam my way into becoming a touring musician.

THE OBVIOUS PLACE TO run for a young drummer with dreams seemed—at least in spring 1979—to be Hollywood. So the day after Nick called the house, I packed my drums into the trunk of my 1964 station wagon, grabbed a pound of weed to sell and live off for a while, and headed straight to LA.

Like so many others, I did a couch-surfing tour of friends' living rooms and spent my evenings at the clubs on Sunset Strip. I played with Prophecy in some of them. One night, after gigging at the Starwood on the corner of Santa Monica Boulevard and North Crescent Heights Boulevard, I was in the VIP bar upstairs when I suddenly spotted Rob Halford. I elbowed Jeff, who didn't seem particularly impressed when he followed my line of sight. Slightly disappointed by his reaction, I raised my glass but didn't have time to drink before I froze and mumbled, "Holy shit!"

Walking straight toward me was a tall, stick-thin figure with spectacular jet-black hair, black-and-white striped tights and high-heeled shoes. Until that moment, I'd thought I looked pretty cool in my red latex pants, Mom's silk shirt, and white Capezio dance shoes. I was skinny and had big hair and a ring in one ear. But compared to this guy, I was suddenly nothing. It was the first time I ever saw Nikki Sixx, who had started a band called London a few years before. It's true, London wasn't particularly well known outside of LA, but in my eyes at that moment, he was as much of a rock star as a man could be.

As I stood there gaping, Nikki took an awkward misstep that caused the heel of one of his shoes to break. He stumbled, paused, looked down at his shoe, and yelled, "Oh no! Goddamn it, I broke my heel!"

There were plenty of colorful, interesting figures at the Starwood back then—it was the main rock club in LA in the 1970s, owned by the gangster Eddie Nash. Just a few years later, he would become infamous for the Wonderland murders, in which both the porn actor John Holmes and coke played a starring role.

After Nikki had hobbled off with his broken shoe in one hand, I realized that Eddie still hadn't paid us for that evening's gig. So I turned to Jeff and Dave and said, "Come on, we need to get our money."

The three of us left the bar and walked down a dark corridor of half-open doors. In the rooms we passed, I saw people taking drugs. The whole place felt incredibly seedy. Eddie Nash's office was at the very end of the corridor, and when I knocked on the door he immediately said, "Come in!"

It was so dark that when we first stepped inside, we could barely make out Eddie behind the huge desk. "Hey," I said. "We're Prophecy. We just played here."

Eddie studied us for a moment with a cigarette hanging from one corner of his mouth, and said, "You kids want some quaaludes? You want some sherms? Or d'you want the cash?"

Jeff was very much against drugs, so there was no question of us not taking the money. But I still couldn't help but ask, "What's a sherm?"

"Well, kid," said Eddie, "that's a cigarette blended with PCP."

As we left with our money, heading back downstairs, we bumped into Kevin DuBrow, who asked if we wanted to buy any ludes. He was the singer in Quiet Riot, but like me needed to make money selling drugs.

Farther down Sunset from the Starwood was a place called the Rainbow. It was *the* place to hang out if you wanted to meet the right people. I wasn't actually old enough to get in, but I went over there anyway and loitered outside until the owner, Mario, came over one evening, held out his hand, and asked who I was and what I was doing there.

"My name's Matt Sorum, I just moved here."

"Well, what do you do, kid?" he asked.

"I'm a drummer."

"Yeah, you look like you might have it," he said after giving me a searching look. "I like you, but you look skinny. Follow me."

He walked in ahead of me, sat me down at one of the tables, and told a waitress to bring me chicken soup and bread. Shortly afterward, I was served an enormous bowl with what looked like half a chicken in it, and half a loaf of bread. I really was emaciated at the time, and ate like I'd never seen food before. Mario smirked as he watched me, and said, "It's on me, kid." He fed me like I was a chick that had fallen out of its nest, and he continued to do it for several years.

I quickly realized that "everyone" gathered in the parking lot outside the Rainbow after two in the morning to find out where the parties were up in the hills. I made sure I was there too—and on one of the very first nights, I was genuinely starstruck. As I stood there, a white Rolls-Royce limousine suddenly pulled into the parking lot. The conversations stopped, and all eyes were drawn to the limo as the door opened and Queen's Roger Taylor climbed out. I felt my jaw drop.

Roger was wearing an elegant white suit and had a model-like girl on each arm. He held a glass of champagne in one hand, which he sipped from as he absentmindedly looked around. That left a lasting impression on me, because I realized right there that he was everything I had ever wanted to be.

A few nights later, I gathered my courage and headed to the Central Club, farther down Sunset Strip, because I knew they ran a jam night every Tuesday.

"Hey, you wanna play?" the guy at the door asked. He ran the list that you had to add your name to if you wanted to jam.

"Well, I'm a drummer."

"Great, and can you bring your drums here?"

At the time, I had a really big drum kit with eight toms, but since I saw this as my chance to show off what I could do, I dragged the whole kit over there every week in the hope I would get to play. Two or three weeks passed with no luck; instead, I had to watch a bunch of other drummers playing on *my* drums. But then, on the third or fourth Tuesday night, as I stood there watching these guys fuck up my drums, the door guy finally came over and said I could play if I wanted to.

It was around one forty-five in the morning, but there were still plenty of people around. I heard the host shout, "Matt Sorum from Orange County, are you here?!"

I felt my heart start to race, took a deep breath, and quickly made my way up onto the stage, where the black, left-handed guitarist Gregg Wright and his bassist, Tim Solas, were waiting for me. I was probably better on the drums then than I am now. What's certain is that I'd been waiting weeks to play, and now that I had been given a chance, I gave it my all.

Immediately afterward, Gregg took me to one side and said, "Dude, you play fucking great."

"Thanks," I said, smiling a little bashfully.

"What are you doing?"

"Well, I just got here...I just came to Hollywood."

He raised an eyebrow slightly and then said, "Do you wanna go on tour?" I was so surprised that I didn't know what to say, and Gregg explained with a shrug, "We lost our tour drummer, you see."

"When do we leave?" I managed to blurt out, quickly adding, "Who's your bass player?"

"He's right there." He pointed to Tim, who nodded at me. "Where do you live?" Gregg asked.

"I don't...I mean, I'm sleeping on a friend's couch."

"Okay, great. We start rehearsals the day after tomorrow, and we leave in two weeks."

The very next day, I moved in with Tim in his tiny apartment in Glendale. It only had one bedroom, so I slept on the couch there too. The morning after that, we started rehearsals in Gregg's garage.

Across the alley on Ventura Boulevard was a place called Charles's Restaurant, which was actually more of a coffee shop than anything. During our first rehearsal, the door to the garage opened and none other than Leon Russell strode in.

"Hey, Leon!" Gregg said, in a tone that suggested they knew one another.

"I was having a sandwich at Charles's and heard you playing," Leon said.

I later found out that all kinds of artists and musicians hung out at Charles's while they were at the nearby recording studios in the Valley. Among others, the CBS studio was just around the corner.

Leon shamelessly sat down to listen, and though I was starstruck, I managed to give everything I had. Partway through the song, I heard him yell, "You guys got a good sound!" Then he left as quickly as he had arrived.

That wasn't the only unexpected celebrity visit to the garage. Just two days later, the doors opened again and Narada Michael Walden came strolling in midway through a song. He was most famous for being the super drummer in Mahavishnu Orchestra and for playing with Jeff Beck, but he would later become a big name in his own right as a producer. I recognized him immediately, of course, and wondered what he was doing there. I was also struck by an acute performance anxiety.

But rather than just sit down in front of us with a cocked head and a critical expression, he grabbed a couple of sticks from the floor and started ripping on a small fan in the garage, like he was playing percussion with us.

"Holy shit!" I mumbled to myself, barely believing that it was happening.

47

The very next week, it was time for us to head south, where Gregg was famous enough for us to fill clubs. Gregg and I were to drive down in a Ford Econoline van while Tim and a crew guy would travel in a wood-paneled station wagon. The instruments all ended up in the station wagon, and the PA speakers were loaded into our van.

I was still only nineteen, and the whole thing felt slightly surreal as I loaded my drums into the car. I guess Gregg must have noticed, because he said, "Are you ready, Matt?" and placed his big hand on my shoulder with a smile.

I looked up, met his eye, and nodded.

10

On Tour in the South

*I get my first taste of southern hospitality,
and then have to run from the Ku Klux Klan.*

OUR FIRST SHOW WAS in El Paso, but I don't remember much of
that or any of the other gigs in Texas; all I really remember is that
I caught crabs from one of the shabby hotels we stayed in. As luck
would have it, we mostly stayed with friends of Gregg, and their
places were both cleaner and more comfortable, especially after
we arrived in Louisiana and played at a club on the outskirts of
Lafayette. Yet again, we were staying with someone Gregg knew,
and as usual, since I was youngest, I got the couch. It didn't really
matter to me, and after the gig that evening I was asleep before
I had even managed to stretch out properly on the couch. Suddenly,
a sound woke me, and I could make out a young girl stooping over
me. After a few seconds, once my eyes had adjusted to the half-light,
I realized she was completely naked.

"I just wanted to welcome you to Louisiana," she said softly in a
singsong voice.

She pulled back the covers and straddled me. I was naked too,
and the minute I felt her warm skin against mine, I got an erection.
She tipped her hips slightly, and I slipped inside her, and she started
fucking me—slowly at first, then quickly speeding up. I had no idea
who she was or what her name was, but it made no difference. She
was the first Southern belle I had ever met, and I remember thinking
how great it was to be in a band.

Once she was done having sex with me, she went out into the kitchen and opened the refrigerator.

Not long after, she came back with a plate of food.

"I thought you might be hungry."

She put the plate on a chair next to the couch, along with a cold bottle of beer.

It felt like I was in heaven, and all I could do was give the girl a lame smile.

When I saw Gregg the next day, I excitedly told him about my nighttime visit.

"I know," he said, blowing on the cup of hot coffee he was holding in front of his lips. "I set it up."

I stared at him as he sipped from the cup.

"I just wanted you to experience a little southern hospitality."

I laughed and said, "I think I'm in love."

Gregg gave me a serious look and said, in his deep, slightly drawling voice, "Don't fall in love... We're moving on to the next town now."

A few hours later, we arrived in Baton Rouge, where we had borrowed an apartment that would serve as our base over the next few weeks while we played various places in New Orleans.

After our first gig, we went to a bar called Crazy Shirley's on Bourbon Street, and I had yet another kind of awakening. Like usual, I was at the bar, drinking like there was no tomorrow, and listening to the killer band playing up onstage. Suddenly, an unbelievably attractive woman came over and sat down on the stool to my right. She was black, and I immediately started chatting to her, buying her drinks. We were laughing, and she kept pressing herself closer and closer to me.

It felt good, and even better when she suddenly put an arm around my shoulders.

Next thing I knew, I was making out with her, but a hand on my shoulder quickly put a stop to that. Gregg had come over, and he pulled me over to one side. "Matt, what are you doing?"

I didn't know what he meant and just wanted to get back to the girl before someone else got his hands on her. "Come on, man, she's beautiful."

Gregg sighed. "Look at the Adam's apple."

"What? What do you mean?"

"The Adam's apple...and the hands."

"Wow, that's a guy?!"

"Yes!"

I glanced over to the girl who was no longer a girl and thought, *Oh, shit, I was just making out with a guy! I'm gonna be so traumatized!* Then I snatched the beer from Gregg's hand and took a deep swig.

The next morning, as we sat on the mattresses on the floor in our unfurnished apartment, Gregg turned to me. In what was probably a well-meaning attempt to drag my thoughts away from what had happened the night before, he said, "I'm gonna take you to the middle of Baton Rouge, where it's all black." He looked me straight in the eye. "You okay with that?"

I was instantly curious, so I said, "Yeah, let's go!"

So later that evening, we made our way into the black part of town to play at a club that seemed like it was straight out of some film. The room fell silent as I entered, and I realized how it must feel to be the only black face among a sea of white. I thought, *Wow, I'm the oddball here.*

Two men in suits came over to us, and one of them said, "Who's the white boy?"

"He's a badass little drummer," Gregg told him.

"Yeah, right," said the other dude.

Right then, a dirty blues band started playing up onstage. After a few songs, they spotted Gregg, and the singer took to the mic: "We've got a local hero here tonight...Gregg, come on up and play something for us."

Gregg took his guitar up onstage and asked the guys in the band, "Is it okay if I bring my drummer with me?"

The band grinned and the singer waved to me. "Well, come on up, white boy."

So I went up onstage too and took my place behind the drums. Gregg nodded and counted me in, and then we started playing a slow blues one-four-five. I remember playing with an intensity that surprised even me. The guys glanced at one another and nodded. Everything I did from then on was cool.

The next day, the tour moved on to some of the more scary parts of Louisiana, like Shreveport, eventually reaching the small city of Hammond. It all seemed very provincial. The stage at the place we were playing seemed kind of weird, and when I looked out at the crowd that night, I was genuinely scared. The eyes staring back at me were hard and suspicious, but a couple girls near the front differed from the majority and were giving Gregg the eye. In any case, we didn't draw out the set like usual, and when we finished the barman came over to us and said, "You guys need to leave by the back door—like, *now.*"

He turned to Gregg. "There are some guys here who want to have a word with you." He nodded discreetly toward the bar, where a group of white men were standing. I realized immediately that they were KKK dudes, really hardcore.

The barman continued, "Why don't you play it safe and get an escort out of town?"

To be blunt, those men by the bar wanted to kill us. They were all like, "Let's kill that nigger. Let's kill that Mexican."

I felt anger mixed with fear and couldn't stop myself from staring back at them. They noticed me and started yelling at us. The atmosphere quickly became so threatening that we had to take shelter in the cubbyhole that served as the changing room, and not long after that the cops showed up to escort us out of town. I don't think I've ever felt racial tension as clearly as I did that day.

11

Drinking Games in Hawaii

*I do a bump with Robin Williams
and almost die from alcohol poisoning in Hawaii.*

THE TOUR WITH GREGG went on for so long that 1979 had become 1980 by the time we returned to Hollywood.

Gregg, Tim, and I continued our jam sessions at the Central Club on Tuesdays, and one night when we finished playing and I slumped down at the bar, I realized that Robin Williams was sitting just to my right. I looked down and saw that he was holding a small mirror beneath the overhanging bar and that there were several lines of powder on the glass.

Robin realized I was looking and quickly glanced up. "You want one?" he asked.

Next thing I knew, I had done a bump with Robin Williams, and then he said, "You wanna do a shot?"

We did a few shots of Jack Daniel's, followed by more coke, and then Robin asked me to follow him down to the basement. These days, there's a bar down there, but back then it was just a storeroom, and when we got down there I could hardly believe my eyes. Standing in front of me, sharing a joint, were John Belushi and Angie Bowie. They greeted us warmly, and John handed me the joint. Angie took out a small silver case from her handbag and said, "Would anyone like one of these?"

She held out the case to us, and I saw that there were a large number of quaaludes inside. I hadn't tried them before, but as the four of us started to make our way back upstairs a while later, I was so high that it easily topped every other experience I'd had with drugs up to that point.

I was still aware of John climbing up onto the stage and singing with the band, but I have no idea how the night ended. All I remember is that Buddy Miles, Jimi Hendrix's drummer, joined us as we left the Central Club and that I turned to him with wide eyes and thought, *Hollywood, man! This is cool!*

A few nights later, I met John Belushi again. This time, it was in the VIP room of a club on Hollywood Boulevard. John was everywhere back then, and he knew everyone. On this particular night, he introduced me to the comedian Sam Kinison, who—if possible—was even crazier than John and who immediately wanted us to go back to his place to continue the party. Not long after, a small group of us—the Who bassist John Entwistle included—headed off there together.

Back then, Sam was borrowing a house close to the Comedy Store on Sunset Strip, and we realized, on arriving, that he had unimaginable resources. In all honesty, I'd never seen that much cocaine before. It was like being in *Scarface*, and I ended up staying there for several days. Every time I thought about leaving, I realized I would regret it if I did.

When I wasn't partying, I was gigging with Gregg, but I had begun to realize that it was difficult to make ends meet on those club gigs alone. More or less by chance, I started playing with a Top 40 band. A keyboard player friend of mine named Dan called me up one day and said, "I've got a gig in Hawaii, at the naval base in Pearl Harbor. It's three hundred fifty bucks a week, plus a place to live. You'll only have to play, like, three hours a night."

"Cool," I said. "When do we rehearse?"

"We're not gonna rehearse."

A few days later, I received a plane ticket in the mail. I don't remember the names of everyone in that band, but the singer and bassist was Jason Scheff, who later made it big in the band Chicago.

I also remember that we came up with the set list on the plane. One of the main reasons I was able to support myself just by playing drums from early on was that I was a very quick learner. I never wrote down any bars, verses, breaks, or anything; I just learned by listening to the songs and memorizing everything. As time passed, I only needed to hear a track once to be able to sit down and play it back.

When we landed in Hawaii, the promoter came to meet us—wearing, of course, a Hawaiian shirt and smoking a cigar—and drove us to the house where we would be staying. It was in a place known as Samoan Town, purely because the only people who lived there were Samoans—really big guys who looked angry all the time.

I remember that on our first night there, I woke to what sounded like screaming. When I rushed outside, I saw several Samoan guys chasing a terrified pig with butcher's knives. There was no way I could get back to sleep after that, so I took off for the liquor store a few blocks away, feeling their hostile glances. When I got back to the others, I immediately said, "We've gotta get the fuck out of here."

The next morning, we called the promoter who had hired us and asked whether there was anywhere else we could stay.

"Yeah, but the house is on the other side of the island, so you'd have to drive forty-five minutes every day."

"Okay, so where is it?"

"Waimea Bay."

We moved into that new house the same day. It was on a cliff with views out to sea. The house was owned by Mark Foo, a famous surfer, and he was there when we arrived. He was watching himself surfing a huge wave on the big screen TV when we came in.

"Check it out, that wave's fifty feet," he said enthusiastically, gesturing to the TV with his whole hand.

After we got settled in, we took the car we were borrowing and drove to Pearl Harbor and the venue for the upcoming gigs. It was a pretty big club where all the Navy guys hung out. Given that they had to stay on the base, they didn't exactly have much choice in the matter.

Aside from a few Navy women, everyone there was a dude.

On either our first or second night at the club, we started playing a drinking game. I can knock back an entire beer without breathing, and when we played for the Navy guys someone bought me a pitcher. They all started yelling to drink it, and I downed the whole thing and counted in the next song. It was something I started doing every night as the crowd yelled, "Chug, chug, chug!"

A week or so later, the whole fleet arrived at the base, which meant suddenly around six thousand guys were there. It was pretty crowded, and not just with the Navy; there were also a whole load of Army guys, too. The Army was on one side and the Navy on the other, and they were all pretty competitive.

The beer trick had become a routine by that point, and after a few songs Jason would announce into the mic, "Time for Matt! Time for a pitcher of beer!"

I downed the pitcher they brought me and we played a few more songs before an Army guy suddenly climbed up onto the stage. He had a huge brandy glass in one hand, which he handed to Jason and said, "Tell your drummer to drink this."

Next thing I knew, the glass was in my hand.

"What is it?" I shouted to the Army dude, who had now jumped back down from the stage.

"Bacardi 151 and Drambuie," he yelled back with a grin. "Chug it, you motherfucker!"

I sniffed the contents of the glass. It was pure alcohol, but I chugged it all the same.

I then kicked off the song "Working for the Weekend" by Loverboy but didn't make it any further than the intro before the entire club and everyone in it started to spin. A second later, I fell back off the drum riser.

When I woke up, I was on a bench in the dressing room, and as I raised my hand I realized that my head was bleeding. I could also hear an incredible amount of noise coming from the club itself.

"What's going on out there?" I asked Jason, who was leaning over me with a concerned frown.

"They're fighting," he said. "Apparently the military cops are on their way." He straightened up and added, with a sigh, "The gig's off tonight. We're going home."

We left the club by the rear entrance, and I had to lie down on the backseat while someone drove us back to Waimea Bay. Throughout the journey, I had to sit up at regular intervals to throw up out of the open window. The road was flanked by pineapple fields, and whenever I gasped for air I breathed in the sweet scent of the crop. Even now, I can't smell pineapple without feeling like I need to barf.

When I got back to LA with some money in my pocket, I realized that I could support myself as a drummer. I put together my own Top 40 band with Dan, the keyboard player who had gotten me the job in Pearl Harbor. We called the band Metro and were soon booked five nights a week for a month at a restaurant called the Black Angus. We played five sets each night and earned between $200 and $250 a week, which was pretty good money for a musician in the early 1980s.

The great thing about it was that if I needed to be at another gig somewhere, I could just call one of my drummer pals and ask him to step in for me. Actually, I was moving between different Top 40 bands all the time back then.

During this period, my hair was pretty crazy. I was also skinny and often wore bright red pants and makeup. Guys used to come up to me all the time and ask, "Are you a guy or a girl?"

"Well," I would say, "what do you want me to be?"

I'm guessing that they were just homophobic and jealous, because girls used to come up to me all the time, and I got laid every night. I remember one night in particular when I was chatting to a few girls after a show. One of them suddenly turned to her friends and said, "We need to fuck Matt."

I thought she was kidding at first, but she dragged us all to a small hotel around the corner, where she paid for a room and then sat in a corner, watching while I had sex with her friends. During it all, I kept thinking, *This is really weird!* I'm sure there was alcohol and coke in the picture, but still…

At roughly the same time, I met another girl who, after our first night together, told me, "I'm bisexual."

"What's that?" I asked.

"I like girls, and I like guys."

"Oh…okay."

"Have you ever tried a threesome?" she said.

"No, but I always wanted to."

I was renting a room in a house near the garage where I used to rehearse with Gregg, and she brought one of her girlfriends over. The friend seemed a little shy at first and said, "I've never been with a guy before. I'm a lesbian."

Rather than bumming me out, it got me even more worked up, and as I slept with both of them I noticed that the lesbian kind of liked it, so I said, "So does this mean you're not a lesbian anymore?"

"No, I'm still a lesbian," she said. "But I guess I'll have to consider calling myself a bisexual."

Those two lesbians who were actually bisexual stayed with me for two months. I remember thinking, *This is really cool—I've got two girlfriends.*

But then they started fighting over me—or, more accurately, over the fact that one of them thought I was spending more time with the other one than with her. They fought practically all the time, and eventually I got sick of it and calmly and firmly asked them to move out. It was so much easier to break up in those days. It was easier to live back then in general. I didn't have a lot of money, but I had a lot of fun. I was in a band, and I was getting laid.

One day, a recording engineer friend of mine named Dan Nebenzal called me up and said he was working with a producer named Michael Lloyd who needed a drummer for a studio job. I had never planned to become a studio musician, but I thought it sounded exciting, so I drove over to Michael's place in Beverly Hills the next day. He had a studio behind his house, and I immediately got to work adding drums to a couple of tracks.

"I really like your drumming," he said. He clearly meant it, too, because just a few weeks later he called me up and booked me for another session, with Belinda Carlisle, who had left the Go-Go's by that point.

Still, the coolest session I got called in for was with King Solomon Burke (one of the best gospel singers). I felt a little nervous as I drove to the studio that day. I was just some white kid, but luckily I had my experiences in Louisiana behind me. So when I stepped into the studio and saw the skeptical looks from the whole gang of black guys inside, I knew I just had to focus and do my thing.

The first track we were due to record was a slow blues shuffle kind of thing, and Solomon sang something like, "I'm gonna burst your bubble, baby."

It only took a few takes before we had the song down. We recorded two more tracks after that, and once we were done for the day, Solomon came over to me. He was wearing a slick three-piece suit and smelled like a mix of Hennessy cognac and Hai Karate cologne.

"That was pretty funky for a white boy," he said with a smile.

"Thank you, Mr. Burke," I said.

Still with a smile on his lips, Solomon pulled a fat money clip from his inner pocket and teased out three hundred-dollar bills, which he then handed to me.

"Pretty funky," he repeated, before slowly turning around and leaving the studio.

12

The Neptune Society

I do Mom a huge favor and get nothing but guilt in return.

WHEN MOM AND LEE finally got home from their long sailing trip, Lee was seriously ill with a terminal case of colon cancer. He was given all kinds of drugs but still got worse and worse, and one morning Mom called me up and said, "Matt, I think it's best if you come home. Your stepfather is in a bad, bad way."

I admit that I didn't really have warm feelings toward Lee. Not that I would wish that terrible illness on him, but I wasn't exactly lying awake at night worrying about him. Still, I obviously wanted to be there for my mom. So when I finished up a studio job later that day, I headed straight over to Mom and Lee's house in Orange County.

As Mom met me in the hallway, I could tell that she was pretty torn up. Her eyes were red, and she was trembling as she hugged me. We went into the kitchen and sat down at the table.

"I don't think he has much time left." She glanced up at me with a kind of pleading look in her eyes. "I'd like you to go in there and tell him you love him."

I squirmed as she said it. What Mom asked me to do felt anything but natural, but I couldn't say no. I took a deep breath, got up, and went into the bedroom, where Lee had been bed-bound for months. The room was gloomy, and at first I could only make out the shape of him in the double bed. But as I got closer, I saw that his eyes were closed, and there was no reaction on his face as I said, "Hey, Lee, it's Matt. I'm here to…uh…"

I didn't know how to continue, and I also didn't know whether there was any point, as Lee seemed to be in some kind of coma. I assumed that the cancer meds might be responsible for his condition and could see a thin string of saliva glistening its way down his unshaven chin.

I cleared my throat but still couldn't see any signs of life from my stepfather. I pulled over a chair and sat down, then I thought about what Mom had asked me to do. Saying "I love you, Lee" didn't just feel fake, it also felt impossible. So after thinking for a while I said, "Thank you for raising me." Even as I said the words, they felt false to me. But Lee probably hadn't even heard me. The most important thing was that I had, to an extent, done what Mom had wanted.

As I went back out into the kitchen, the doorbell rang. Mom went to answer and returned with a middle-aged woman in a nurse's uniform. Mom introduced us to one another and explained that the nurse came twice a day to check on Lee and give him painkillers.

The nurse went in to see Lee, and I had no choice but to lie when Mom asked whether I had told Lee I loved him. The words I had recently said to Lee were also a lie, and I realized that this was one of those situations that left no room for the truth.

A little later, when the nurse came back out, she had a serious, concerned look on her face. She thoughtfully fiddled with her well-filled blue bag and said, "He's not going to make it; he's in a lot of pain…I think that if you really want to help the process along, you can help him on his way. All you have to do is turn up the morphine drip, and he'll be gone."

For a few seconds, I saw that Mom had stopped breathing. Then she composed herself and followed the nurse out. When she came back, she looked me straight in the eye and asked whether I thought I could do what the nurse had suggested. "I can't handle it myself," she explained.

I was completely floored and didn't know what to say. At first, I didn't even know if she was serious. But then I saw how much she was suffering, and I said, "Of course, I'll do it."

I stayed over at her place that night, and we ate breakfast in silence the next morning. As I finished my coffee, I said, "I may as well do it now." I glanced at Mom. She didn't protest, just looked down at the table. I got up and went into the bedroom, over to the bed where Lee lay in the same position as the day before, with roughly the same blank expression on his face. I studied him for a moment before turning up the morphine drip and going back out into the kitchen.

"It's done," I said, slightly surprised that I didn't feel much at all.

Mom, on the other hand, suddenly seemed upset. She raised her hand to her mouth and stared at me, making me feel guilty even though I hadn't done anything wrong. After that, she hurried over to the telephone on the wall, dialed a number, and said, "I need to tell your sister." My "sister" was, in fact, my stepsister, someone I had never really had much of a relationship with.

"Bonnie…" I heard Mom say in a voice that sounded like it might break. "He's going today. He's going to pass away today."

She hung up and stared at me with a terrified look in her eyes. Before she had time to say anything, I knew she had changed her mind. I raced into the bedroom, but I knew it was too late the minute I saw my stepfather.

I was twenty-three and had never seen anyone die before. The sight that met me was awful. I'd had no idea that a person's bodily fluids seeped out like that, but that's what was happening to Lee. He was also making all kinds of strange noises, and I had to listen to them; I couldn't just walk away. The worst was the last rattling breath that filled the room just as Bonnie came rushing in with Mom right behind her.

Bonnie had clearly been nearby and had driven like a madwoman to make it in time. Seeing her father lying lifeless in front of her, his mouth open, she screamed.

In some kind of misguided attempt to comfort her, Mom started to explain what had happened, how the nurse had told us to increase the morphine to end Lee's suffering. Bonnie fell silent and stared at Mom as she continued, "So that's what Matt did."

Bonnie looked possessed as she turned to me and screamed, "You killed my dad!" In that moment, I realized she would never be able to see that I'd done her father a huge favor.

Later that day, I called my brother Mark and told him that Lee was dead. His spontaneous reaction was "good!"

Lee was a cheap man. No one liked him. I don't even know if Mom did. What I do know is that her kicking out my dad and marrying an asshole fundamentally shaped my view of women and the relationships I had with them. The anger and disappointment I felt about Mom and Dad often made me spiteful toward the women I lived with.

When Mom and I were left alone in the house later that day—you couldn't exactly count Lee as part of the family anymore, lying dead in the bedroom—I asked her, "So what happens with the funeral and everything?"

She had been staring straight ahead for quite some time, but she turned to me and said, "There won't be a funeral."

I gave her a questioning look.

"They're coming to collect him," Mom said.

"Who are?"

"They're just going to dump him in the sea."

"Mom, who's gonna dump him?"

They turned out to be a company called the Neptune Society. They arrived later that day, taking Lee away in their van. I asked one of the guys what was going to happen to my stepfather's body, and he said, "First we cremate him, then we take him out to sea in one of our boats and scatter his ashes in the waves." With that, the name of the company suddenly made sense.

As they wheeled Lee out on a gurney, loading him into the van, I couldn't help but think it felt odd that he wouldn't have a funeral, any kind of memorial, or anything—just into the crematorium and then straight into the sea.

As the van pulled away, a dog started barking in one of the neighbors' yards. I saw the man I had disliked so much—and whom I had more or less killed—disappear down the street, and that was it.

63

13

Tori

I start a band with Tori Amos and experience my first heartbreak in the reality of the music business.

THE EARLY-TO-MID 1980S SAW the arrival of the New Wave period in LA, with bands like the Plimsouls, the Knack, and 20/20 doing the rounds. The competition between musicians was brutal, and though I'd become a kind of local drummer people could call on, I had the nickname Matt the Mercenary: I really had to fight to bring in money. That's one of the reasons I couldn't have been happier when our Top 40 band Metro was lucky enough to become the house band at the Marriott by LAX.

We played there every night on a small stage in the hotel lounge, and though the audience might not always have been paying much attention to us—they couldn't care less what we played, in other words—it was a decent job in a comfortable environment.

One night, while we were taking a break after our set, I heard someone playing in the piano bar next door. It sounded incredible—the voice in particular—so I went in and saw a red-haired girl at the piano. She was playing a cover of a Bad Company song, and when she paused before the next song, I took the opportunity to go over to her.

"Who are you and where are you from?" I asked, completely astounded by her.

"My name's Tori, and I'm from Baltimore," she said.

"You sound great. You're amazing."

"Thanks." She smiled.

"Do you play with any other musicians?" I asked her.

She shook her head.

"I know some guys," I said. "We're gonna start a band, and I want you to come jam with us."

It was true that a few of us had talked about starting a band, but the plans had always been pretty loose—until I heard Tori, that is. I immediately thought about the guys. There was Brad Cobb, a bassist I'd met while I was on tour with Gregg Wright in Louisiana, and Steve Caton, a guitarist who was a kind of a Hollywood Robert Fripp and whom I'd seen play with a band called Skin. Brad and Steve were both the esoteric kind of musicians, and to my ears, Tori's style was like Kate Bush meets Peter Gabriel. I thought, *Those are the right guys for her.*

Two days later, I introduced Tori and Brad in a rehearsal room, and Steve Caton came down to listen. After playing for a while, I said, "I think this could be really great."

Tori seemed more doubtful. "Well, yeah..." she said. "But where do you think I fit in?"

"Do whatever you want," I told her, because I was convinced her talent could take us places.

We started rehearsing, and before long we were booked at clubs like Madame Wong's West on Wilshire Boulevard, and Madam Wong's East, in Chinatown. We called ourselves Y Kant Tori Read and were a pretty typical New Wave band both in terms of sound and style.

In those days, you couldn't carry a grand piano around with you, so Tori had a little keyboard. The only problem was that she was really scared of crowds—during the first few songs, at least. But as a rule, she generally relaxed and got over her stage fright, and toward the end of the gig she sometimes even left her keyboard and ran out into the crowd to grab people. She was very intense.

In any case, we were really banking on our music but earned hardly anything from the shows. Whenever one of us had no money, we would all share food. Other times, whoever had money would buy food for the rest of the band. Tori was unbelievably productive and wrote at least four or five songs a day. One morning, she called me up and asked me to come over to her place, a small cottage behind the church on Franklin Avenue in Hollywood. I thought she wanted me to listen to her new songs, but the minute we were sitting on her tiny couch in the room she used as both a living room and studio, she said, "Matt, I don't have any money. I'm broke."

I didn't really know what to say to that. It was hardly news that the guys in the band sometimes ran out of money, and I knew that Tori had no interest in doing any Top 40 gigs, so there weren't many other options. I shrugged slightly, at a loss.

"I got an offer to be in a Kellogg's cornflakes commercial."

"Don't do it," I said before she had even finished her sentence. Tori looked at me with a blank expression, and I continued, "It'll come back to haunt you. You're gonna be huge. You're gonna be famous."

"Yeah," she said, "but they said they'll pay me ten thousand dollars."

"So?"

But Tori had already made up her mind, and not long after, she did the Kellogg's commercial.

Around the same time as it aired on TV, we did a number of shows at a club called Sasch on Ventura Boulevard. Bands like Mr. Mister had gotten signed after playing there, and people from various record labels came down there to watch us too. It meant there was a certain sense of expectation in the band, and one night, a young guy came into our dressing room after the gig.

"Hey, I'm Jason," he said, greeting Tori first.

The guy was Jason Flom. He was in A&R at Atlantic Records and had relatively recently given Twisted Sister its big break. He said that he really liked us, and added with a smile, "So I wanna sign you to Atlantic."

I was the first to react: "Awesome!"

The others looked completely shocked, but once Jason had gone, the celebrations started. I finally, finally felt like all my hard work had paid off.

After that, the final two shows at Sasch went off without a hitch. We didn't have any more gigs booked, but it didn't bother me because I knew we would soon be making a record.

A week passed, then another, and I heard nothing from Tori or anyone else. I tried to call her, but she never answered. Things no longer felt so good, and it got much worse when a musician friend of mine told me that Tori was in the studio with a bunch of session musicians. I didn't understand what was going on, so I called Tori again. This time, she picked up. "Tori, what's going on?"

I heard her sigh, or take a deep breath before she answered. "Here's the thing. Atlantic wants to sign me, not the band."

"What are you talking about?" I said. "I'm the one who put the band together. I discovered you!" I remember feeling like I'd really been screwed over in that moment. "So that's it, you're taking the deal solo?"

There was another sigh down the line, and then she practically whispered. "Yeah."

"So what are you gonna call it?"

"Y Kant Tori Read."

"Fuck that, that's our band."

I hung up.

That betrayal genuinely broke my heart. I'd devoted almost two years to the band, but once the dream of making a record became a reality, Tori decided to do it with a bunch of studio musicians instead. It was a bitter lesson—but also a great reminder of just how the music business worked.

I tried to keep my thoughts away from Tori and the record, and after two months I had almost managed to forget about the whole thing. Then Tori called.

"I need you to come down here, Matt. It just doesn't feel right."

I knew right away that she meant the recording, and had a strong urge to say, *Yeah, tell me about it.* But I held my tongue, partly because I didn't want to sound bitter and partly because I could see an opportunity to turn things around in my favor. I thought, *For once, I'm going to make sure I get paid. This is when I finally learn how to negotiate.*

"How many songs do you want me to play?" I asked, as though it was any old job.

"The whole record."

I thought for a few seconds, and then I said, "Give me ten thousand dollars and I'll do it."

"Okay, I just need to speak to Jason," she said.

She called me back later that same day and said, "I've got the money."

I headed down to the studio and played drums on that record. The way it was recorded was really weird. I was hired as a studio musician in my own band, and the same applied to Steve, who also played on the album. Brad wasn't there, however; he had been replaced by a number of different bass players. I never saw Jason Flom down there at all, but I quickly realized that it had nothing to do with him being ashamed of his behavior.

Once we were done with the recording, I thanked everyone and picked up my check, and I never heard from Tori again.

14

Rock 'n' Roll Smuggler

*After being kicked out of two bands, I start
smuggling large quantities of cocaine to Hawaii.*

AROUND THIS TIME, THE whole New Wave thing started to lose ground
and rock made a comeback. I let my hair grow and started going to
auditions for various bands, all without much success. I actually missed
out on gigs for the simple reason that my hair wasn't long enough.

Still, one day I got a call from a guy named Geoff Lieb, who said
he had talked to a friend of mine, Pat Torpey (who later became the
drummer in Mr. Big). I knew Geoff a little and knew that he played
typical Sunset Strip rock. "I need a drummer for my new record," he
said. "Pat says you're awesome."

Geoff recorded and performed under the name Jeff Paris, and
the producer for his record was a British guy named Tony Platt,
who had worked with bands like AC/DC, Motörhead, and Cheap
Trick. It was my first experience with a real asshole producer. I once
touched the board in the control room, and he hit my hand and
yelled, "Don't you ever touch my console again, you wanker!"

In any case, one of the tracks on the record was called "Saturday
Nite," and I was also in the video, which meant I got to watch myself
on MTV's *Headbanger's Ball*. The song sucked, but I proudly told all
of my friends, "I'm gonna be on MTV."

We went on tour in autumn 1987, which meant I was on the
road with Geoff. Since we were sharing both our bus and crew with
another band, sixteen of us were on board.

Even then, I used to stay up all night talking to the driver. What little sleep I eventually got was on the floor of the bus, since all the bunks would already be taken by that time. Still, I didn't care, because Geoff had put together a really great band. Gary Moon was a part of it, for example; he would join Night Ranger just a few years later. The only problem was that Geoff was more of a songwriter than a rock star. He didn't know how to move around onstage, and I remember having to dress the guy because he had no style at all. On top of that, he was also a huge dick.

During one of our gigs, he shoved the keyboard player out of the way so that he would be more visible while he played a guitar solo. It could have looked cool, like he was saying, "I'm taking over now," but he pushed the guy so hard that he went flying. I was really pissed off about it when we left the stage that evening, and I told him, "That's the most unprofessional thing I've ever seen."

Geoff and I got into a fight, and he said, "Well, if you don't like it, you can go home."

"Okay," I said. "See ya!"

I was living at Geoff's house at the time, so I took my shit and moved over to Burbank to live in a warehouse that Gary from the band had told me about. There was no heating there, and I had to sleep on the floor in a tiny room. There was also no shower or kitchen, but the worst part was that I now also had no job. I tried selling drugs in West Hollywood, but I didn't have the right contacts there, and almost no one I knew ever had enough money to buy.

Then, one day, I bumped into my musician friend, Steve Caton, who had also left Tori by that point. He said, "I know a guy who just moved to LA and wants to start a band. And here's the best bit: he wants to pay people a salary."

I stared at him, not understanding a thing. Eventually, I managed to blurt out, "What? A salary?"

"Yeah, he'll pay us three hundred fifty bucks a week to be in his band, but we only have to play once a month."

"I'm in!" I said. "Where are we playing?"

"Mostly here in LA," he said.

It sounded too good to be true, but just a few days later I met the guy, who was named Bill, at a rehearsal space. He was a good-looking dude, and very charismatic. He also turned out to be a terrible singer. Still, what did that matter when he was offering us such generous terms? There was another benefit to working with Bill, which became clear between songs one day, as he went over to a huge boom box on the floor. He turned it around, pulled off the back panel, and grinned at me and Steve. We smiled too when we saw the plastic pouches of blow he had stashed inside.

The three of us sat down on the worn couch unit in one corner of the studio and each did a few lines. It was the best coke I had ever tried, and Bill seemed to have unrestricted access to it. He also drove a brand-new BMW and always had huge quantities of cash, but no job. To put it bluntly, it wasn't hard to figure out that Steve and I were being sponsored by a drug dealer.

After rehearsing for the third time, Bill turned to us as we were doing lines on the couch: "I thought we could call the band Question 16. I've booked us a studio to make a record, and I want you, Matt"— he turned to me—"to be the producer."

I had just bent down to do yet another line, and the shock almost made me blow it away. "What?" I said.

But Bill had clearly made up his mind, and a few weeks later we headed down to Baby-O Studios in Hollywood, in the conservative Hollywood Athletic Club. It was a great place, where bands like Kiss had recorded, and Bill was renting the biggest studio there.

We had access to it from midday on, and the first thing we did was head down to Bogie's Liquor Store to buy a ton of booze. We had a party after that, with girls and friends stopping by. The recording itself started midway through the party, and we kept at it until the small hours.

With every day that passed, we started recording later and later. At first, we had begun at two in the afternoon, but before long it was five, and not long after that it was eight in the evening. Eventually, we were pulling all-night shifts. I seem to recall that we continued like that for a long time, a month at least. We were mostly fucking around and didn't get much done. Often, when we got to the studio, we were convinced we had recorded a masterpiece the night before, but when we listened back it always sounded like crap, so we had no choice but to start over.

"You can come stay with me in Long Beach if you like," Bill said once we were finally finished and left the studio for the last time.

By that point, I was tired of living in the warehouse, unable to take a shower, so I moved into Bill's house on Second Street in Belmont Shore the very next day. It wasn't too far from LA, but far enough to be out of the loop. Still, plenty of people came over there to hang out with me and Bill, and the band often played at a couple of clubs in Long Beach. One of them was called Bogart's, and it was on Pacific Coast Highway. The other, Fender's Ballroom, hosted a whole load of bands I'd never heard of before. I explored that new music scene, and got increasingly fucked up on cocaine, which was more accessible to me than ever before.

One day, I opened the closet door in the hallway and saw a bucket with a lid inside. When I lifted the lid, I saw eight kilos of cocaine. One of them had been cut open, and I heard Bill's voice behind me: "Take as much as you want."

I bent down and picked up what looked like a white rock. It was the purest cocaine I had ever seen.

On several other occasions, I opened doors in that house and found myself staring at paving stone–sized blocks of cocaine wrapped in paper and marked "COLOMBIA" plus something in Spanish. There would often be an open pack on a table somewhere, with a small silver spoon pushed into the powder, ready for you to help yourself to as much as you liked.

One day, Bill turned to me and said, "Hey, man, do you wanna make a couple grand?"

"What do I have to do?"

"You just need to transport two kilos of this coke to Hawaii." He nodded toward the open closet doors.

"How am I meant to do that without getting busted?"

"You tape it to your body and board the plane like normal."

I thought about it for a few seconds—a.k.a. no time at all—and said, "I'm in!"

A few days later, we opened one of his two-kilo packs and then repacked it all into smaller pouches that we taped to my body. Once that was done, I put on an exercise belt to hold everything in place. I then pulled on a large shirt and jacket over the top. We went through everything in minute detail, and Bill said, "No taking any of it out to do a line in the airport bathroom, because if anyone sees that you're high, you're screwed."

Naturally, I was nervous as hell when the time came. I remember I had a surfboard with me so that I looked like a real surfer.

Back then, the security checks weren't anything like they are now, so in principle all I had to do was walk straight through and board the plane. Though it felt like the longest five hours of my life, I managed to keep myself relatively calm.

When I got to Honolulu, I followed Bill's instructions and checked in at the Waikiki Hilton. The minute I got into my room I did a line to compose myself. I had been given permission to take a quarter of an ounce for my own use—strictly speaking, it was part of my payment. Then I waited, and waited, to do the drop. Eventually, I heard a knock at the door. Standing outside was an ugly Asian dude with an acne-scarred face. He stepped inside without saying a word, and I handed him the bags, which he weighed on a small set of scales he had brought with him. He stashed everything in a silver briefcase and handed me a few stacks of $100 bills, which I used the scales to weigh rather than counting them. Each bill weighs one gram, so it's easy to do the math.

The bills amounted to my pickup of $25,000, which I then put into the hotel safe. The Asian dude's ugly face broke into a smile. "First work—then pleasure," he said.

For a moment, I didn't know what he meant. Or rather, I was completely paralyzed with nerves, because I didn't know this guy and had no idea what he was capable of. All I knew about him was that he was a high-ranking dealer of some kind. But it turned out he wanted to take me to a special nightclub that night, and since I wasn't flying back to LA for another two days, I couldn't say no.

The club, called the Wave, was in Waikiki. I quickly realized that this was where all the local party people hung out. I also noticed that my pockmarked friend had no problem getting hot young girls to follow him around. No doubt they were there for the coke. I took a couple of girls back to the hotel with me both that night and the next; we had sex, I got a few hours' sleep, and then I went down to the tanning salon next to the hotel to work on my tan before heading to the airport. I didn't want to raise any suspicions by looking too pale.

I flew back to LA with the money taped to my body, just like the drugs had been, and handed it over to Bill when I got home. He gave me my share, and I was pretty happy with it—despite the obvious risks I had taken.

I did another five or six smuggling trips to Hawaii after that, following roughly the same pattern as the first time; I was still happy with my payment and continued to have fun in Honolulu. The real problem was the very thing I was smuggling: I could do as much coke as I wanted, and since the quality was so good, I took far too much and became totally paranoid to boot. So when I got home after the sixth or seventh trip, I was completely convinced I was being followed and bugged by the police.

"Bill," I said, cautiously peering out through the living room window, "I can't do this anymore. I know they're onto us."

"Bah," he said, counting money and stacking the bills into neat piles on the coffee table. "You're just paranoid."

"I swear," I said, feeling my blood drum in my temples and beads of sweat on my forehead. "I know they're tailing me. I've been over there too many times."

"So you don't wanna do another run?" Bill said.

"No." I shook my head and peered nervously outside again.

Another guy was living with us at the time, Dave, and he was basically Bill's right-hand man, though he wasn't the sharpest. In any case, when he heard us talking, he offered to do the next run, setting off two days later. The police were waiting for him when he landed, and he was given twenty years in prison.

With Dave being arrested, I quickly realized that he could easily rat us out. Bill had come to the same conclusion, so we moved into his girlfriend's house instead. That's where everything really started to spiral out of control. A few days after moving in, I was looking for Bill, and eventually found him in the garage. He had a piece of aluminum foil in one hand, a lighter in the other, and a small straw in his mouth. I asked what he was doing.

"Oh, just smoking a little something."

"Wow," I said.

"You wanna try?"

"What is it?"

"Heroin," he replied.

"Wow," I said again, but I tried it all the same.

I'd heard that people generally feel ill after their first time, but that's not how it was for me at all. I was completely euphoric and thought that I got the whole point of it, so I continued smoking heroin with Bill. Despite that, I had a huge amount of respect for the drug—maybe because I knew that this shit was too good. I felt like I could handle coke, but heroin was a completely different beast, and I could tell that Bill was really getting into it.

All of a sudden, Long Beach felt more like a one-way street than anything, and I realized I had to get out. As luck would have it, that was when Pat Torpey (the same guy who had gotten me the job with Jeff Paris) called and said, "The Cult need a new drummer, and I recommended you.

15

The Audition

I do what I can to blend in among the deadly serious Brits.

I HAD BEEN LIVING with Bill for almost a year and a half by the time
I returned to LA. Still, I didn't make it any farther than the record
store in my old neighborhood before I bumped into more musician
friends who said they had recommended me to The Cult.

I don't remember whom I was staying with back then. I also
have no idea whether I contacted the band or they contacted me,
but I do know that we agreed I would go over to their rehearsal
space at Mates Studios in the Valley the very next week.

I also know that I was determined to get the job, and I listened to
The Cult's earlier stuff from dawn until dusk in order to memorize
it. I even listened to their first EP, recorded when they were still
known as Death Cult.

I spent quite a lot of time thinking about my appearance too.
The look on Sunset Strip at the time was all skinny jeans with
cowboy boots. The Cult were more sophisticated than that, dressed
in black and with biker boots, so that's how I dressed on the morning
I headed to their studio. I even fixed my hair—straightened it a little
to blend in. When I arrived at Mates in North Hollywood an hour
later, I felt completely prepared.

We had agreed to meet in Studio A, so I immediately started
carrying my big double bass kit inside. Only Billy Duffy and
Jamie Stewart were there at the time—there was no sign of Ian
Astbury.

They came over and said hello to me, and Billy gave my drums a skeptical glance and said,

"What's with the other drum?" I looked down at the bass drum, but didn't have time to reply before Billy continued, "Definitely no double bass."

A few years earlier, I had auditioned for David Lee Roth and lost out on the gig because I didn't play double bass. (This was right after he left Van Halen.) So after that, I had really gone in for learning how to play that way. But here, it was just a case of taking the bass drum away. We played a couple songs. It felt good, and after we finished Billy turned to me and said, "Sounds good, mate. Sounds really good."

Jamie gave him an approving nod.

"When will I know if I got the gig?" I asked.

"Ian will be back in about two weeks," Billy said, "so we'll do one more rehearsal to get his approval. But just between us, you've got the gig."

Obviously that sounded hopeful, but when my friends asked how it had gone, I gave vague answers. I didn't want to jinx it by saying anything before I had signed on the dotted line. I wanted everything to be right first.

Another two weeks passed before Ian returned from London, and I was asked to go to another rehearsal studio in the Valley. I felt a little tense, of course, because everything now hung on what Ian thought.

He still hadn't arrived when I got to the studio. Just like the time before, Billy and Jamie were the only ones there. I said hello to them and then went and sat behind my drums to wait. After half an hour or so, Ian showed up. Like the rock star he was, he was in full regalia: black flares, a black hat decorated with a skull, sunglasses, and a huge silver cross hanging from a thick chain around his neck. He glanced at me but didn't say a word, and I thought, *Uh-oh...*

Next thing I knew, we had kicked into "Fire Woman," following it up with "Sweet Soul Sister" and "Wildflower." Once we had played "Lil' Devil" too, Ian turned to me.

"You've got the gig, but stop smiling so much."

16

The Cult

*I meet Steven Tyler and Tommy Lee, blow two weeks' wages,
and eat Jason Newsted's crab legs.*

ONCE I HAD IAN's blessing, it wasn't long before I found myself being
called into Howard Kaufman's office. Howard was the legendary
manager of bands like Aerosmith and Def Leppard, and at that time
he also looked after The Cult.

His management company was called HK Management, and its
offices were in Universal City at the time. A cute blonde receptionist
welcomed me in and showed me into a conference room. I had to sit
and wait for a pretty long time, but eventually a guy who was only a
few years older than me came into the room.

He introduced himself as Jimmy. I'd later find out that he was
Howard's right-hand man. Since I didn't have much experience with
that kind of meeting, I didn't really know what to expect from the
conversation. Jimmy began by saying, "So…we're gonna give you
fifteen hundred bucks a week."

I felt a flutter in my chest. It was like I'd just won the lottery.
Jimmy continued, "We're gonna fix it so you have Yamaha drums
too. Just let us know what sizes you want."

At that point, I really should have shown him some kind of poker
face, but instead I broke into the biggest grin and heard myself say,
"That's awesome!"

A few days later, I packed up all of my possessions into
one suitcase and set out on the road with The Cult, supporting

Metallica on their "And Justice for All" tour. Our first show was in Vancouver. That's where all the bands were in those days, because of producer Bob Rock. Mötley Crüe, Bon Jovi, and Aerosmith had all recorded their latest albums with him at Vancouver's Little Mountain Studios.

We were staying at Le Meridien, which was a sweet hotel even then, and arrived the night before the show. I'd never toured at that level before, so everything felt new and exciting, even something like the guys from the band checking in under fake names. I remember I picked "Dr. Lingus" for myself, a name I would go on to use for many years to come.

Before she handed me my room key, the girl at the front desk asked, "Do you have a credit card?"

"No, I don't," I said, because I hadn't owned a credit card in my life.

The girl frowned then, and said, "In that case, I can't give you the key to the minibar."

"Okay," I said with a shrug, simultaneously wondering how I was going to open it without one.

As it happened, a screwdriver worked perfectly. When I got to my room not long after that, I undid the screws on the back of the little refrigerator and grabbed all the tiny bottles of vodka from inside. I downed them, refilled them with water, and put them back.

A while later, we went out to a cool rock club farther down the street. I think its name was Metro. When that place closed in the early hours, a whole load of people followed me back to my room at the hotel.

I was really drunk, which might be the main reason my imagination ran wild. My room was on the tenth floor, and as I looked at the four pillows on my bed, I suddenly found myself wondering what it would look like if their insides fell to the ground.

Next thing I knew, that thought had become reality. I opened the windows and yelled, "Let's see how many feathers are in these pillows!" Then I sliced them open one by one and shook out the feathers, making them swirl around like snowflakes in the night.

I woke the next morning to someone pounding on the door. I was still fully dressed, but everyone who had come back to my room was gone. I struggled to my feet and went to open the door.

Two guys from hotel security were outside. They peered behind me and saw the feathers all over the room.

"Mr. Lingus," one of them said firmly, "please look out of the window."

I did as he said, and saw that the entire pool down below was covered in feathers. The hotel manager came into my room and said, "We're going to have to charge you for this."

That was when they noticed that the minibar was broken. They took $400 from my fee to pay for the pillows and $1,200 to clean up the street and the pool. And then there was the damaged minibar. Somehow, I'd managed to blow two weeks' wages before I even stepped onstage with the band. When I met the other guys in the lobby later that day, they laughed so hard that they cried, and I couldn't help but join in.

We traveled out to the Pacific National Exhibition (PNE), where we were due to play. Oddly enough, I don't remember being especially nervous. What I do remember is that Tommy Lee and Steven Tyler were hanging out backstage when we got to the arena. It was the first time I had met either of them, and when Steven came over to introduce himself, I heard myself say, "Hey, I saw you guys play when I was fourteen."

Steven just stared at me and said, "Thanks for making me feel old." Those words put an immediate end to any further conversation.

The whole backstage thing was new to me, and what fascinated me most was that there was always so much food and drink available. I almost felt like I was in heaven, and when I got up onstage I must have been a little nervous after all, because our set felt like it went at double speed. Afterward, I could barely process what I had just done.

Tommy Lee was the first person to speak to me after I left the stage, and he said, "That was awesome! I love your band!"

Metallica started playing soon after that, and Tommy and I hung around one side of the stage, watching them. After a few songs, he shook his head and said, "I don't get it at all." He meant their music.

We were booked to play shows all over Canada, and we left the next day for Edmonton, followed by a gig in Calgary. No matter where we were, I went out on the town and invited people to our shows—not just girls, but random guys too. If I saw a couple of young people in town, I would go straight over to them and ask if they wanted to be on the guest list. They would always say, "Are you in the band?"

"Yeah, I'm in The Cult," I proudly replied.

"No way!"

"So you wanna come to the show?"

It meant that I had a guest list of ten, sometimes twenty people every single night. The other guys in the band couldn't understand it. "How come you know people everywhere?" they asked. But the thing was, I just liked making people happy.

Throughout the tour, we had two buses. Billy traveled in one and Ian in the other. Those guys really didn't get along.

Ian and I, on the other hand, got along very well and started drinking together a lot. The truth is, our bus was one constant party.

On the whole, I got along well with the entire band. They liked me, aside from my Californian sense of humor. They were really British in that respect.

Before we crossed the border back into the United States, I noticed that Lars Ulrich had started to watch me play from the side of the stage. I played pretty straightforwardly with The Cult, but every time I did a little fill, he asked me afterward how I'd done it, and after our last show in Canada he invited me over to Metallica's dressing room.

The first thing I noticed when I arrived was the insane amount of food and booze. There was always plenty in The Cult's dressing room, too, but Metallica had everything you could ever want in there, and my eyes immediately focused on some crab legs.

Lars, James Hetfield, and Kirk Hammett were in the dressing room; I had no idea where Jason Newsted was. Lars was looking at me, and I said, "These crab legs look great."

"Yeah, have 'em," he said, and James joined in: "Yeah, go for it."

So I sat down with the band and started to eat the crab legs. There wasn't a single one left by the time I was finished.

Suddenly, Jason came in, and the instant he saw me he yelled, "No fucking way! You ate my fucking crab legs?!"

James and Lars glanced at one another and grinned, and I didn't know what to say. I mean, they were hazing him. They gave him shit and wound him up all the time.

17

Fight Fire with Fire!

Ian tries to shit on the floor in my hotel room,
and I manage to set off the fire alarm.

SINCE IAN AND BILLY were mainly drinkers, I'd cut down my consumption of blow since I joined the band. We didn't know one another yet, and I didn't want to seem like I wasn't serious. The fact we didn't know each other also meant that I didn't know what to think after our gig in Cedar Rapids when Billy came up to me and said, "Whatever you do, Matt, don't let Ian into your room after one in the morning."

I looked at Billy and smiled, the way you do when you think someone is just messing with you. But Billy looked dead serious.

A couple of hours later, I was on the phone to my brother in my room; I was wearing underpants and a wifebeater when I suddenly heard someone roar in the corridor outside. Next, I heard loud knocking on one of the doors. The people inside clearly didn't answer, because the banging moved on to the next door, then the one after that. Eventually, the madman was at my door, practically kicking it down. He roared, "Let me in, you fucking wanker!"

"Hold on," I said to Mark. "I gotta get the door."

I put down the phone and went over to the door. I opened it—Ian was outside. He had a kind of crazy look in his eyes, and before I had time to say anything he had pushed past me and started to break everything in his path. Paintings and bedside lamps were ripped down and smashed on the floor. Chairs and tables were destroyed. Shards of glass and fragments of wood were literally flying through the air around him.

I was overwhelmed, of course, but eventually managed to get some air in my lungs and shouted, "Hey, what the fuck?!"

It was like Ian was in a trance, and he grabbed the broken lights from the floor and threw them out the window. Next thing I knew, he had the bed on its side and was tearing off the sheets.

They disappeared out of the window too.

I picked up the phone and said, "Mark, I'll call you back."

Ian was suddenly standing still, flicking through a glossy magazine. He spotted something, and when he turned the page slightly I saw that it was a whole-page portrait of a well-dressed man.

He put the magazine on the floor, open, and started to unbutton his pants. They dropped, along with his underwear, and he crouched down. He quickly looked up at me and yelled, "I'm gonna shit on this man! I hate the way he looks."

"Oh, no!" I shouted back. "You're not gonna shit in my room."

In a panic, I ran out into the corridor. I spotted a fire extinguisher in a cabinet, tore open the little glass door, and hurried back to my room with the canister under my arm. Ian was straining over the open magazine, his face crumpled.

"Don't you dare shit in here!" I shouted, pointing to him with the nozzle of the extinguisher.

"I'm gonna shit on this wanker!" Ian roared back, straining even harder.

"Don't do it!" I squeezed the handle on the extinguisher, and white powder sprayed all over Ian.

It was in his hair, his mouth, his eyes, everywhere.

"*Aaaaahh*...I'm blind!" he roared, waving his arms as he squatted with his pants down.

The next thing I knew there was a sharp, robotic, prerecorded woman's voice coming from the little speaker up by the ceiling: "Fire on the sixth floor. Please evacuate."

Both Ian and I froze, and he quickly pulled up his pants as he tried to rub the powder from his eyes.

I rushed over to the door and peered out through the peephole. The corridor had filled up with guests in no time, all wearing bathrobes and hurrying toward the stairwell in a line.

Ian pushed past me and looked out into the corridor. "Shit," he whispered. "What're we gonna do?"

Rather than reply, I rushed toward the closet and grabbed the two bathrobes from their hangers. I tossed one to Ian. He immediately knew what I was thinking, and we threw them on, brushed the powder from his hair, snuck out into the corridor, and joined the stream of people. We tried to look as innocent as possible as we followed the others down the stairs and through the lobby, and the minute we got outside Ian whispered to me, "Quick, let's hide!"

We managed to sneak over to the tour bus without being seen, each fetched a beer from the refrigerator, and then sat drinking and listening to the commotion and the sound of sirens from the emergency vehicles outside. People soon began to shout for us, and we realized we had no choice but to confess.

When we eventually crept out of our hiding place, we were quickly faced with the fire marshal. "Hmm," he sighed, looking us up and down before opening his black imitation leather briefcase. "This is going to cost you a pretty penny, guys." He was right about that—ten grand, to be precise. Since the tour had just begun, I had to hand over everything I'd earned so far.

But when I shouted at Ian, he just moaned that I'd ruined his eyes. "You fuckin' blinded me!"

I shook my head in irritation, but the next morning he did actually have to go to the hospital—it turned out the powder in the extinguisher had damaged his cornea. When he came back to sound check, he had a patch over one eye.

18

Family Gathering in Minneapolis

Dad, my cousins, and even Aunt Dale start to realize exactly what I do.

I HADN'T HAD A whole lot of contact with Dad since I was a teenager, but as we approached his old stomping grounds in Minnesota, I got a sudden urge to call him.

He knew I was a drummer and that was how I made my living, but he'd never bothered to find out whether I had any talent for it—just like he'd never really bothered to ask what I wanted to be when I grew up. As far as I could remember, he had only seen me play twice. The first was when I was fourteen and did a gig with Prophecy; the second was years later, when I had a Top 40 gig at some place in Orange County. He came over from Norwalk, where he lived at the time, and had my younger half-brother Dave Jr. with him—whom I'd never met before. It was a really odd experience.

A few days before our show in Minneapolis, I called him from a pay phone on the road. "Hey, Dad," I said. "I'm coming to Minnesota. I'm with a band now, they're called The Cult."

He had no idea who The Cult were, of course; my mom didn't either. When I told her about my new job, she said, "The Coo? What does that mean?"

"No, Mom, The Cult."

But then I told Dad, "I'm playing the Met Center."

"The Met Center? You mean *the* Met Center?"

"Yeah, Dad. The Met Center."

"But that's an arena. It's a really big place, isn't it?"

"Yeah, it is."

"I want to bring your Aunt Dale," he said then.

Dale must have been almost eighty, so I explained to Dad that our gigs could be pretty loud, but he just said he'd bring some earplugs for her.

We chatted for a while longer, and by the time the call ended, I'd also invited my aunt Karen, my cousins Zibby and Amy, plus a couple other relatives. There were eight of them in total, and I'll never forget Dad arriving at the arena that June evening, at the head of their little gang. I met them by the backstage entrance, and they all seemed a little unsure and expectant—happy to see me all the same, and I was really happy to see them too. I'd always liked Dad's side of the family; they were so down-to-earth and genuine, pretty much the opposite of everyone in Hollywood.

When we went backstage, the first thing Dad saw were the cases for my drums. There were huge white letters on each of them reading MATT SORUM, THE CULT. Dad practically stopped dead and said, "Oh."

My aunts and cousins were chatting more and more; they were relaxed and thought the whole thing was really exciting. Old Aunt Dale in particular seemed invigorated and curious about everything awaiting her. I noticed that she'd dressed up a little for the occasion.

From where we were standing, we could see that the arena had started to fill up with people. The Met Center held fifteen thousand, and the gig was sold out. Dad suddenly started talking again.

"Are all these people here to see you?" he asked.

"Yeah," I said. "Partly. Metallica's headlining."

"Who?"

I explained that they were a big band and that we were the supporting act.

He looked out at the crowd and said, "Wow, that's a lot of people."

We still had a while before the show was due to start, so I took the whole gang down to our dressing room. There was nothing special about the room; other than a couple of couches and a low coffee table, there wasn't much inside. On a slender table by the entrance were some drinks, snacks, and fruit in a huge glass bowl.

"Wow, is this your dressing room?"

"Yeah," I said, not quite understanding why he was so impressed.

I could see that the others thought it was all pretty cool too. It was like they had only just put two and two together and realized what I actually did—where I was in my life and career. Dad in particular seemed taken aback, and though he tried to be subtle about it, I noticed him glancing at me with a look of genuine surprise, as though he was thinking, *Is* my *son really a* star?!

Dad, whom I'd barely seen in years, suddenly started calling me all the time, wanting to hang out with me in every possible and impossible scenario and to come to our gigs.

The amount of effort he put into seeing me was like he was now my biggest fan. After all my boyhood years of pining for my father and not having him around, I would take what I could get at this point in my life. I liked having him around. Now it was my turn to show my Dad the great adventure I was on. Like I dreamed about from his postcards when I was a boy. He was actually a bigger troublemaker than me. We drank a lot together, and he was quite the charmer with the ladies. Like father, like son.

19

Me and Lars

I manage to piss off Billy and Ian and organize it so Metallica get laid.

METALLICA'S FANS WERE ALMOST exclusively guys, but we always had quite a few girls at our shows. On tour, it's the roadies' job to get girls for the band once the stage is ready, but for Metallica's roadies, that was a near-impossible task. Billy and I, on the other hand, had no trouble finding girls. Ian had brought his girlfriend on tour, and Jamie—our bassist—was married and unshakably faithful to his wife. It meant Billy and I were the dogs in the band. I used to go out into the crowd after our set. If the girls had black hair and red lips, you knew they were Cult fans, and I often had a dozen or so of them backstage with me.

Someone who noticed this early on was Lars Ulrich, and one evening right after a gig in Minneapolis, he pulled me to one side and said, "Matt, you can stay, right? We'll party?"

Lars and I had become friends by this point. He often invited me to Metallica's dressing room, which bothered my bandmates.

"So you're going over there again, are you?" they muttered. "Fucking traitor."

I glanced over at Ian and Billy, who were having one last beer backstage before it was time to clear out. We generally had to travel overnight to make it to the next location in time for sound check the next day. "I don't know, we're about to leave," I said, noticing that Billy had cast a disapproving glance in our direction.

"Come on, you can hang with us in our plane," Lars said, boxing my shoulder a little. "We'll fly you to the next show."

I hesitated, because I could just imagine how Ian, Billy, and Jamie would react. All the same, it was too good an offer for me to turn down. "Okay," I said to Lars, almost feeling like I'd decided to cheat on my girlfriend.

Not long after that, I went over to our tour manager and explained what was happening. "I'm flying to the next place with Metallica. You don't need to worry, I'll be at sound check tomorrow." He gave me an incredibly skeptical look but said nothing, just nodded.

I hung out in Metallica's dressing room after that, while my own bandmates set off on a twelve-hour bus ride through farm country and dead small towns. Still, if I had a bad conscience about it, that vanished pretty quickly, because the Metallica guys and I had a great time that night. The girls I found for them were hugely appreciated, of course, and the appreciation was entirely mutual. These were your typical small-town girls, and for them it was the biggest thing to ever happen.

The morning after, it was time to head to the airport and fly on to the next place. I have to admit that I felt far more like a rock star on that plane with Metallica than I ever did in the bus with The Cult. Metallica didn't even have to worry about making sound check; they had a so-called crew band to do the check for them—guitar technicians, drum technicians, and so on. I, on the other hand, had to get straight to the arena the minute we landed.

I hadn't heard a thing from the guys since the previous night, but I could feel the bad vibes the minute I set foot onstage. I wasn't late, but all three were already waiting, and they didn't exactly greet me with happy faces or shouts. In fact, both Ian and Billy deliberately avoided looking in my direction.

Yes, I'd known it might be tough, but their behavior still made me uncomfortable, and I realized it would be a while before they forgave me. I turned around to sit down at the drums, but stopped dead when I saw the enormous rubber chicken they'd put on the stool behind the kit.

I heard Jamie laughing behind my back, then saying in an affected voice, "Ooooh, friends with Lars."

A few days later, Billy and I were at a bar together, and I'll never forget what he said to me. "I don't think it's a good idea for you to take that plane again. Better to stick with us in the band, okay?"

"Sure," I said, "but is it okay if I go over to their dressing room to chat sometimes?"

"Nah," he said. "I think it'd be better if you didn't."

20

The Goldfish Sory, Part I

Ian and Renee start a family, and I meet Axl for the first time.

IT WAS NOW JULY, and we were doing an outdoor gig somewhere north of New York City. I remember we went out onstage early in the afternoon, and the sun was really beating down. Between two songs, I quickly bent down to grab one of the bottles of Corona I always kept to the side of the drums, and out of the corner of one eye noticed something come flying toward me.

Whatever it was landed with a thud, just a few inches from my beers. I realized that it was a plastic bag filled with water, and that there was an obviously shaken and terrified little goldfish swimming around inside. *That's weird*, I thought, pulling the bag over with my drumstick so none of the others accidentally stood on it.

Once the gig was done, I took the bag backstage with me. The first person I ran into was Renee, Ian's girlfriend.

"What's that you've got?" she asked.

"A goldfish," I told her, holding up the bag.

"Ahh," Renee squealed (she was cute and young and often squealed). "Let me have it!"

I handed her the bag and, once we were back on the bus not long after, I could hear Renee's high-pitched voice: "Oh, Ian, we've gotta get a fish tank for the fish."

Ian and Renee slept in the back lounge on the bus, while the rest of us slept in the bunks. I heard Ian's much lower voice: "Okay, we'll sort something out."

A few minutes later, he had asked one of the crew to find something to put the fish in. Half an hour or so after that, the guy came back—drenched in sweat. He wasn't carrying a goldfish bowl, like you might have imagined, but an enormous tank.

Renee was delighted and rushed off to buy some "nice things" for the goldfish to look at as it swam around its new oversized home. I had to help carry the tank (it weighed a ton) to a shelf at the back of the bus, strapping it into place so it was somewhat secure.

Renee was soon back from the same pet shop the aquarium had come from, and she filled the bottom with small round stones. She spread out the other things she'd bought: an underwater rock, a treasure chest, colorful corals and shells.

We filled the tank with water, and once that was done Renee told us all to gather in a semicircle around it. She held up the plastic bag with both hands, glanced at us, and solemnly announced, "I name thee Lennon." She quickly emptied the bag into the aquarium, and the little goldfish found itself swimming around, as confused as it had been onstage.

When we finally got on the road, we realized that a tour bus might not be the best place for a huge aquarium. The water sloshed about so much that it spilled onto the floor, leaving little puddles everywhere—not that Renee cared. She just seemed happy that she'd been able to make a safe, beautiful world for her new pet.

But give me an example of happiness that lasts. Not long after, she suddenly came running to the front of the bus where we were drinking beer and chilling out.

"I think Lennon's freezing," she said, her little face so worried it was practically crumpled. "He's not well. We need to turn off the AC." The minute she finished, she rushed off back the way she'd come.

Billy and I exchanged a dubious glance, not really knowing what to think. But then Ian said, "Right, boys. We do as she says."

The sun was still beating down on the black asphalt and the metal roof of the bus. But before we had time to argue, Ian had vanished, and next thing we knew the dull hum of the AC had fallen quiet.

"Fuck that woman," Jamie muttered.

"What's she need that goddamn fish for?" Billy asked.

I kept quiet because Ian had come back.

It didn't take long for the temperature to rise inside the bus, quickly reaching eighty degrees.

"Come on, Ian, turn the AC back on," Jamie panted, sweating out his beer as quickly as he was drinking it.

But Ian wouldn't budge. Apparently it was more important to make the fish comfortable than ensure the band survived until their next gig.

That was when Renee came running back out to us.

"Lennon's not swimming anymore!" she shouted, looking upset. "He's just floating around on the surface. Ian, you have to do something!"

We were driving through Poughkeepsie at the time, and Ian told the driver to pull over. He followed Renee to the back of the bus. A few minutes later, they both returned, this time with the goldfish in a jar of water.

"We need to try to find a vet," Ian shouted to us before they left the bus.

Jamie, Billy, and I just looked at one another. We left the bus too, heading into an air-conditioned diner to wait for them. I called Lars.

"Dude, you won't fucking believe what's happening." I told him the entire story.

"What?!" he shouted back.

"Yeah, they took it to the vet. More precisely—they took Lennon to the vet."

It was only after I insisted for a second time that I wasn't making it all up that he believed me.

We must've sat in that diner for two hours before we saw Ian and Renee walking back to the bus. Sure enough, they'd found a veterinarian who had given them some kind of medicine for

94

Lennon—and the little fish was now swimming around his tank again, albeit with slightly listless movements.

It meant we could get back on the road to New York City and our hotel, the Mayflower by Central Park. I'd never stayed there before, and the first person I saw as we stepped into the lobby was Sean Penn. Next thing I knew, Robert De Niro strolled past, and I saw Nick Nolte sipping a drink at the bar. The Mayflower was a typical rock 'n' roll hotel—even in the sense that anything seemed possible. As I handed my bags to the doorman, he whispered, "You know, anything you need…just call down and say you need another bag."

Ian and I headed to the bar, but we'd barely been served our drinks before Renee came running with a handkerchief in her outstretched hand.

"He's dead!" she shouted before bursting into tears. She seemed inconsolable.

I craned my neck a little and saw that Lennon really had given up the ghost this time.

"Oh, I'm sorry, darling," Ian said, stroking his tearful girlfriend's arm. It didn't make the slightest bit of difference, of course.

"I want to bury him in Strawberry Fields!" Renee sniffed.

"Of course, darling," Ian said, as though it was the most natural request he'd ever heard. Next thing I knew, the two of them were heading out into the summer's evening to bury the goldfish at John Lennon's memorial in Central Park.

Later that evening, Ian called me in my room, where I was drinking and watching TV. "Hey, Axl's gonna swing by and pick us up."

"Axl…Rose?"

"Yeah, see you in five."

I had never met Axl before, even though we moved in the same circles in Hollywood. Anyway, in the elevator a few minutes later, Ian explained that Axl and Izzy Stradlin were in New York to find inspiration for Guns N' Roses' second record.

Because the Mayflower attracted a certain type of person, there was constantly a feeling that seedy stuff was going on. It's why

I probably shouldn't have been surprised to see Christopher Walken the minute Ian, Jamie, and I left the elevator. He was just standing in the lobby, and he flashed me a smile as we passed him on our way to the limo waiting out front.

The suit-clad driver opened one of the rear doors, and there was Axl Rose. What immediately struck me is that he genuinely did have a rock star aura around him. He was super skinny and dressed in full regalia, with the bandana and everything. But before I had time to say hey, I heard an unmistakable voice behind me.

"Hey, where are you guys going?" It was Christopher.

"We're gonna hit up the Scrap Bar in the East Village," said Axl.

"Can I catch a ride?" Christopher asked.

Shortly afterward, I found myself sitting in that limo with such unlikely company that it took me a while to shake the feeling of being in a Federico Fellini film. Aside from Ian, Jamie, Christopher, Axl, and me, Izzy Stradlin was also there, sitting diagonally opposite me. If Axl was the obvious star, Izzy was the definition of cool. He was sitting quietly, smoking, and watching life on the street.

"So how're things going?" Ian asked, looking at Axl.

"Well, you know, we're working on the next album," Axl said with a quick glance at Izzy, who hadn't said a word and also didn't seem to give a damn about the conversation. "But I'm also seriously thinking about funding the Nicaraguan army and arming my own militia. You know what the situation's like for the people and the government down there."

I just looked at Axl and thought, *What the fuck is he talking about?*

"Wow, that sounds great," Ian said, genuinely looking impressed.

Axl nodded, his face serious. Izzy still didn't speak.

We reached the Scrap Bar, which was in a pretty rough neighborhood. For some reason, Christopher didn't want to come in with us. Maybe he had somewhere else to be. In any case, he started walking down the street, held his hand up in goodbye, and shouted back to us, "See you later, guys!"

I looked at the brownstone in front of us and wondered how you got inside. Axl took charge and led us down a staircase and through a basement entrance, and I quickly realized that *everyone* inside was wearing leather. They all looked like they listened to punk rock and Motörhead. The downside was obviously that the girls weren't all that attractive. At most there were a couple who looked okay. We sat down, chatted, and drank, and before any of us knew what had happened, it was four in the morning.

"What're we doing now?" Axl asked.

"I wanna jam!" said Izzy.

Not long after that, we left the Scrap Bar for another place called the Loft, where Izzy, Axl, Ian, Jamie, and I started jamming almost straight away. We kept drinking, and the hours ran away from us. When I next checked the time, it was ten fifteen. It was already morning, in other words, and I remembered something I should've thought about a long time before.

"Fuck!" I shouted. "We have a photo shoot in Central Park at noon!"

I looked around but couldn't see Ian anywhere. Jamie had bailed a few hours earlier to head back to the hotel, but Ian and I had kept drinking, like usual—only now he was gone.

"You seen Ian?" I asked Axl, who was deep in conversation with a guy with a dark beard I didn't recognize.

Axl shook his head.

"Fuck," I said, getting up and rushing out through the nearest doorway.

The bright daylight blinded me, and it took me a few seconds to realize that I was in the alley behind the Loft. I spotted Ian's boots sticking out from behind an overflowing dumpster.

I rushed over and saw Ian lying on the ground with his cowboy hat beside him and puke all over his T-shirt. At first, I thought he was dead, but when I got onto my knees and shook him, a horrible rattle came from his mouth and his eyes twitched slightly. I was absolutely wasted myself, but still nowhere close to Ian.

I shook him harder and shouted, "Ian, we've gotta go! We have a photo shoot at noon! And then we have a show tonight!"

He was moving a little by then, and mumbled something inaudible. I grabbed him under the arms and dragged him onto his feet. Ian's eyes were two small holes, and he swayed like he was about to collapse at any minute. Despite that, I somehow managed to get him out of the alley and into a taxi, which took us back to the hotel, where the staff told us the others had already left. After a quick trip to the bathroom, where I splashed cold water onto our faces, we staggered back out and into the park on the other side of the road. It took us a while to find them, but Ian eventually spotted the guys on top of a small hill.

Even from a distance, it was clear from their body language that they'd been waiting for us, and as we came closer, I saw Billy's expression change from relief to alarm to anger in just a few short seconds.

21

The Goldfish Story, Part II

Ian goes off the rails, and I get my revenge on Renee.

THE PROBLEM WITH IAN was that he started to destroy himself around this time. There he was, performing for huge crowds every night as the front man in one of the world's coolest bands. Our new album, *Sonic Temple*, had made it into the Top 10 on the *Billboard* charts, selling better than any Cult album before it, and the single "Fire Woman" also did well around the world. The band was on the verge of being really big, in other words, but Ian's drinking was out of control, and he'd put on a load of weight. It affected his voice too. Things were so bad that he even asked me to sing his parts on certain songs.

"Oh man, could you sing the high harmonies?" he said to me. "I'll go low."

I had no problem doing it, because in a band you step up for one another. But we had a singer who seemed to have lost interest in performing. That, in turn, caused a lot of friction between Ian and Billy, and the day before we were due to perform in Houston, Billy came up to me and said, "Hey, man, maybe you shouldn't drink so much with Ian."

I stared at him, trying to see whether he was messing with me. When I realized he wasn't, I said, "Come on, it's hardly my fault Ian's going downhill."

I was partying pretty hard at the time, but unlike Ian I didn't front a band, and it didn't affect my ability to perform.

After New York, the tour continued through the southern states. We went west after that, ending up in Portland where we would be playing our final show with Metallica. Band members always had to deal with more or less crude pranks during their final gig, and inevitably the headliners would try to fuck with the support act.

We went out onstage, and I couldn't help but notice that Ian really did look like shit. Maybe even he was aware of it by that point, because between songs he started muttering a whole bunch of bitter remarks and alienating the crowd with rude British jokes no one understood. It didn't exactly help that from the very outset, large chunks of the crowd were against us—for the simple reason that they were there to see Metallica.

Suddenly, I saw Lars, James, Kirk, and Jason coming onto the stage in tight black shirts, long black wigs, and carrying small vacuum cleaners. You could interpret the vacuum cleaners any way you like, but there was no mistaking the fact that they were dressed as Ian. All four had shoved pillows under their shirts so that it looked like their stomachs were bulging.

Next thing I knew, the guys in their crew had thrown a bunch of stink bombs onstage, and the smell of rotten egg spread through the air. White talcum powder rained down on us, and we were left looking like ghosts. I tried to rub the powder off my face with my arm as I kept playing. Two of Metallica's crew walked over to me then, taking my floor toms away.

They came back and carried off my cymbals next. It was getting hard for me to keep up the beat. I also suspected something else was going on, because when I intuitively looked up, I saw two of Metallica's crew had climbed up into the lighting truss and were standing above us with buckets in their hands.

Next thing I knew, they had emptied them onto the stage. It wasn't just water that hit me, I realized. There were goldfish—hundreds of goldfish. They were everywhere, floundering in the pools of water. There were even a couple flapping around on what was left of my drum kit.

Suddenly, I saw Renee come running out onstage. She stopped dead in the middle—apparently unaware of the audience—and held up her hands, waving them as she looked around with a dismayed face at all the dying fish. She shouted, so loud that I could hear her over the music, "Oh, my God! Oh, my God!"

Then she turned and rushed backstage. A moment later, she was back with a full bucket of water, and started to rescue the now mostly dead fish. She was so busy trying to save them that she didn't initially seem to notice that twenty thousand people were watching her efforts.

We kept playing during her rescue operation, but when the song came to an end I grabbed a Corona from the floor next to me and jumped over one of my drums. I was in the middle of the stage, a few feet from Renee. I saw Ian staring at me in surprise, and Billy gestured as though to say, *What the fuck are you doing?*

I was so focused on what I felt like I had to do that I didn't care about them or anyone else in the arena. I bent down and picked up a goldfish by its tail. It flapped, trying to get free. When I managed to catch Renee's attention, I held the goldfish right in front of my mouth and opened wide.

Renee stared at me, like she was frozen, then shouted, "Oh, no!"

I mimed *Oh, yes!* and smiled at her, opened my mouth wide again, and dropped the fish into my mouth. I took a swig of beer and felt it slip down my throat, then burped and smiled.

22

London

I introduce Zakk Wylde to drag queens, meet Lemmy for the first time,
and sing "Beth" pantless in a bar.

SONIC TEMPLE WAS THE Cult's breakthrough record, and we were
suddenly able to go on our own world tours. The $1,500 a week
I made at the start of the tour with Metallica increased to $3,500
by the middle of the tour; now that we were headlining, I was
making $5,000.

This was the late 1980s, a strange time fashion wise, if you ask
me, but compared to lots of other bands, The Cult actually looked
pretty cool.

In any case, the plan was to start the tour on the guys' home turf,
in England. But first, we had to do some promo work in London.

I had never been to Europe before, and thought it was
kind of cool to check into the Holiday Inn in the Swiss Cottage
neighborhood. I quickly saw a whole load of clubs and bars there,
but I didn't have time to visit any of them before the promo work
started. Ian and Billy were the band's front men and did virtually
all of the interviews. That said, it was clear to them that Jamie and
I should be present for any photo shoots. As I stood in front of the
camera, I thought, *Wow, I'm really part of this band!*

Still, that generosity from Ian and Billy didn't change the natural
pecking order. It was the first time I had noticed how it worked in a
band at that level. Ian and Billy were the classic rock 'n' roll duo of
singer and lead guitarist, like Plant and Page, Mick and Keith, Axl

and Slash. While Jamie and I put on a good show as well, we were the rhythm section and there to support them.

One of the first things we were booked to do was perform on a famous British TV show called *Top of the Pops*. When we found out that we had to be in the studio at nine in the morning, I remember saying, "Nine AM? Is this a joke?" In my world, that didn't sound very rock 'n' roll.

The studio, at the BBC, was pretty sterile, with linoleum floors and strip lighting. It looked a bit like a government agency. But when we got to the cafeteria next to the recording studio, my jaw dropped—Tom Jones was sitting at one of the tables. I'd always thought he was pretty cool, which I obviously had to tell him. The guys from Take That were there too, with Robbie Williams. I didn't know Robbie at the time, but we'd later work together.

That night, Ian and I went to the Hippodrome, one of London's biggest clubs. A sign above the entrance said ROCK NIGHT, and as we went to the bar to order some drinks, I checked out the crowd. The place was like a rock 'n' roll version of Studio 54, and I was pretty comfortable there until the guys from Sigue Sigue Sputnik came over. They seemed to be friends with Ian, who introduced me to the bassist, Tony James. He had previously played in Generation X with Billy Idol.

"Matt's our new drummer."

Tony looked me up and down and said to Ian, "Was that really the best you could do?"

I bit my tongue and thought, *What a fucking wanker!* That superior English attitude could be annoying, but I went into the club and partied through the night.

When I got back to the hotel and went down to the lobby the next day, I was surprised to spot my drummer pal Randy Castillo checking in at reception. "Hey, Randy! What're you doing here?" I yelled.

"We're here with Ozzy," he replied, pointing to the guy next to him. "This is Zakk."

It was the first time I had ever met Zakk Wylde, but both he and Randy looked really cool at the time: skinny and dressed in black leather. They were badass rock 'n' rollers.

We talked for a while, and I felt so excited to have bumped into them that I said, "We should all go out!"

Both Randy and Zakk thought it sounded like a great idea.

"Matt, you've been here a while," said Zakk. "Where do you think we should go?"

"We should go to the Hippodrome!" I said. "It's a killer club. I was there yesterday."

The problem was that the Hippodrome often had different themes, with different club nights on different days of the week. When we arrived a while later, I immediately knew that something wasn't quite right.

We went over to the bar, in any case, but I noticed both Randy and Zakk glancing around a little dubiously. "Are you sure this is the right place?" Zakk said to me.

"Fuck yeah, let's get some beer."

We each ordered a beer, and just as we were handed our glasses a girl came over and stood next to Zakk at the bar. I thought there was something odd about her, and when I glanced around I realized that it wasn't just her: all the girls in the bar were actually guys. I'd managed to take Randy and Zakk to a drag night.

Zakk stared at the drag queen and said, "Hey, what the fuck!" He was from New Jersey, and in New Jersey there were no drag queens. "What's the deal with you? Are you a dude or a chick?" he asked, as loud and as wide-eyed as before.

The drag queen just smirked at him.

Zakk then shouted, "If you came to Jersey like that, we'd kick your ass!" He turned to us. "We need to get the fuck outta here."

"I'm sorry, Zakk," I said. "I picked the wrong night."

We headed to St. Moritz, a famous rock club on Wardour Street in Soho. We had to go down into the basement to get in, and I had only just made it over to the bar when I spotted Lemmy Kilmister sitting by a slot machine at one end. I'd heard that he loved those machines, but I had never met him before.

Randy, on the other hand, knew him, and he said, "You wanna talk to Lemmy?"

"Sure!" I said.

Zakk had disappeared somewhere, so Randy and I went over. "Hi, Lem," said Randy. "This is Matt Sorum; he's the new drummer in The Cult."

Lemmy stared at me and said, in his gruff voice, "Well, I guess that's a good thing. The new guy—the drinks are on you, then?"

I quickly lined up a few Jack Daniel's shots on the bar, and Lemmy barely said a word as we drank. Much later, when I really got to know him, I realized that that was just how he was—a man of few words. Also, we didn't speak much more that night because of a woman who caught his attention. It wasn't long before Lemmy had left with her.

Randy and I stayed behind and continued drinking shots. When we got back to the hotel, it was after four in the morning. Despite that, neither of us felt much like sleeping. Instead, we headed straight to the hotel's so-called residents' bar. The guests could hang out there for as long as they liked, and the bartender had to stay until the last guest had left. Maybe that was why he gave us a weary look when he saw us. Still, he politely asked, "Would you like another drink, gentlemen?"

"Yeah!" we said.

Right then, Zakk appeared, and the night immediately felt young again, because he started telling us all kinds of funny stories. We drank and laughed, nodding at the bartender from time to time whenever he tried to make us leave by pointing out that he had small children to take care of and needed to sleep.

Eventually, it got so late that a maid arrived to start sweeping the floor—not that we cared about that. Instead, Randy glanced at the piano in one corner and said, "Zakk, play 'Beth' by Kiss, will you?"

"Oh, okay, you wanna hear that?" Zakk said, emptying his pint. "But then I'll have to do it with my drawers off."

He went over to the piano and pulled down his pants and underwear before sitting down. He glanced over to us and yelled, "You guys need to drop your drawers too!"

Randy and I shuffled down from the bar stools and went over to Zakk, where we also dropped our pants and underwear. Zakk had started playing and singing "Beth," and we joined in. From the corner of one eye, I saw the maid staring at our bare asses as she swept the floor. It was a great moment, and one of my very best memories.

But tell me what kind of magic lasts forever. Before long, a young male receptionist in a dark suit appeared. He came over just as we were singing the chorus. He cleared his throat several times, and we ignored him. Then he cleared it again, so loudly that he began to cough. As we temporarily fell silent and turned to look at him, he politely said, "Please, gentlemen, I think it's time you retired to your rooms."

Zakk smiled indifferently and then firmly hit the keys and shouted, "Hold on a minute, man. Last chorus!"

I put one arm around Randy, and the three of us gave it everything we had:

Just a few more hours
And I'll be right home to you.
I think I hear them calling,
Oh, Beth, what can I do?

23

Sonic Temple Tour

I see Ian get headbutted and get stuck a few feet above the stage.

AFTER THE NAKED SINGING, I didn't get much sleep before it was time to leave for our first UK show. I guess I was still drunk when I went down to the lobby to check out, but I remember that there were a whole load of dark-haired dudes on the couches down there, playing like crazy on their acoustic guitars while one of them sang at the top of his voice in a language I didn't understand.

"Who are they?" I asked the receptionist.

"Gipsy Kings, sir," I was told.

When I turned around, I noticed that people had stopped to listen both in the lobby and out on the street.

The band and I flew up to Edinburgh, where I quickly learned not to talk about an *English* tour, since doing so was seen as a real insult. The people in Edinburgh weren't Englishmen; they were proud *Scots*! Another unique thing about that city was the drinking culture. Ian was the one who told me about it when he and I went out to a bar before the show.

"You need to be careful when you go out drinking here," he said. "These guys, they like to headbutt you. You've got to watch out for the headbutts!"

"Okay," I said, not entirely sure what he meant.

We went to a typical local bar and had barely been served our beers before a dude came over and started messing with Ian. "Are you in a band or what?"

"Yeah, I'm in a band," said Ian.

"You look like a fucking girl. Are you a girl?"

As though this was an everyday occurrence for Ian, he grabbed his glass and smashed it against the bar, ready for a fight. But the guy was already about to headbutt him—I saw it coming before Ian—and then *crack!* He managed to land a perfect headbutt that floored Ian.

"Holy shit!" I shouted, bending down to Ian, who was flat-out on the beer-soaked floor. I shook him, slapped his face, and started pulling him onto his feet. But just as Ian unsteadily opened his eyes, the guy hit him hard on the back of his head, and he dropped to the floor again.

"Fuck!" I shouted, bending down to him again. Ian was on his back, seemingly unconscious. That was when I noticed that something strange was going on around me, and next thing I knew a full-on fight had broken out in the bar. I didn't know why, but I knew that Ian and I should get out of there pronto.

"Ian!" I yelled, hitting him harder than before. When that failed to work, I poured beer on his face, and he finally came to. I managed to get him onto his feet, and we fled the place, ducking beneath flailing arms and flying glasses. As we were in the doorway, I glanced back at the fight we had somehow caused. It was like the Wild West in that bar. People were hitting one another with bottles and chairs, and I saw one guy land a perfect kick in the balls on another.

I rushed to drag Ian farther down the street, and when we stopped to catch our breath, I realized he was bleeding from a nasty gash in his forehead.

"What the fuck happened?" he asked, his eyes crossed.

"Well," I said, "you started a fight."

If the Scots were the wildest, craziest fighters I ever encountered, they were also the most passionate fans. In fact, I'd never seen such a devoted crowd as when we gigged in Edinburgh that night. It was a whole other level of barbarian rock 'n' roll—very, very intense. People were acting like they were wild animals on speed.

Another thing that distinguished the Scots in Edinburgh from other fans we played to was their near-incomprehensible dialect. Still, that was nothing compared to how difficult it was to understand what anyone said when we recrossed the border and arrived in Newcastle upon Tyne. I don't know what country we ended up in, but there's no way it could have been England. A characteristic of the English is surely that they speak English, but when people in Newcastle opened their mouths it was something entirely different that came out. "Excuse me?" was practically all I said while we were there.

The tour continued down through the country, and eventually we returned to London for our last two gigs at Wembley Arena, which we had sold out for two nights in a row. The feeling of going out onstage and seeing more people than you could really take in was totally mind-blowing, and I almost felt high as I sat down behind the drums on those nights.

During our second gig at Wembley, we recorded a video for "Sweet Soul Sister," the third single from the *Sonic Temple* record. (We'd recorded the video for the second single, "Edie (Ciao Baby)," in New York right before we came to England.) It was November 25, 1989, and the band sounded better than ever, but we didn't use the live music from the gig; we used the album version in the video. I had always been sensitive to tempo, but I thought that the music synced really well with the images. Two months later, when "Sweet Soul Sister" came out, it was a hit.

By then, we were back in the United States and on the American leg of the tour—with Jason Bonham's band as support.

Jason was Led Zeppelin drummer John Bonham's son, and the record they had just released was called *Bonham*, like the band. It sounded pretty similar to Zeppelin, and it sold really well—not as well as *Sonic Temple*, of course. Our record had gone platinum by that point, which meant that for the rest of the tour we were playing to arenas of twenty thousand people or more. Very few bands can cope with such heights without suffering from hubris. We were no exception.

For some reason, we suddenly decided that we wanted an elaborate stage with an enormous iron cross that kind of came down from the heavens. This is where one of us should have taken a step back and thought about a certain satirical film about an imaginary British rock band that had come out a few years earlier. Instead, I said, "Wouldn't it be cool if I had some timpani drums and a gong?" The others wholeheartedly agreed. Above all, they thought a gong would work in our song "Sun King."

Along with the floating iron cross, I came up with another equally out-there idea. Why not also fix it so that my timpani drums looked like they were floating high above the stage?

I found out that you could use forklift trucks for precisely that purpose and suggested the idea to Ian, who nodded thoughtfully and said, "It sounds great—so long as it doesn't cost too much."

It didn't, so I organized the forklifts and was pretty happy when I realized it would work out. I rose toward the ceiling with my timpani drums, and my gong was like a big glittering sun.

Our first US gig with the new staging went off without a hitch—for us, that is. The same can't be said for Jason Bonham, who turned up at the arena with a beer in one hand and the other arm in a cast. It was the first time we had met, and I just stared at him and said, "Your arm's broken! How're you going to play drums?"

He smirked, seemingly unconcerned, and said, "I've got to figure that out, mate."

As it happened, he had brought along a small drum machine that he positioned next to his kit, and he played that with the fingers sticking out of the cast. He also used his good arm to play his usual kit like normal. The whole thing looked crazy, but it worked surprisingly well, and he kept it up for the entire tour.

In any case, Jason and I quickly became good friends, and we started drinking together. He always drank until he blacked out, and I would help him into bed. I remember one particular occasion when I struggled to get him up to his hotel room after a gig, dumping him on his back in bed. The phone started ringing and continued to ring while I took off his shoes and turned him onto his side so that he wouldn't choke on his own vomit during the night.

I undid the top button of his shirt and opened the window slightly to let in some air, closing the curtains to stop the sun from streaming in on him in a few hours' time. All this time, the phone kept ringing, and I wondered who could be trying to reach him so late at night.

Eventually, my curiosity got the better of me, and I answered. "Yeah?"

"Is Jason there? This is his mother. Is he all right?"

I sobered up a little then; that's the effect that anxious mothers have on drunk men. "Yes, he's asleep," I said, making an effort not to slur.

But I could hear that she was worried about him, and I understood why. Jason's father had lived hard and died young, and when I ended the call I looked down at Jason, who was now snoring loudly. It was clear that he was following in his father's footsteps in more ways than one. The guy was hardcore.

Jason and I had a really good time on that tour, and I got a real kick from the shows we played—especially the big arenas. On December 13, 1989, we were due to play the SkyDome in Toronto, and the place was sold out, all fifty thousand tickets.

I felt the familiar rush in my body a few hours before the show began, but that was nothing compared to how it felt to see the audience later. As the two forklift trucks raised me and my timpani drums—and my gong—into the air, I felt like Robert Plant when he yelled, "I am a golden god!" from the balcony of Riot House on Sunset Boulevard.

But, as they tried to lower me down, one of the trucks stopped working. I desperately looked down at the driver, who peered up at me and held out his arms in resignation. *Oh no,* Spinal Tap! I thought.

24

The Last Show

I hear Ian claim that Axl stole his look, get chronic diarrhea,
and see Slash and Duff tumble out of a limo.

WE STILL HAD SEVERAL months of the American leg of the tour left
to play when I got sick—really sick. I developed diarrhea, and while
that kind of thing normally blows over, it didn't this time. I was
shitting day after day after day. As a result, I lost a whole load of
weight, so even though I felt like crap, at least I no longer looked so
swollen from all the alcohol.

It wasn't just my body that was falling to pieces—the entire
band was on the verge of falling apart. Things had been tense
between Ian and Billy ever since we went out on the road with
Metallica, but Billy continued to tell Ian that he was getting fatter,
he partied at the wrong times (e.g., before important TV shows),
and he didn't bother singing all the lyrics. I was pretty annoyed
at Ian myself, because we were playing great in those days, and
the band was really on top of its game. If he hadn't sabotaged the
whole thing for us, we could have been insanely big. But it was like
Ian lacked the self-confidence to be the kind of superstar he had all
the prerequisites to be.

Still, even though I fundamentally agreed with Billy, I didn't say
a word. I just wanted to play drums; I didn't want to get dragged
into their constant bickering. I was perfectly happy just being in the
band and had no problem at all hanging out with Ian offstage, even
if he could be pretty bitter and whiny at times.

On one particular occasion when he and I were alone in one of the two buses, he suddenly said, "You know I'm the one who gave Axl his first headband?"

"Nah, I didn't," I replied honestly. What I did know was that Guns N' Roses had been the support act for The Cult on their The Electric tour a few years earlier, and I had heard Billy claiming that he had taught Slash how to work the stage. According to Billy, Guns had only played clubs before and had no idea how to make use of a bigger stage. There might have been some truth in it, because in the early days they did spend a lot of time just standing around the drum kit. But this whole thing about Axl's headband was new to me, so I said, "Tell me more!"

It was like turning on a tap. Ian claimed that he and Axl had hit it off during the tour together, and when Axl—who, back then, had a kind of crazy Mötley Crüe hairstyle going on—came backstage after the Guns' set, Ian said to him, "Hey, Axl, why don't you try this headband?"

Ian held out a bandana. He had the whole Native American look going on himself, with his long black hair and a headband. He was also with Renee at the time, and she was some kind of stylist.

She combed Axl's hair and tied the bandana.

Axl studied himself in the mirror and said, "Okay, cool." He clearly liked the look, because he wore the bandana at the next show, with a baseball cap over the top.

"I gave him a fucking headband," Ian whined. "He stole my look!" It was a story I would hear over and over again.

Billy had become increasingly irritable on the road, and he and Ian were barely speaking. Billy was hard on the crew; once he fired the guy who looked after the monitors—just a few hours before that evening's show. "The guy didn't even have the chance to do the show," I said to Billy as I sat behind the drums and did my sound check. "What happened?"

"I didn't like the fucking wanker," Billy said.

So although I was annoyed at Ian for the way he behaved, it also made me sad that Billy always seemed so unhappy. Billy and I are still close and both of us have reflected on those days together; it was harder on Billy looking back because it was his band from the early days and he just wanted to rock...which really should be a simple concept, but Ian wanted something else.

That was the main reason for Billy's frustration in retrospect.

Yes, we had a lot of fun together, but unless everyone in the band is heading in the same direction, unless everyone wants it equally, it makes no difference how much potential you have. It will only ever end one way. I still consider Ian one of rocks premiere frontmen and Billy's guitar style and tone one of the best in rock.

My stomach was so bad that as soon as we made it to the arena, I desperately went off in search of the restrooms. Not that it helped having turned my stomach inside out before we went onstage—in the middle of the show, I suddenly felt an urgent need to take a shit, and without warning the others I threw my sticks down and rushed offstage.

I ran like a madman down the corridors backstage and managed to find a free toilet at the very last minute. The relief was indescribable. As I began to make my way back to the stage, I got completely lost in the dim passages and corridors. I had no idea where I was, but in the distance I could hear Ian shouting into the mic, "Our drummer has gone for a shit!" The guys in the band knew all about my stomach troubles by that point, and now so did several thousand others.

Eventually, I managed to find my way back, and after the show we were all due to travel to Los Angeles, where we would finish off the tour with two sold-out shows at the Universal Amphitheatre. I had assumed that the entire band would be flying together, but Billy suddenly announced that if I wanted to fly with them, I would have to pay for my own ticket, because he and Ian weren't going to do it. As I saw it, this was the end of the whole all-for-one-and-one-for-all thing that I think is the entire point of a band. I could have bought my own plane ticket, but it wasn't about that—it was the principle.

So while Ian and Billy headed to the airport, I stood backstage and pictured the two-day, cross-continent bus journey that I had ahead of me. I must have looked pretty down because Jason Bonham came over, put a hand on my shoulder, and said, "I heard. I'll ride with you. We can take an eightball."

I gave him a questioning look and asked, "Is that enough?"

We bought five grams of blow, in any case, and managed to make it last the whole way.

When we eventually arrived in LA, I had decided to make the two final gigs into something I could look back on with pride. I had a really good drum sound in The Cult and had worked hard to make it fat and thunderous like Black Sabbath or AC/DC. I was very professional in that respect, often turning up early to sound checks and spending at least an hour getting the sound how I wanted it. The first show, on April 1, 1990, went well. I was on form that night—I was wearing my headband and my hair was slicked back. I'd also switched to a smaller drum kit by then. I had one rack tom and was playing really tough.

Two days later, when the time for the very last show of the tour came around, I was standing in the outdoor section of the backstage area with my girlfriend MAURA.

The Cult had been on the road for a year and a half, and the energy in the band had gotten worse and worse along the way. At some point, I had even asked Billy, "Why are you guys so miserable? We're living the life out here." At the same time, it felt kind of sad that I had gone from the pinnacle of my life, when I joined the band, to now being a bit unhappy with the outcome of the tour. But when I looked out at the expectant people milling around with glasses of wine and beers in their hands, I thought, *No damn way I'm gonna let Billy and Ian ruin this evening for me.*

Suddenly I noticed that security was rushing to open the gates in the outdoor section of the backstage area. A huge limo pulled up not far away from us. The door opened and Duff McKagan of Guns N' Roses climbed out of the car; he was so lanky it was more like he was being tipped out. His bandmate Slash appeared next—in a cloud of smoke, dressed like classic Slash: with the hat and everything. Four super hot, scantily clad girls climbed out next, and with one on each side of them, Slash and Duff walked straight past us with a bottle of liquor each, heading straight into an area that had been cordoned off for them backstage.

It was such a rock-star moment, and I jokingly said to Maura, "Maybe I should join those guys instead."

All that being said, The Cult was probably the most perfect fit for my drumming style, and there have been times when I've pondered how my life would have been different if I had stayed with one of rock's coolest bands.

25

Slush Is on the Phone

I join GN'R.

WHEN THE TOUR FINISHED, I suddenly got even sicker. Yes, I'd had diarrhea during the entire latter part of the North American leg, but since I'd been drinking and doing drugs constantly I just chalked it up to that. But now my entire body started aching, and I had so little energy that when I got back to Mom's place in Mission Viejo, I could barely make it up the stairs to the guest bedroom. The reason I had to move in with Mom was because I didn't have a place of my own while we were away on tour.

Shortly after I moved in, I came down with a fever that refused to go away. It was like my entire body had just given in. Mom got so worried she eventually took me to a doctor, who gave me an X-ray.

"Hmm," the physician said, frowning in the way you don't want a doctor to frown when looking at an X-ray. He looked up at me and said, in a serious tone of voice, "One of your lungs is half full of liquid. I'd guess you've had a walking pneumonia for a good while now. It's actually a miracle you can even stand."

"What should I do?"

"Well, you need to rest."

That evening, I developed a crazy rash all over my body and had to slather myself in camphor ointment just to soothe the itch enough to sleep. I was completely white; I looked like a ghost.

I'd been bed-bound for four weeks when the phone rang. It was an early afternoon in mid-May, and Mom came into the guest room to say there was someone named Mike Clink on the line for me.

I knew who Mike Clink was, of course—a producer who'd worked with bands like Whitesnake and UFO—but I'd never met him. I dragged myself into the kitchen and picked up the receiver.

"Hi, Mike."

"Hey, Matt, I got your number from Lars," he said. "Someone's gonna be calling you from a band pretty soon."

"What band?" I asked, but he wouldn't say.

An hour or so later, the phone rang again, and Mom stuck her head around the door and said, "Someone called Slush is on the phone."

Again, I hauled myself out of bed and into the kitchen, where the phone was on the wall. "Hey, Matt," I heard down the line. "It's Slash."

"Oh, *Slash*," I said, feeling my stomach turn as I cast an irritated glance at my mom, who was flicking through a magazine at the kitchen table. "What's up?"

"Well, Steven, our drummer, is in rehab. It doesn't look like he'll be able to get it together to do this record."

By that point, it was almost three years since *Appetite for Destruction* was released—that was a long time; bands generally released a record a year. But as Slash now complained, GN'R were struggling, and Steven just couldn't play. "He can't even get through a song anymore," he said.

"I'm really sorry to hear that."

We were both silent for a moment, then Slash said, "You think you could come play with us?"

"Sure," I said. "When do you want me up there?"

"Can you come up tomorrow?"

I was still so sick and weak that I could barely stand, but I heard myself saying "yeah" without hesitating.

Slash sounded pleased and said, "Cool. We'll put you up in the Oakwoods."

The next day, I threw my bag into the backseat of my Datsun 280z and drove up to Hollywood, where I met GN'R's tour manager, who gave me the keys for the apartment. As soon as I'd dumped my bags there, I headed straight to the rehearsal space, Mates Studios, which was at the end of a long driveway in North Hollywood. I knew the place well; I'd played there with a whole bunch of bands since the early 1980s. Still, as I climbed out of my car in the parking lot outside, I had to take a couple of deep breaths before I headed inside.

I walked down a long, dark corridor, passing two smaller studios and a lounge with a pinball machine flashing away, and opened the door at the end. It was like stepping into an opium den. The only light in the room was from a couple of lamps in one corner and on the little stage.

Almost every surface was covered with a Persian rug, and there was a refrigerator against one wall. Slash and Duff were sitting on an old leather couch in the middle of the room.

"Hey, how're you doing?" Duff said.

"You want a drink?" Slash asked.

It was obvious that they had already drunk quite a bit, so I said, "Yeah, I'll have a beer."

I took the cold bottle Slash pulled out of the refrigerator and noticed that my drum technician, Timmy Doyle, was already busy setting up my kit onstage. In the gloomy areas where the light of the lamps didn't reach, I could make out a couple of roadies who just seemed to be waiting on orders.

Neither Izzy nor Axl were there, but that didn't seem to bother Slash or Duff. After chatting for a while, they said we might as well get started.

Izzy turned up not long after. He said hi to me and then played a couple of demos he'd brought with him—small cassette tapes of acoustic versions of "Dust N' Bones" and "Bad Obsession," among other things. They sounded really raw.

After we finished listening, the four of us went onstage—which was really more a raised platform in the middle of the room—and went through the chords for one of Izzy's pieces, electrifying it. I noticed that Slash and Duff built on the foundations and did something to the chord changes to come up with an ensemble riff. They copied one another, essentially—on guitar and bass—with Izzy Stradlin's roots rock rawness going on over the top. It struck me suddenly that this was precisely how the GN'R sound was made. What filled the studio at that moment really was the band's sound.

Something else I quickly noticed was that the songs varied hugely in length. Some were only three minutes or so—an ideal length, in my opinion—whereas others seemed never to end.

"Locomotive" was one of those songs. It lasted over eight minutes, and though I was new behind the drums, I couldn't help but ask, "Does this song really need to be so long?"

Slash looked at me, a cigarette hanging out of his mouth like usual, and said, "Yeah, man, it's cool."

It was, in a way, but at least I said what I thought, and no one seemed to mind. The mood in general seemed really open and tolerant.

The four of us kept rehearsing like that, and by the fourth day I couldn't avoid the question I'd wanted to ask for so long: "Who's that guy on the couch?" I nodded discreetly in the direction of a dude sitting quietly on his own. "He's been here every day."

Slash rolled his eyes a little and said, "Oh, that's Dizzy, Axl's friend. He plays *keyboards*."

Something else I had been wondering was, of course, whether the band's singer would be coming to any of our rehearsals. I got the answer to that unspoken question the very next day, when Axl suddenly turned up midway through a song. I remember that I kind of froze—Axl had that effect on people.

He walked slowly, in a wide arc, through the studio. It was like he was just wandering randomly and didn't really have any reason to be there. As he passed the stage, he cocked his head a little and glanced at me with an intense look. Then he turned to Slash, nodded gently, and left the studio without saying a word.

We finished the track, and Slash turned to me and said, "Hey, man, you wanna come up to my house after? We can have some barbecue."

Thirty minutes or so later, Duff, Slash, and I headed to his house up in Laurel Canyon. Izzy had stopped drinking by that point, and I guess he wanted to avoid temptation, because he went home.

But I had a feeling it wasn't just the alcohol he was avoiding.

In any case, Slash's house was really funky, a kind of hippie style. Actually, the whole of Laurel Canyon had a real hippie vibe.

I went through a gate and passed a pool. I felt kind of on edge because of Axl and the weird atmosphere at the studio—but also because I didn't know what was going on.

As I came into the house, my jaw dropped; every wall was painted dark purple, the rustic furniture looked like it was straight from Bali, and the whole place smelled shut in. It seemed to have been a while since anyone last cleaned.

I went into the bathroom to take a piss. Everything was purple in there too. The shower was built around a terrarium, and as I tried to relax and do my business, I saw an enormous boa constrictor slither up one of the branches inside.

When I got back to the living room, Slash and Duff were sitting on a large, dark velvet couch with a huge table in front of it—also Balinese in style. There was a carved wooden box on the table, and it was full of blow. Duff was drinking a vodka cranberry, and he mixed one for me.

There was so much vodka and so little cranberry juice in it that the drink was barely even pink, and when I took a sip and tried not to grimace, I realized that it tasted about as good as it looked. Slash made himself a Jack and Coke. Then he turned to me and asked, "So do you wanna join the band?"

I felt my heart skip a beat but managed to stay calm as I said, "Well…I thought I was just doing the record…" Slash and Duff sat in silence, like they were waiting for me to go on, so I said, "Yeah, make me a member!"

They both raised their glasses and toasted me, and Slash smiled and said, "You should come meet our manager, Alan Niven."

The next day, when we were done with rehearsal, Slash, Duff, and I headed off to a place called the Hamburger Hamlet on Sunset

Boulevard. It was a famous burger joint, but it was actually more of a coffee shop than anything.

As we stepped inside, it took a moment for my eyes to adjust to the darkness. We bought a couple of beers from the bar and took them over to the corner booth. It was only then that I noticed the big, long-haired guy in a black leather jacket already sitting there. He was dressed like a rock star playing manager, and he introduced himself as Alan Niven. All I knew about him was that he was from New Zealand and that he wanted to be the new Peter Grant (Led Zeppelin's legendary manager).

One thing he had in common with Peter Grant was that he was really loud. Alan practically yelled when he greeted me, and he squeezed my hand excessively hard.

Slash, Duff, and I sat down at the table with him.

"The boys want you in the band," Alan shouted in his thick New Zealand accent. "What d'you think?"

Before I had time to say anything, he looked me straight in the eye and shouted a number at me, even though I was sitting right next to him.

I stared at him and then glanced at Duff and Slash, who were sitting all dumb-faced, not saying anything. Right then, I realized that it wasn't a joke and that they genuinely thought I would accept their bullshit offer.

I started laughing and said, "Are you outta your mind? I make three times that with The Cult."

I had actually just been called into a meeting with The Cult's manager, Howard Kaufman, a few days earlier; he had offered me a percentage of the band. It meant I was in a pretty good negotiating position with this Peter Grant wannabe at my side. I shook my head—still laughing—and said to Alan, "Not for that money."

I saw Slash give Alan a quick look, and Alan frowned his big forehead and sidled over to me like he was trying to crush me in the corner of the booth. "Okay, we'll give you a percentage of the band."

That sounded more reasonable, so I said, "I've heard you guys are doing pretty well, so I'll take that."

Alan said he would draw up a contract, and he welcomed me to the band.

So I took the deal on offer, which meant I would also have a share on the record. But as I was grabbing a cold beer from the refrigerator at the rehearsal studio the next day, Slash walked by, mentioned some different terms, and said, "That cool?"

I was so floored that I didn't really know quite what to say, so all I could come up with was, "Yeah, cool!"

Much later, I realized that my "yeah, cool!" probably cost me a few million dollars—and that it was Slash, not Axl, that I should've watched out for.

26

Use Your Illusion

I become a regular at Crazy Girls and get "initiated" into GN'R.

AFTER WE REHEARSED ALL the new songs, Mike Clink came down to Mates to listen. We had managed to pull together thirty-six songs, and after playing all of them for Mike, we decided to record the lot and then pick out the best thirteen or fourteen.

I remember liking several of them, especially the killer tracks like "You Could Be Mine," "Dust N' Bones," and "Pretty Tied Up." Then there were the tracks like "Coma," which I just didn't get at all. I mean, a ten-minute rock song? But Axl just said, "Look, Queen did it, the Stones did it. We can do whatever the fuck we want. Let's push it, let's go as epic as we can. Let's not make the same record again."

Axl wanted to take the band to a stadium level, and he knew that with epic songs, epic videos, and larger-than-life imagery, we could do it. So at some point in June 1990, we began recording *Use Your Illusion* at A&M Studios on La Brea Avenue in Hollywood.

The idea was to meet at the studio at twelve every day, and at first we were actually pretty good at showing up on time. Or, more accurately, Slash, Duff, and I usually turned up around twelve. Izzy arrived just after, and Axl came and went as he pleased. In the beginning, he generally showed up at some point during the day, but after just a few weeks he stopped appearing before evening, by which point several of us were tired and wanted to go home. Before long, he stopped showing up at all.

I generally started the day with coffee, but Slash and Duff drank booze, and by the afternoon they had already had a fair amount.

We had booked into Studio A, which included a large recording room in which *We Are the World* and a whole bunch of other epic records had been made.

We really did have carte blanche: plenty of food that was swapped out several times a day, private parking, and unlimited alcohol. We could also order whatever we wanted, and if I got tired and wanted to leave the studio for the day, I could just order sushi. Slash hated fish so much that he preferred to leave as soon as he saw my food. I can still picture his face—he looked horrified.

Izzy had set up his own little room in the studio, in a vocal booth, and he had a thick Persian carpet, a chair, and a lamp. From where I sat in the smaller recording room, I could see him in the glow of it. Duff was in front of me and Slash on a chair to one side. Through a window, we could see Axl's piano in the middle of the bigger recording room.

Since he never showed up, we recorded the tracks without him. For many of the songs—Izzy's excluded—we still hadn't heard the lyrics. We didn't overanalyze anything; we were just shaping the songs, and recorded a maximum of three a day.

We sometimes got into discussions, about the tempo among other things, but there weren't many retakes. Once we were done with one track, Mike Clink immediately said, "Let's do another one."

We didn't get much direction from him. If I'm honest, I thought of him more as a babysitter. He just didn't have any musical influence on what we were doing, and looking back now I wish he had said things like, "Hey, do a different fill there." But it never happened.

We used to take a break in the middle of the day and head right across the street to a strip club called Crazy Girls. It worked well to begin with, but as time went on we started spending longer and longer there, and when we finally got back to the studio Mike would just sigh and say, "Go home." On a few occasions, he managed to get something good out of us despite the state we were in, but for the most part we were just too drunk. Mike had a mysterious ability to tell, just by looking at us, whether there was any point in trying to get anything done, or whether it was just a case of giving in for the day. If he chose the latter, we went straight back to Crazy Girls and got even more fucked up.

We occasionally went to another strip club called Star Strip, but for the most part we were at Crazy Girls, hanging out with the strippers there. A few of the girls sometimes even came back to the studio with us. There were always other girls there too, and one of them came over to me one day. She said, "I need to initiate you into the band."

I didn't get what she meant, so I said, "What does that mean?"

"I need to give you a blow job."

So we went off to the amp room in the main studio. The doors were open, and there were a bunch of amplifiers in there. We moved behind the speakers and she immediately dropped to her knees and started sucking. I was hard right away, and before long I started fucking her.

Once we were done and went back out to the others, I saw through the window into the control room that the entire band was inside, roaring with laughter. The microphones on the speakers in the amp room were all turned on, and I realized that they'd probably recorded the entire thing.

When the doors into the control room opened—they were like something from *Star Trek*, double doors that parted with a swooshing sound—everyone shouted, "Welcome to the band!"

Then they played the entire tape over the speakers. It was all "Oh, baby, oh, baby, I love your pussy!"

"Okay, you got me," I said, feeling my face turn red.

Slash ejected the tape from the DAT player and said, "I'm gonna be keeping this."

"Fuck you!" I shouted, but I couldn't stop myself from laughing.

While all this was going on, I was still in a relationship with Maura, but I really had transformed into the worst scallywag ever—a transformation that had begun way back when I was in The Cult.

One night, when we got back from the girls at Crazy Girls, we were really, really drunk. Mike was still in the studio and wanted us to record "You Ain't the First."

The only problem was that I was so drunk I couldn't even sit up straight behind the drums. It meant that my drum tech, Timmy Doyle, had to play for me. I was on the tambourine, but I played it really loose, so it had a cool feel to it.

We were all sitting in a row by the window into the control room. Izzy and Slash were playing acoustic guitar, me the tambourine, Timmy Doyle the bass drum. Izzy had been waiting for us in the studio the whole time, so he might not have been in the best of moods. It was also one of his songs. But if you really listen to that track on the record, it sounds a bit like pirates on a ship.

That really was the spirit of what we were back then.

Even at that stage, there were three levels within the band. There was me, Slash, and Duff; then Axl; and then there was Izzy. We were going in three different directions, but I rolled with Slash and Duff; we were on the same party train and had the same ideas about how to live our lives. Axl lived his life in a different way. He was drinking champagne, eating caviar, and smoking cigarettes he'd rolled himself.

In that regard, Axl was genuinely playing a part. I don't think he'd ever really seen money before. After all, they hadn't seen any of the money from *Appetite* until just before we began recording *Use Your Illusion*.

When you're a guy from Indiana—like Axl—that can really affect your psyche. Suddenly you're a millionaire, and that makes you feel powerful.

27

The Record Plant

Mike Clink builds a bedroom for Axl,
Slash is too shy to play guitar while the rest of us watch,
and Duff finds me coked out of my mind in his closet.

DURING THE RECORDING OF *Use Your Illusion*, my friend Mike Fasano
and I were living at Duff's house on Sunshine Terrace, in the foothills
of Laurel Canyon. It was a cool little house with a pool and a Jacuzzi.

Once we reached a certain point in the recording process, I was
constantly coked up. I'd often done blow during our visits to Crazy
Girls, but things really started to escalate at this time.

Maybe it had something to do with the pressure I felt in the
studio, as a result of the huge amount of material and the difficulties
we were having recording songs like "Breakdown." Slash and Duff
couldn't get their heads around that song, and Izzy had already left.
He couldn't get his head around "November Rain," so he only really
came in for the overdubs. One exception was when he pulled out
his cool Telecaster and started playing "Double Talkin' Jive," which
is really simple in its construction. As he played, I came up with a
drumbeat and we got it down in one take. It's only three chords.
Slash was playing that live.

But with "Breakdown," things were far more complicated. We
couldn't get it right, and eventually both Slash and Duff got fed up
and headed home. I couldn't really figure out where it was going
either. It had all these weird breaks and no consistent beat. But Axl
had finally showed up, and he asked me if I would stay, so I said,

My first family photo. Left to right: my brother Mike, Dave
(Dad), Joanne (Mom), me, and brother Mark.

Left to right: my brother Mike, me, and brother Mark.

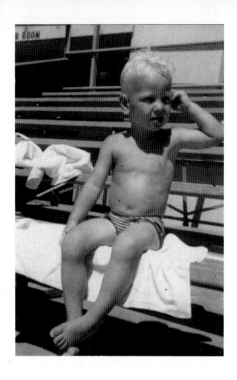

My first swimming lesson.

Junior All-American Football team.

Junior high school band in seventh grade.

Ninth-grade photo.

Gregg Wright Band, 1979. Left to right: me, Gregg, and Tim Solis.

Drumming drinking games, early 1980s.

My mom, Joanne, and me, early 1980s.

With Tori Amos in Y Kant Tori Read, 1985.
Left to right: Brad Cobb, me, Tori, and Steve Caton.

The Cult's *Sonic Temple* Tour. *Photo by Jim Marshall, courtesy of Beggars Banquet.*

The Cult, London, 1989. Left to right: Jamie Stewart, Billy Duffy, Ian Astbury, and me. *Photo by Russell Young, courtesy of Beggars Banquet.*

Loft jam, New York City, 1989. Left to right: me, Ian Ast-bury, Axl Rose, and Izzy Stradlin. *Photo by Dana Frank, courtesy of the photographer.*

With Iggy Pop at the release party for his album *Brick by Brick*, 1990. Left to right: Duff McKagan, Iggy, me, and Slash.

Me and Izzy in Istanbul with Guns N' Roses, 1991. *Photo by Gene Kirkland, courtesy of the photographer.*

Use Your Illusion Tour with
Metallica, 1991. *Photo by Gene
Kirkland, courtesy of the photographer.*

Me and Duff backstage at the Tokyo Dome, Japan, 1992.

Photo by Gene Kirkland, courtesy of the photographer.

Guns N' Roses 1993 Skin N' Bones Tour. Left to right: Gilby Clarke, Dizzy Reed, Duff McKagan, Axl Rose, Slash, and me.

Photo by Gene Kirkland, courtesy of the photographer.

Session with N.W.A., North Hollywood, 1993. Left to right: me, Slash, Eazy-E, Jimmy Z, DJ Yella.

Neurotic Outsiders photo shoot, 1996. Clockwise from upper left: me, John Taylor, Duff McKagan, and Steve Jones. *Photo by Chris Cuffaro, courtesy of the photographer.*

Velvet Revolver live, 2004. *Photo by Karl Larsen, courtesy of the photographer.*

Velvet Revolver promo shoot during
filming of "Fall to Pieces" video.
Photo by Karl Larsen, courtesy of the photographer.

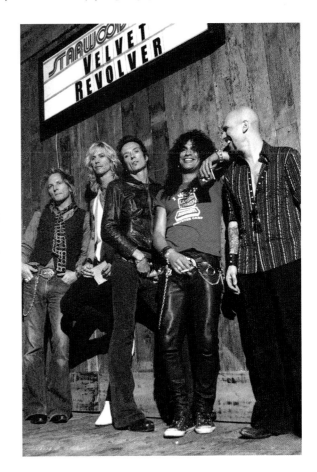

Slash and me outside Lillie's Bordello bar, Dublin, 2006.

Photo by Ray Senior/VIPIreland.com, courtesy of the photographer.

Ace and me outside Lillie's Bordello.

Photo Ray Senior/VIPIreland.com, courtesy of the photographer.

Motörhead US tour, 2009. Left to right:
Phil Campbell, Ace, Lemmy, and me.

Kings of Chaos tour of South Africa, 2014. Left to right: Duff McKagan, me, Steven Tyler,
Billy F Gibbons, Gilby Clarke, Robin Zander, and Nuno Bettencourt.

Photo by Kamal Asar, courtesy of the photographer.

Ace and my engagement photo shoot
at the Roosevelt Hotel, Hollywood, 2013.

Photo by Michael Segal, courtesy of the photographer.

At our wedding in Palm Springs,
October 12, 2013.

*Photo by Michael Segal, courtesy of the
photographer.*

Ringo Starr and me, Los Feliz, Los Angeles, 2014.

Photo by Danny Clinch, courtesy of the photographer.

Hollywood Vampires, 2016. Left to right: Johnny Depp, Alice Cooper, me, and Joe Perry.

Photo by Ross Halfin, courtesy of the photographer.

On the Big Bad Blues tour
with Billy F Gibbons in 2018.
*Photo by Brendon Weyers,
courtesy of the photographer.*

In Palm Springs with my '62
Galaxie named after my wife, Ace.

"Yeah. If you wanna get this done, I'll stay here all night or all week. I don't care."

Axl smiled and seemed to like the fact that I had the work ethic, because he said, "There's this place called Greenblatt's Deli over the road, and they have caviar. You ever had caviar?"

"No, I haven't," I said as I thought about how decadent it sounded. I felt like I was on a whole different level of rock 'n' roll excess.

With The Cult, it was a case of getting on the bus and drinking beer with my buddies, playing five nights a week. That was a normal rock band experience, but this was different: the energy was intense. People's reactions were different when they found out that you were in the band too—the truth is, my life changed in that moment.

Not long after, Axl and I were back in the studio, eating caviar and doing shots of chilled vodka. We were on the floor, kind of Indian style, when Axl suddenly grabbed a pen and paper and started drawing a diagram, a kind of circle. He said, "So, Matt, do you know much about publishing?"

I shook my head. "Eh...no."

"Okay...Here's how it works. This is a pie."

He pointed to the circle. "Let's say that half of it is called publishing, over here. Right? And these are the writers of the song. Now, this slice of pie right here goes to Izzy. Izzy wrote the riff."

Axl pointed to the pie he had drawn and said, "I'm gonna cut you off this slice right here." The section was roughly 10 percent, and he said, "That's for you." He took my hand and shook it. "That's for all the things you do, and I think we owe you for these songs."

But just two or three days later, something went down. I think I mentioned it to my lawyer, but he got back to me and said, "Slash doesn't agree to that, so that publishing agreement isn't going to happen."

At the time, it didn't affect me as much as it does now, when I look back and think, *I could have had a conversation, I could have asked Axl again.* But I never did. I just accepted it. I later realized that Slash was a real cunning businessman. He played the role of the quiet guy who acts like he's drunk all the time (or is drunk all the time), but there's something else going on in the background. He's a lot smarter than he looks.

Once Axl had finished drawing, he said, "Let's try the song again."

He sat down at the piano and I went into the other room and got ready behind the drums. Before long, we were playing again. Axl seemed to like what I was doing with my tom-toms and shouted down the microphone, "I like the sound of your toms." Then he suddenly cut off the take and said, "I'm gonna play this chord, and you're gonna hit that cymbal. Play that cymbal for me!"

He played the chord, and I hit the cymbal, and we kept that up for what felt like an eternity. Eventually, I tried to gently suggest a different arrangement, because his was a little wacky. It was all over the place. "Axl," I said, "what do you think about trying that three times before we—"

I didn't get any further before he slammed the lid of the piano and rushed out of the studio. Before long, he was back. He sat down at the grand piano and said, "Let's try this again?"

We worked on that song for three days, and reached a point where Slash and Duff came back and tried to learn what we had done. And then they overdubbed their parts.

The more time passed, the worse the performance anxiety became, which meant I started doing more drugs, more coke. I guess the others were thinking, *Great, we got another drug addict!*

In my bedroom at Duff's place was an enormous walk-in closet. I had a landline phone with a long cable, and one morning when we only had three or so tracks left to record, I took it with me into the closet, where I lay down in the dark and tried to sleep. It didn't really work, though, because I was completely coked out. I could feel my heart beating, or rather, I couldn't just feel it beating, I could hear it, which made me panic. So I called my friend Mike, who was in the next room. He had his own phone in there.

The minute he answered, I said, "I can't make it. I can't go down there anymore."

"Okay," Mike said, still half asleep. He called the studio and explained the situation to Duff.

An hour or so later, Duff came back to the house and found me there in the closet. "What's going on?" he asked.

I held up my hands and said, "Duff, I have no idea." I was so coked out I could barely speak. My mouth was like sandpaper, and my lips felt like they were about to split. But I still managed to say, "Duff, I can't do it. Can we take a break?"

Up until that point, we had been in the studio every day. Duff didn't speak, so I continued, "Or can I come in later?"

I have almost no memories from the recording of those last three tracks, but I do remember thinking, *These tracks can't possibly make it onto the record.* As a result, I kept my part incredibly simple.

Later that day, Axl came charging into the studio in his full regalia—headband and everything. We hadn't seen him for some time, but he must have heard the recordings, because he said, "I love it all, it's all great. Here's what we're gonna do… We're gonna make two records and release them simultaneously." Before any of us had time to speak, he energetically continued, "We can have the same cover art for both records, but distinguish between them by doing them in different colors. I found a perfect image by the artist Mark Kostabi."

The rest of us just glanced at one another, and I thought, *What?*

Axl could probably see that we weren't entirely convinced, because he went on, "Why? Let me tell you. Double albums cost over twenty-five dollars, and that means the record stores have to keep them behind the counter." Axl knew this because he had worked in Tower Records on Sunset Strip. He continued, "We don't want our fans to have to go and ask for our record. We want them to be able to go to the bin, touch the record, and then buy it."

I remember thinking, *This guy is a fucking genius.*

"And," Axl continued, "we're gonna go back to Geffen, and we're gonna renegotiate for two albums."

After that, he went to fetch the album artwork. It was a huge painting on canvas, and he had placed it by the entrance to the studio. He pointed to a detail in one corner and said, "That's the cover. Blue and red." In other words, we used a tiny section of the painting, which was copied from a famous work by Raphael, the Renaissance artist.

It was August when Mike Clink suggested we move the whole recording process to the Record Plant. I asked Slash about it as we were in the control room: "What's going on at the Record Plant?"

"I wanna do all my guitar overdubs there."

"Didn't you do the guitar already?"

Slash squirmed. "I wanna do a lot of other stuff, like solos."

I hadn't realized that he did overdubs; I had always thought he was done with his part.

During the recordings, I occasionally said things like, "I think I wanna do a fourth take," and Slash had always said, "No, why? Do you wanna suck the rock 'n' roll right out of it?" But now he was going to add more guitar himself despite the fact that we had already been recording for three or so months.

I guess he could see that I was confused, because he said, "We're gonna move down to the Record Plant, but I don't want anyone else to come down there, I'm gonna record my guitars by myself."

I nodded and didn't bother asking any more questions. Still, a few days later when I swung by the Record Plant to pick something up (I don't remember what), I saw the sound technician at the mixing desk and Slash playing guitar with his face to the wall. He couldn't handle anyone watching him because it made him so nervous. He got really funny about people looking at him—not when he was playing in arenas, but in smaller settings like this.

I thought, *Wow, that's really fucking weird.*

We rented two studios at the Record Plant, Studio A and Studio B. Eventually, Mike Clink decided to turn one of the studios into a place for Axl to sleep. Mike reasoned that if we could just manage to get him down to the studio, there was a good chance he would sleep there. Mike hoped that Axl would then record the next day.

The plan worked to an extent, but we had over thirty songs to record, so even if Axl worked from some point in the afternoon until late at night, we would still be pretty far behind schedule.

In the early 1990s, renting a studio like that cost somewhere around $2,500 a day, so the production really had started to hemorrhage money. Maybe that was why we decided to record a few cover versions too. Among other things, we recorded the Damned's "New Rose" and the Sex Pistols' "Black Leather."

Axl's idea of releasing *Use Your Illusion 1* and *2* wasn't just about avoiding a double album; it was also meant to ensure that we had enough recorded material to be able to tour for two years without having to produce anything new. We could just release new videos instead. What we didn't know at the time was that even the covers we were recording would later be released on a record called *"The Spaghetti Incident?"*

28

I Turn Thirty

I have to carry Lars Ulrich to his hotel room,
and Axl gets to know my mom.

"HEY, MAN, I'M IN LA. Can I swing by the studio?"

Lars Ulrich and I had been in sporadic contact ever since we toured together, and during one of the recording days at the Record Plant, he called me up out of the blue.

I covered the phone with my hand and glanced at Slash. "Lars wants to swing by?"

Slash shook his head.

I spoke to Lars again. "I'll meet you down the street. By the burger place on the corner of Sunset and La Brea."

When we met outside the studio an hour or so later, he asked me almost right away, "What does the album sound like, man?"

"Well, there's some epic shit and ballads."

"Ballads?!"

"Yeah, and some piano."

"Piano?!"

"Yeah, piano."

We went into the burger joint. Lars ordered a grilled cheese sandwich, and we sat down at one of the window tables. I tried to ask how it was going with Metallica, but he just gave me short answers and then returned to his questions about our recording sessions. He really was a little nosy when it came to GN'R.

"Well, man," I said, "there are all these long ballads." I gestured with my hands. "I'm almost running out of drum fills."

134

Right then, Lars's sandwich appeared. He took one bite and pulled a face, because the guy serving him had forgotten to remove the paper from the slice of cheese.

"Fuck!" Lars said, leaving the sandwich on the table.

"Sorry," I said. "I haven't checked out this place before."

Lars shrugged and continued his questioning: "What d'you mean, you're running out of drum fills?"

"Well," I said, "there are like thirty-six songs."

Lars's eyes widened. "What?"

Lars and I knew one another pretty well by that point, so I knew that he was curious and inquisitive by nature. But above all, he was competitive. He wanted Metallica to be the biggest band on earth, but at this point no one was as big as Guns and there would be nothing stopping the band. In retrospect Axl was just as driven and wanted nothing more than to be at the top. Ever since I joined Guns N' Roses, I had become pretty protective of the band, so I didn't say much more.

By November 19, when I turned thirty, we still weren't done with the recording sessions, but I decided to organize a decent birthday party for myself and booked a Moroccan restaurant called Dar Maghreb on Sunset Boulevard. I invited around seventy people, among them a few childhood friends like Darryl Brooks. My mom was also there, as were Slash and Duff.

It was the kind of restaurant where you sat on the floor and ate with your hands, and I remember that the atmosphere was good during the whole meal. Axl showed up toward the end, coming straight over to me.

"Happy birthday, man!" he said, glancing around the place. "Who's paying for this?"

"Well, I am," I said.

Axl shook his head. "No, no, I've got it."

I just stared at him. The meal cost around $3,500, but Axl really did pay the check. Unlike Slash, he was a giver like that. The fact that he later became more controlling was probably largely do to how

135

Slash was. It really pissed off Axl that Slash would hang out with people like Michael Jackson. And I think he had a point; no one in Metallica would have done that. But Slash would just disappear from time to time and end up playing with Billy Joel or someone like that.

He never asked the band for permission. Slash did what Slash wanted to do.

Once Axl had paid, he and my mom started talking, and they really hit it off. Mom knew nothing about rock 'n' roll, but she liked Axl because he was intelligent. Axl was also a guy who knew how to control a conversation. We actually had a nickname for him—Mark Twain—because he was a real storyteller. Slash, Duff, and I would always just sigh and say, "He's Twaining again." But the truth is, people were totally mesmerized by him. And this was his heyday, when he looked like *that* guy and had *that* presence. He just had to walk into a room and people would be all "ohhh…"

Suddenly I heard Axl say to Mom, "You should come down to the studio." He turned to me and said, "I wanna play your mom some of our stuff."

Was he joking? Apparently not, because once dinner was over twenty or so of us took a couple cars down to the Record Plant, including me, Mom, Axl, Darryl, a few other friends, and some girls.

Izzy was still working in the studio, but when we came storming in he just rushed out without saying a word. Next thing I knew, I saw Axl and Mom sitting at the mixing desk to listen to the tracks. I thought, *What the fuck is going on?*

Then I saw Axl take out a small glass pot pipe and smoke it in front of my mom. He passed it to her and she took a hit, and I thought, *Now they're smoking weed together?!*

The next morning, I woke to the phone ringing. It was someone from management. "Axl lost his pot pipe, and he thinks your mother took it." The person on the other end of the line explained that Axl loved that particular pipe and that he needed to get it back.

"My mom lives in Orange County," I said, "but I'll give her a call."

"Just find that pipe!" said the person from management.

I immediately called Mom. "Mom, look in your purse."

She did as I said and found the pipe right away. "Oh, what a wild night!" she said.

"Mom," I said, "you smoked weed with my singer."

"But I don't even smoke pot."

"Well, you do now."

Mom lived eighty miles away, but I said, "Mom, you need to get that pipe up here right now." I didn't want Axl pissed at my mom, of all people. So later that day, she really did drive all the way to LA to drop it off with me.

A few days later, Lars called me again, trying to do more snooping. "Hey, man," he said. "Meet me at the Sunset Marquis Hotel." I had nothing better to do, so I headed over there, and Lars and I sat down by the pool and had a few drinks. Though it was November, it was still pretty warm, and I remember we were talking tour memories and laughing when Lars suddenly said, "Call Axl."

So I went into reception and asked to borrow a phone. I called Axl, who immediately said, "Come up to the house!"

At this time, he had an apartment on Sunset, in a place called Shoreham Towers. It was pretty close to Tower Records. He lived on the twelfth floor and actually wrote the song "Right Next Door to Hell" about his neighbor. She was this crazy bitch who used to scream at him; at one point she even attacked him with a wine bottle.

Lars and I headed over there, and we had only just arrived when Lars said, "Axl, you wanna get some blow?"

Axl thought for a moment, and then he said, "I know a guy."

He called this guy, and after just an hour or so the doorman buzzed and the guy came up to the twelfth floor. I remember that I was the one who answered the door, and I was genuinely surprised to be standing face to face with a rabbi—an orthodox Jew. He must have been around sixty, and without saying a word he walked past me and placed Axl's order on the table. A moment later, he was gone.

We tipped the coke onto a regular dining plate, and Axl fetched a razor blade and the snorting straw from the next room.

Lars and I were sitting down, and when Axl came back he sat down opposite us. We each did a line, and before you could count to ten Axl had started Twaining. He talked and talked and talked. All Lars and I could get in was the occasional "yeah" and "cool."

After a while, Lars and I did another line, and we asked Axl if he wanted more, but he just kept talking. As far as I can recall, he only did the one line. Lars and I, on the other hand, did a whole bunch of blow. We also drank a fair amount of alcohol, and after listening to Axl for a solid three hours, Lars was so drunk he could no longer sit upright. It was three in the morning, and Axl said, "I've gotta go to the studio today."

I called a cab, grabbed Lars, and dragged him to his feet. I got him into the elevator and down the hill into the cab I had ordered. Since he still couldn't stand when we reached his hotel, I had to carry him right up to his room and put him into bed. I went back down to the cab and headed home to Duff's.

The next day, I got a call from management. "Axl canceled the session." Even the band was angry with me.

Slash called me up and said, "What the fuck are you doing, going up there and doing a bunch of blow with Axl?"

"Please, Slash," I said. "He did one line—*one* line."

"Well, he says his voice is gone, and he has to cancel a week of sessions."

"That's bullshit," I said. "He did one line. Ask Lars."

"Lars was there?!" Slash didn't like Lars. He didn't trust him, and his tone changed completely. "What were you guys talking about?"

"I don't know," I said. "The only one talking was Axl. Lars and I said nothing except 'yeah' and 'wow.'"

For Slash, this was all about money. He was thinking about how he would have to pay for the canceled sessions, and he said, "Meet me down at the studio. We're gonna record some shit."

29

Rock in Rio

I buy seven grams of blow from a cop
and see Spider-Man climbing the walls outside my window.

By EARLY 1991, WE still weren't done at the Record Plant. Axl had four tracks left to add vocals to, and then everything needed to be mixed and mastered. Still, we had a world tour scheduled, with the first date at "Rock in Rio"—and we only started rehearsing with a week to go. It was the first time I had played the songs from *Appetite for Destruction*, and I stuck to the script. I played Steven Adler's fills, even trying as much swing as he did, but that's not really my style. In my opinion, it was a bit sloppy, but I did my best version of it. In any case, I learned "Mr. Brownstone," "Welcome to the Jungle," "Paradise City," "My Michelle," "Rocket Queen," and "Sweet Child o' Mine," but I also learned songs like "Mama Kin" from *Lies*.

There was no sign of Axl, however. He didn't show up until it was time for us to fly to Rio.

This was my first gig with the band, and I felt shocked when we landed at Galeão International Airport in Rio some time in the after-noon. Around three thousand fans had come to meet us at the airport, and we had to be escorted out of some kind of VIP entrance by the police and the military. It was insane. People were screaming, and the air was thick and damp. Izzy and I were in the same van. It had cur-tains over the windows, and when we opened them the kids started throwing themselves at the vehicle, hitting the windows as hard as they could. Then they ran after us, shouting, *"Guns N' Roses!"*

Izzy glanced at me and said, "Welcome to the band."

"Fuck," I said. "It's like being in the Beatles."

Izzy smirked. "Yeah, man."

When we arrived at the International Hotel, right by Copacabana Beach, there were several thousand more kids outside. Some of them already seemed to know who I was, because they yelled my name the minute they caught sight of me.

We were escorted into the hotel and up to the floor that had been reserved for us. I don't think we even had to carry our luggage ourselves, because as I remember it, we got our keys and then Slash, Duff, and I headed straight to the hotel bar to order drinks. I said, "Give me the most popular Brazilian drink!"

The barman made me a caipirinha, which tasted incredible, and as we drank I turned to look at the guys standing around us. There were security guards, cops, dudes in bulletproof jackets, and everything. It was all pretty hardcore.

One guy, who seemed to be a cop, looked back at me and said, "Is there anything you need?"

"Yeah," I said. "We need cocaine."

"I'll take care of that," he said.

I turned to Slash and Duff. "Okay, guys, I'm gonna get this shit delivered to my room. Come over, and we'll hang out."

A few hours later, someone knocked on my door. Outside was the police officer, who had brought me seven grams of the highest quality coke.

This was January 17. Our first gig was due to take place on January 20. In other words, we had one day to recuperate, one for the sound checks, and then the gig. We were playing in a huge stadium called the Maracanã, which holds 145,000 people. Every seat was sold out.

I did a few lines and then called Duff. "Dude, I've got the stuff."

"Oh, man," Duff sighed. "I can't come. I had a fight with Kim."

Kim was Duff's girlfriend, or some kind of friend that he'd brought on the road with him, at least. Slash was already with his first wife Renée at the time, and he'd fought with her too, meaning he couldn't come either. I had brought Maura along, so we carried on and before long I was coked out of my head and a day and a half had disappeared.

I have no idea what we did, but I know that I still hadn't slept when our tour manager called.

"We're leaving," he said.

"What? What day is it?"

Not long after, I was sitting next to Izzy in the van, and the minute he saw me he groaned and said, "Oh, no!"

I felt like I had climbed on board a pirate ship, and that meant waving the pirate flag with all the other pirates. With The Cult, it was more a question of the English style of drinking and the occasional bump, but with GN'R, things had quickly become very different.

After we finished our sound check, I headed straight back to the hotel and continued to do blow. I kept at it until I saw a guy climbing up the outside of the hotel. Maura and I were on the sixteenth floor, and I yelled from the balcony, "Spider-Man's coming up here!"

I turned to Maura and repeated myself, "He's climbing up here. There's a guy climbing up the building!"

Maura was in bed and she just shook her head. "There's nobody climbing up the building."

But I was totally paranoid and stood my ground, and the situation hardly improved when I stayed awake afterward. I don't think I slept for three days straight, and on the morning of our first show, Axl's guy, Earl Gabbidon, called me up and said, "Axl wants you to do a drum solo tonight so he can take a break."

I cleared my throat. "A drum solo…in which part of the show?"

"He'll let you know. There's no set list."

My brain was so feverish and jacked up on coke and a lack of sleep that I could barely take in what he was saying. Still, I managed to blurt out, "Okay, I'll do it."

When we got to the stadium, I still hadn't rehearsed once with Axl. In fact, the first time I ever heard him sing live was a few hours later, when we stepped out onstage.

We opened with a new track called "Pretty Tied Up" that no one in the crowd had heard before. We were the headliners, so it must have been around one in the morning, and as I started playing the intro I looked out at the audience and thought, *Holy shit!* There were so many people there, and when they started jumping, the whole stage shook.

Axl soon came out, wearing a white jacket and a bandana. He had a crazy look in his eye, and I knew we were all on point.

Partway into the gig, Axl introduced me as the new guy in the band; he called me an assassin and said I wore cement underwear. He pointed to me and I started playing a crazy drum solo that lasted almost twenty minutes. I thought that if I had to do a solo, it should be as aggressive and stadiumesque as possible, so I really went all in—right until I saw Axl standing to one side of the stage, watching me. I stopped then and stood up. I kept hitting my bass drum, and showed the audience the beat with my hands. When I looked up, 145,000 people in front of me were clapping in time.

When I look back at pictures of myself at that gig, I look so bloated and puffed up from all the alcohol I drank during the preceding years. So fat—except I wasn't fat, I was just bloated. These days, people often tell me I look better now than I did then. I've got Norwegian heritage, so I can handle my alcohol, but it immediately shows on my face.

Ahead of the next gig, which was due to take place a few days later, I hung out with Maura and Izzy and his then-girlfriend Victoria. Maura and Victoria immediately hit it off and decided they wanted to go shopping for bathing suits. So along with a couple of bodyguards, we headed to the mall. It probably wasn't the best idea we ever had, because as Izzy and I stood there in that store, waiting for our girls, I happened to look out of the window. Several hundred kids were pressed up against it outside, some of them even climbing over the top of one another. "Holy shit!" I said. "They found us!"

Next thing I knew, the whole store shut down, and we had to escape up a ladder to the roof. We went down via another staircase and then out of the staff exit.

30

The Warm-Up Shows

I come up with a system for getting girls that's so good
Duff and Slash don't understand a thing.

AROUND MARCH OF 1991 we all met at Mates Studios in North Hollywood. When we arrived, Axl was already there, sitting on the couch with our manager, Doug Goldstein, and our tour manager, John Reese. "What do you think about this?" Axl asked when he spotted us. He nodded to John, who brought over a model of the stage for the upcoming tour. He put it down on the coffee table in front of us.

Everyone but Axl, Doug, and John looked down at it with skepticism.

"Look," Axl said, "it's like a crashed bomber plane. The wings are gonna be the ramps."

The whole stage genuinely was an enormous plane wreck, and when I took a closer look I realized it was actually pretty cool—especially since the drum riser was the nose of the plane.

Slash and Duff didn't like the idea at all, however—not that it seemed to bother Axl, who calmly continued to explain his vision to us. "Each of us gets a room beneath the amps," he said, "where we can hang out during breaks."

I thought that sounded like a pretty good idea and immediately began thinking about what I wanted my room to be like. I knew I wanted a bar and some stools—with a Persian rug on the floor and soft, subdued lighting.

Before I got any further, Axl interrupted my thoughts. "Okay, so let's talk about the airplane."

The rest of us glanced at one another and assumed he was still talking about the stage. In actual fact, he meant the plane we would use to fly between shows, and John spread out a couple of photos of a turbo prop plane in front of us.

"No fucking way," we all said, practically in unison.

John produced a picture of a G4 jet instead, and Axl said, "Don't Mötley Crüe fly in one of those?"

"Yeah, they do," John told him.

"Hmm," said Axl. "I want a bigger plane."

I noticed John sigh to himself before quickly flicking through his folder and pulling out another picture. "This is the 727 MGM Grand," he said, explaining that the plane had four private cabins, a lounge, five hostesses, and—most important—a bar. There would be room for our entire entourage at the front of the plane, and there was also lounge space toward the middle.

The staterooms—that was what they called the bedrooms—were at the rear, and each one had two couches and a TV.

Everyone but Izzy suddenly looked incredibly happy. "I don't want any part of that airplane. I'm not paying for it. I'm gonna buy a bus, and I'm gonna drive my bus with my girl and my dog."

And that was that.

Since GN'R always played incredibly long shows and we never knew what the evening's set list would look like, we had a huge number of old and new songs to rehearse. Eventually, we decided that we knew everything and that we were ready to set out on what would be one of the longest world tours in history.

The first three shows were unannounced—at the Warfield Theatre in San Francisco, the Hollywood Pantages Theatre, and the Ritz in New York. We grouped them together under the name "The Warm-Up Show," and they acted as a kind of final rehearsal for the tour.

When Axl opened the first show at the Warfield on May 9 with the words "this is a rehearsal!" the audience didn't seem to mind. There was nothing wrong with the way we played, either; I remember we sounded hungry and tight, and when we got back to our hotel later that night, I felt high with happiness that we were finally on our way. "Where's the fucking after-party?" I asked Slash and Duff as we caught our breath in Duff's room.

"What do you mean, man?" Slash asked, swigging his drink.

His answer confused me, because in The Cult, we'd always made sure to have girls waiting for us after our shows. In GN'R, they didn't seem at all tuned in to what they were able to achieve.

I groaned, and said, "Where are the chicks?"

Slash and Duff both continued to stare blankly at me, and I realized it would be down to me to take charge.

"Listen, guys," I said. "We can do whatever the fuck we want. We can get some cameras, bring in some cameramen to film the girls for us."

"Well," Duff said, "obviously we can have cameramen onstage."

"What are you talking about?" I asked him. "We send them out into the crowd with the security guys to get us some girls."

"What do you mean?" Slash said.

I explained, "We run a feed backstage, and connect it to a big TV in our dressing room. That way we can watch what's going on in the audience."

"Man," Duff said, "that sounds really difficult."

"What?! Difficult? All you have to do is find a fucking cable that's long enough. Just find it, get it!"

"But what are we gonna do with the cameras?" Duff asked.

I took a deep breath and said, "We'll have walkie-talkies too, which means we can talk to the security guys. The camera will follow them just like they follow us around onstage."

"And we'll do what?" Duff asked.

"We'll tell them, 'Bring me *that* girl and *that* girl.'"

Our next show was two days later, at the Pantages on Hollywood Boulevard. I had arranged it so we had a feed running down the hallway to a widescreen TV in our dressing room.

We had five security guys by that point, and I'd sent them out into the crowd to find us some girls. Suddenly, I heard a voice over the walkie-talkie. "How about this one, Matt?"

I turned to the TV screen and replied, "Yeah, bring her and her friend to the right, but ditch the one to the left."

"Okay, but they've got a guy with them."

"Lose the guy too!"

I heard the security guard talking to the two hot girls: "You two wanna come backstage?"

They replied in unison, "Yeah!"

Boom! Just like that.

31

The Party Room

Dizzy Reed shows a new side of himself,
and I teach Sebastian Bach how to go down on a girl.

THE IDEA WAS FOR us to have a couple of free days before our first real gig on May 24, but since we didn't have any firm plans, not much came of it. Instead, we holed up in a studio in Alpine Valley and recorded "Back Off Bitch" and "Ain't Going Down."

For some reason I don't remember, Duff and I started fighting in the studio. It couldn't have been over anything serious, because we were fighting more like brothers than anything.

The tour then began, with two sold-out shows at what was, at the time, the largest amphitheater in the US: Alpine Valley Music Theatre in East Troy, Wisconsin. That also happened to be where I discovered who Dizzy, Axl's friend who played keyboards, really was. On one of those two nights, when I got back to the hotel, I heard loud noises coming from down the hallway. I quickly realized it was coming from Dizzy's room, and when I opened the door my eyes widened. I saw ten or so girls and a grinning Dizzy in the middle.

Fuck, I thought, *This guy's a party animal!*

Dizzy had been pretty quiet up until that point, but just a few weeks later—I think it was during our two sold-out shows in Toronto—I went into my carefully decorated room beneath the amps to take a break and spotted him in my leather armchair with his pants around his ankles. Some girl was giving him a blow job.

"Fuck you, Dizzy. That's my chair!" I yelled.

Dizzy only played on certain songs, so he had plenty of time to hang out in my little cubbyhole with my drum tech, Timmy Doyle. I had made it really nice in there, with a cooler for beer. (I used to drink two beers and two shots of whiskey or tequila before going onstage. That was my thing.)

Duff's little room was beside mine, and he used to hang out there with his bass tech, Mike Mayhew. Adam Day hung out with Slash behind his black drapes on the other side of the stage. Axl, who was being taken care of by Tom Mayhew, also had a space on the other side of the stage, complete with a dressing table and oxygen tank (he really loved having oxygen).

I thought the most important thing was to create a good atmosphere in my room, and that also applied to the dressing room. Unfortunately, we couldn't take girls back there, because there were always so many people milling about backstage. So instead we set up a special room full of booze that we all came to call the Party Room. We could usually fit around twenty to thirty girls inside, some picked from the crowd via our TV screen and some picked from the Polaroids our bodyguards took for us.

Once we finished playing and came out into the dressing room, their photos were always set out ready for us in neat rows on a table. "Oh, that's a good one for me!" I would say, pointing to a photo.

After that, I always hurried into the shower. Since we were playing in big arenas, it was usually a big, sterile, wet room with eight to ten showers inside. Izzy always rushed straight from the stage to his bus, leaving the arena as Axl headed over to his own dressing room. As a result, it was really only ever me, Slash, and Duff that hung out after our shows, and they always seemed so confused when I peeled off my sweaty stage clothes.

"What are you doing?"

"Taking a shower," I said.

"Why?"

I just stared at them. Those guys were both so dirty. Slash often wore the same pair of leather pants for a week at a time. He even slept in them—he could've had a hundred pairs of leather pants if he wanted.

While I was in the shower, Slash and Duff would wolf down pizza or something from McDonald's. I preferred to order real food from the wardrobe girls once I was out of the shower. That was something I'd learned from Metallica—the importance of sitting down for a decent meal during the tour. If you ate healthy, you could party like a banshee.

Slash and Duff always used to call me a pompous ass and things like that.

"You should try this, guys," I grinned back. "It would do you good."

Slash would then throw up suddenly. He had a really sensitive stomach, and almost always threw up from sheer exhaustion after our gigs.

"Good show!" I would tell him as he chucked up his guts.

"Yeah!" he said, vomiting again.

After that, he would need to sit topless on the couch for at least an hour to recover, with a towel on his head. I quickly got dressed and headed over to the Party Room.

I could have virtually any girl I wanted in there. I just had to give her a glass of champagne, and the deal was pretty much done—aside from those occasions when I went down there and realized that Sebastian Bach had arrived before me. Skid Row was our support act on that tour, and Sebastian was a real good-looking dude. The girls loved him.

It really pissed me off, so I said to John, our tour manager, "That guy ain't allowed to come into this room until the band has come down. They're opening for us!"

The problem was that Sebastian had made sure to become friends with Axl, who always had his back. Axl came down too, sometimes—which meant I really did have to hurry if I wanted to have my pick.

One evening, I discovered another problem: a load of girls we hadn't picked started showing up. In other words, they had been invited in by the crew.

Uh-oh, this isn't good, I said to myself. The crew guys were pigs.

I went over to the dressing room and turned to Slash and Duff: "I'm worried we're gonna get sloppy seconds back here."

"What d'you mean?" Duff asked.

"Well, how do you think those girls got in here?"

"Oh," Duff said. "Through the truck driver? Giving him a blow job?"

"Yeah," I said. "We need to talk to the crew and tell them to let us know when they get a blow job. If they've hooked up with some girl and invited her back here, I want to know about it—I don't want someone who's sucked off Butch the truck driver!"

I sent for the production manager, Opie. He looked a little confused when I told him what we had been talking about. But right then, I came up with a solution, and said, "I want you to tell the crew that they need to write their initials on the backstage passes of any girls they have sex with: BB for Big Baller, MM for Mike Mayhew. They should do it with a Sharpie marker pen, somewhere easily visible—so the rest of us can tell if they've been there before us. You can tell them that if they send in a girl they've been with but haven't marked, we'll give them a whole load of shit."

"Good!" Slash shouted, raising a thumb in the air.

Opie studied me for a moment and then said, "Okay." With that, he went off to gather the crew and give them the order. My marking system was in use the very next evening.

Some evenings, Slash, Duff, Sebastian, and I amused ourselves by watching the girls do things to one another. We went into the Party Room—the girls were so open and free in those days that nudity and sex backstage seemed like part of the energy, and both we and the girls were happy to be there. They loved getting naked and giving us a show. We would point to a couple of girls and say, "Hey, we found our next two contestants!" The two girls would then play with each other on the floor in front of us as we sat on the couch and drank.

On another occasion, Slash called me from his hotel room and said, "Dude, get up here!" When I opened the door to his room a while later, I saw twenty or so naked girls inside. Slash was lying on the enormous bed with four girls on top of him—two of them actually blowing him. A girl on the couch had her legs spread wide, and Sebastian was on his knees in front of her. He was eating her out, but when I looked at the girl's face, I realized something wasn't right. She looked more bored than anything, and when I took a closer look I understood why. Sebastian was licking her frantically in the strangest way.

"Are you feeling anything?" I asked her, moving over to the bed.

"Well…" she replied vaguely, which convinced me I had to step in.

"Get out of the way!" I told Sebastian.

Sebastian moved, surprised, and I dropped to my knees.

"You've gotta flatten your tongue," I instructed him. "But don't just use your tongue. You gotta use your whole face—like this!"

I calmly and methodically worked away on her in a repetitive forward and back motion, pushing two fingers into her pussy. The girl immediately started to whimper, and before long she was groaning loudly.

I glanced up at Sebastian. "Got it?"

"Yeah!" he said, looking genuinely grateful.

32

Riverport Riot

Axl starts a riot, and we escape in a van.

ON THE EVENING OF June 2, we arrived at the Riverport Amphitheatre in Maryland Heights, outside of St. Louis, Missouri. We had landed at about four in the morning and spent the whole day sleeping and hanging around the hotel. Since Izzy was driving everywhere in his bus, he turned up at some point during the afternoon.

We were late arriving at the arena, which had officially opened only a few weeks earlier. Still, the organizer who came out to meet us was enthusiastic and said, "This is gonna be great!" He would live to regret those words.

Two days earlier, we had played in Birmingham, Alabama, and partway through the show, Axl had suddenly left the stage without warning. We played some kind of blues segment to fill the time, and Slash had to play a solo that went on and on while we waited for Axl to return. Duff and I kept exchanging increasingly anxious glances, wondering, *What the hell's going on?* Eventually Axl reappeared, but I could see from his face that he was annoyed about something.

The memory of that left a tiny nugget of anxiety as we headed out onstage in St. Louis that evening. Twenty thousand people were in the audience, and at first, the atmosphere both on- and offstage felt great. But an hour or so into the gig, Axl disappeared backstage. *Here we go again,* I thought. I was ready for another endless solo from Slash, but Axl reemerged as quickly as he had disappeared, now dressed in his black feather boa jacket. We started playing "Rocket Queen," and

Axl sounded fantastic, but he also seemed to be increasingly distracted by something happening in front of the stage. Before long, he yelled, "Security, come on!" and pointed to someone.

It was clear he didn't like the way the crowd was being handled. Next thing I knew, he had thrown himself out among the fans, aiming for one guy in particular. As far as I could see, they were both going at it with clenched fists, and black feathers from Axl's jacket were swirling through the air.

I remember that my jaw dropped as I tried to keep up the beat. Axl managed to drag himself back up onstage, where he grabbed the mic and yelled, "Well, thanks for the lame-ass security! I'm going home!"

With that, he threw the mic to the floor, causing the speakers to crackle, and then stormed off. I stopped playing and glanced at Slash, Duff, Dizzy, and Izzy; I realized that none of them were going to do anything about the situation, so I got up and followed Axl, turning quickly to look at the crowd. It was obvious that they weren't happy we had stopped the show—they were booing and shouting all kinds of stuff.

Since I thought Axl and I got along pretty well, and since I thought I knew how to talk to him, I went over to his dressing room. I didn't bother knocking, just walked straight in and asked, "Are you okay?"

Axl turned to me and said, "I lost my contacts!"

"What?" I asked, immediately remembering that he usually wore contact lenses onstage. He had lost them during the fight.

"I can't see!" He shook his head and started rummaging through a bag.

"I think we should get back out there," I said.

"Okay. Just let me find some contacts."

"Sure," I said, closing the door and heading back up to the band, who were now standing to one side of the stage, looking out at the crowd. There was no need for them to say anything, because I could see for myself what had happened during the short time I was away: a riot had broken out.

Almost ten minutes passed before Axl returned, and those were some of the longest minutes in my life. When he finally showed up, it was already too late—the audience had started throwing things up onstage: bottles, seat cushions, even entire seats. "We should go back out," someone suggested.

But John, our tour manager, disagreed: "It's not safe."

He was right: the objects being thrown had even forced our security guys to leave the stage, which had now been swarmed by a large angry mob from the crowd, which was letting loose on our equipment. I heard someone shout, "Call the cops!"

"Maybe we could make an announcement?" I suggested.

"No, let's just get out of here," said John. "We've gotta get you guys out of the venue."

By that point, Izzy had already left the amphitheater. The atmosphere was so threatening that I felt sure shit was going to get fucked up. I saw my drum tech Timmy Doyle fighting with a guy who was trying to steal my drums. Another guy had already run off with Slash's amp.

I yelled to Timmy, "Don't worry about the drums! They were free!"

We ran from the stage and hurried down to the cars that were waiting for us outside. The original plan was that I would share a limo with Duff, and Slash would ride with Dizzy, while Axl had a car of his own. But when we came out into the parking lot, John yelled, "Fuck the limos! We ain't got time for that. Get in the van!"

We all hopped into the van. Axl got into the front seat, and I sat down beside Duff in the back, with Slash, Dizzy, and John in front of me.

"Let's go to the hotel!" John shouted to the driver.

As I glanced out of the side window, I saw that the parking lot had suddenly filled up with men from the crowd, and several of them had started banging on the windows. Slash was still wearing his hat.

"Slash, come on!" I said, batting it off of his head. "Lose the hat! We need to be incognito if we want to get out of here!"

"No way!" Slash groaned, grabbing it just as the van tore out of the parking lot.

We headed to the hotel first, where our bags were ready and waiting for us in reception—we had been planning to fly out of St. Louis that evening anyway. As the others rushed inside to grab them, I stayed in the van and glanced nervously around. It felt like they took forever in there, and when Duff finally came back, he said, "They're saying on TV that Axl started the riot and that the cops are looking for him!"

John, who was still sitting opposite me, looked unusually dogged. "Okay, let's get the fuck out of here!" he shouted to the driver.

St. Louis is on the Mississippi River, which forms the border with Illinois, and our plan of escape was built on being able to cross one of the bridges without being stopped by the state police. If we could just cross the river into Illinois, we would be home free.

We were still wearing our stage clothes, and Axl was in the front seat in his headband and black feather boa jacket. I glanced at him and said, "I think we should duck down, 'cause the cops are looking for us."

"Yeah, everybody get down!" John yelled as the driver floored the accelerator.

Everyone but John did as he said, and we drove that way for at least forty-five minutes, until suddenly he said, "You can sit up now, boys; we've been in the state of Illinois for at least twenty-five minutes."

"Thanks a lot, John," I muttered.

We were driving along Interstate 55 toward Chicago and had just passed Bloomington when Axl started saying he was hungry. Axl usually ate pretty well after the show, and since he was an Indiana boy, that meant he was a meat and potatoes kind of guy. Right then, we all spotted a familiar sign and shouted, "Stop, there's a Waffle House!"

We were used to stopping at Waffle Houses while we were on the road, but I guess we must've been a real sight coming into that particular restaurant, still wearing our stage clothes, because everyone was staring at us. Still, we didn't start laughing about what had just happened until we were sitting with our food. "Man, that was fucking scary!" someone said.

In a way, it was like the escape in the van had brought us together, and I remember thinking, *This is what being in a band should be like.*

There was a TV on the wall in the restaurant, and I asked the waitress to put on the news. That quickly stopped us laughing. We watched as fires burnt outside the amphitheater we had left just a few hours earlier. It was actually pretty hard to take in all the destruction they were showing. The crowd really had trashed the place; it looked like a war zone. With a grave face, the news anchor reported that multiple people had been injured during the riot.

"Holy shit!" I muttered.

Next thing we knew, a picture of Axl had flashed up on screen. The anchor said that the authorities were doing everything they could to have him returned to Missouri. I glanced at Axl, who was trying to process the news.

"Okay, guys," said John. "Let's go to Chicago."

33

Communication

We trick the Chicago police with a doppelgänger and break Bruce Springsteen's record for the longest show at the Forum.

THE FEELING THAT WE were a group of guys on a crazy adventure had completely disappeared by the time we reached Chicago an hour or so later. Everyone was actually pretty subdued as we checked into our downtown Four Seasons hotel. For once, we really did benefit from our fake names. I used the same one as always—Dr. Lingus—and Slash and Duff used theirs too: Phil and Luke Likesheet.

Before we arrived at the hotel, John had said what we had all been expecting: that we would have to cancel at least a couple shows. The most important thing was to get Axl on a plane to LA as soon as possible.

Before we had time to do that, however, the Chicago police found out where we were and came to arrest Axl so that they could extradite him to the authorities in Missouri. John got a call from reception and quickly managed to come up with a plan to get him out of there.

At the time, there was a guy in our crew named Ronnie Stahlnecker. He mostly worked for Slash and even looked a little bit like him with his long, dark, curly hair—though he was actually much bigger than Slash was. We dressed him up in Slash's hat, jacket, and sunglasses, and we made our photographer, Robert John, look like Axl—headband and all. He was simply the one of us who looked most like Axl, and though he also weighed considerably more than his real-life counterpart, the result was still passable.

Once they were ready, we sent the decoys down to the lobby. They hadn't made it much farther than the hotel entrance before several cops ran over, grabbed them, forced their hands behind their backs, and cuffed them. I couldn't help but smile as I looked out through the windows in the lobby and saw them being shoved into separate police cars and driven away.

While all this was happening, Axl had snuck out through a door at the rear of the hotel and jumped into a car that would take him to the airport. He managed to board a private plane to LA without getting busted and spent several days holed up with a lawyer, devising a plan for how they were going to defend him in the lawsuit we all knew was coming.

The rest of the band stayed behind in Chicago, trying to work out how we were going to move on and start over. One major practical problem was that most of our gear had either been stolen or destroyed during the riot.

In just five days, we managed to replace everything we had lost, and, thanks to a team of lawyers, we also managed to ensure that Axl could join us onstage again. By July 8, we were ready to continue the tour with a show at the Starplex Amphitheatre in Dallas. Or, at least Duff, Slash, and I were ready. Like always, we were left waiting for Axl in the dressing room.

After almost two hours without a single glimpse of him, I felt my irritation and anxiety levels rising. I was also worried that some of the audience might wind up getting hurt again. "Fuck, he's doing it again," I said to Slash and Duff. "We're gonna have another riot. We'll have to go get him."

Slash lit a cigarette and said, "Get yourself something to drink. Relax!"

That was pretty much Slash—and Duff—in a nutshell. They never dealt with any problems and preferred to pretend they didn't exist.

"Fuck that," I said. "I'm gonna go get him."

I went out into the corridor and walked over to Axl's dressing room. There was a security guard standing outside.

"Get the fuck out of my way," I said.

"No one's coming in here," he told me.

Though he was much bigger than me, I managed to push him to one side and barge into Axl's room. "Dude!" I shouted.

I scanned the room for Axl, who was sitting on the couch. I was about to yell "Come on, man!" but stopped short when I saw *how* he was sitting—kind of hunched over, with his head in his hands. It wasn't the Axl I was used to seeing.

Confused, I sat down next to him, put a hand on his shoulder, and said, "What's going on, man?"

Axl shook his head and said, "I can't do it. I can't go out there."

"Can't do what?"

"I can't go up there. I just can't."

Axl really was the polar opposite of the rest of us. We just played and didn't worry about a thing, whereas he would take all the shit going on in his life up onstage with him. He was worried about the riot, about the fans, about how he was supposed to step out in front of them and look them in the eye.

"You need to quit putting all this pressure on yourself," I said. "We're a band. Come on!"

"I just can't do it."

"You can," I told him. "You just gotta get up there and leave everything you've been thinking about back here. Have a good time and forget all this shit." Before he could argue, I got up from the couch and said, "You come out when you're ready—but come soon. Otherwise we'll have another riot on our hands, Axl, and we really don't want that. Come on."

He looked up at me and said, "Okay. Just give me a few minutes."

"Okay," I said. "A few."

I went back to the others in the dressing room. "What did you do?!" Duff asked the minute I stepped inside. Both he and Slash looked nervous.

"I talked with him," I replied. Suddenly, I couldn't hold back the irritation I had been feeling for some time, and I added, "You're just enabling his behavior, you know."

"Oh, man," Slash mumbled, looking uncomfortable. Both he and Duff were so passive. Everyone had to tiptoe around to avoid annoying him.

We eventually managed to head out onstage in Dallas that evening, and it was actually a good show—even though the crowd was booing at first. There was so much emotion in the air that it felt like hard work—though maybe not for Slash and Duff, who were just drunk. At the very least, I thought that I'd had a good—if weird—conversation with Axl; it felt like I had finally gotten through to him. Sadly, it didn't make the slightest difference, and just a few weeks later, Axl locked himself in his dressing room—this time at the Shoreline Amphitheatre near San Francisco.

The organizer, legendary promoter Bill Graham, went crazy and started pounding on his door. "I've worked with Jimi Hendrix, Janis Joplin, the Grateful Dead, the Doors," he yelled. "But not once have I ever had to put up with this shit!"

Axl's unpredictable behavior was obviously a challenge for everyone involved, myself included, and maybe that's why I felt so exhausted a few days later when we walked out onstage for four shows at the Great Western Forum in Inglewood. It really didn't help that we always played pretty late into the evening, and we also played for a long time. Ahead of the last show there—which also happened to be the last show of our North American leg—I really felt like shit. That's why, before the show, I went to get some B-12 shots and acupuncture from Steve, a private acupuncturist who followed us around on tour. Our management was willing to do whatever it took to keep us on our feet.

As I lay there on the couch in the dressing room, with needles all over me, Slash came in and said, "Axl wants us to play every song we know tonight."

"No way!" I groaned.

A little later, once I was back on my feet, someone came over to me and said, "Cher really wants to meet Duff."

The crowd was full of celebs that evening—people like Arnold Schwarzenegger, Keanu Reeves, and Johnny Depp. I turned to Duff, who was standing off to one side, and I yelled, "Duff, Cher wants to suck your dick!"

"Oh, no," he groaned.

"Come on, Duff," I said. "Let's go meet her."

Duff seemed to deflate a little, but he mumbled, "Okay."

So we went over to see Cher, who held out her hand to Duff and said "hi" in that deep voice of hers. She was really devouring him with her eyes.

Right then, John came over to tell us it was time to start the show, saving Duff.

To me, it was a huge deal to play the Forum, since I had seen so many big bands there as a teenager. Now I was the one behind the drums, looking out at the crowd. *This is it!* I thought.

It really would have been a perfect end to that leg of the tour if Axl hadn't decided he needed to break Bruce Springsteen's record for the longest show at the Forum—earning himself a Guinness World Record in the process. The gig felt like it was never going to end, and in the middle of "Paradise City," I lost it a little when I saw Keanu Reeves, who was in the front row, headbanging like crazy.

Axl reacted immediately, giving me an encouraging glance and pointing to his watch. "Keep going!" he yelled.

34

Izzy Leaves the Band

We take a vacation in Ibiza,
and I'm forced to talk about my childhood with a therapist.

AFTER TWO GIGS IN Finland, two in Sweden, and one in Denmark, we arrived in the German city of Mannheim on August 24, 1991. We were meant to have played in Norway, but unfortunately for me—with my Norwegian heritage—we had to cancel.

On this leg of the tour, we had Skid Row and Nine Inch Nails opening for us. Axl had personally chosen the latter, which was weird—not only because they were virtually unknown at the time but also because they differed from GN'R in almost every sense. Before they went out onstage, they dressed completely in black and covered any visible skin in white powder. Then they would storm out there like madmen, with their singer, Trent Reznor, at the head.

On this particular evening, we were playing the Maimarkt-gelände, a huge, gray, concrete arena. I could tell right away that the crowd wasn't easily charmed; they wanted to see their band, and didn't give a shit about the opening act. Trent could see that too, and he went over to the front of the stage and did a *Sieg Heil* salute, which caused the audience to boo and Trent to burst out laughing.

Skid Row came out next, doing their thing until it was time for us to go onstage. Like always, we were late. It was as though Axl's mood got worse with every gig. By that point, the smallest of things would make him go absolutely crazy, and on that particular night there was some technical detail that wasn't working. As a result, after just a couple of songs he stormed offstage and left the rest of us up there. I watched as he ran down the ramp to one side of me and jumped into his van. Next thing I knew, Izzy had kicked his amp as hard as he could, then he turned to me and said, "Let's go get him." We rushed down the other ramp and jumped into another van. The whole arena booed. "Follow that car!" I yelled to the driver.

I was really pissed off, really sick of the behavior.

Up ahead, his van had stopped. We pulled up alongside. I glanced at Izzy and said, "Back me up!" So I jumped out and yelled, "I'm sick of this shit."

And when I looked back Izzy was still in the van.

I still remember the surprised expression on Axl's face as he looked up at me from where he was sitting next to his bodyguard, Earl Gabbidon.

"Motherfucker! Get back onstage!" I continued to yell once I had reached the open side door of their van. We were almost ready to go to blows. I raised my fist and was just about to punch Axl when Earl leaped out of the van and picked me up. "Fuck you!" I shouted, trying to get free. From the corner of one eye, I saw Skid Row's manager, Doc McGhee, put his guys into a van, and next thing I knew they had scurried off too. When I finally stopped struggling, Earl let go of me and sat back down next to Axl. They turned around and drove back to the stage. Izzy and I followed in our van.

Though we finished the show that night, something in my relationship with Axl had changed, and it was never quite the same again.

After our show in Germany, we had a week off before the next gig in London, so we decided to take a few days' vacation in Ibiza. We had booked out a boutique-like hotel up on a hill for the band, but Izzy didn't fly with us. When we spoke on the phone a few days later, he said, "I can't do this anymore. Axl's on his own; we can't talk to him. I'm leaving the band."

It wasn't like Izzy and I were close back then, but I think he saw me as someone he could talk to about the problem, and the problem was Axl. Why didn't we address it? Why couldn't we just sit down together and go over everything that was happening? I mean, everyone was definitely upset about how he was acting. We should have sat down like adults and asked what we could do about it—above all, how we could help him.

Regardless, we still had our London show to play, and I said to Izzy, "Just come and play that gig. Get up onstage, play the show, and then go. But play first."

We ended the call, and I went down to the hotel bar. Slash and Duff were first people I saw, drinking at one of the tables. I was really upset, so I went straight over to them and said, "I just talked to Izzy."

Slash lit a cigarette and glanced up at me. "Come on, man. Relax."

Right about then, Axl walked in and took a seat at the bar. He ordered a glass of wine. I turned to Slash and said, "We need to talk, all of us, as a band."

The problem with Slash is that he's not someone who deals well with conflict. He preferred to pretend nothing was wrong, and Duff said, "Come on, man. Just get a drink."

Later that afternoon, I got a call from our management. "We think you have anger issues," they said. "And we need to connect you with a therapist. Otherwise, we'll have to figure out something else, and you might have to leave the band."

So from that day on, I had no choice but to talk to a therapist over the phone for two hours a day. We were talking about my childhood and things like that, and I started to think about the guys in the band. We all had traumatic childhoods. We just didn't know how to talk about it. Emotionally it started getting hard for me at this point. The drinking and drugs only escalated the way I felt and I started feeling depression and anxiety that overwhelmed me. Unhappiness set in so the drinking and drugging got worse and the reason to do it was also different. It was an escape.

After Ibiza, we traveled to play to seventy-two thousand fans at the sold-out Wembley Stadium, which would be the end of that European leg and sadly Izzy's last gig with GN'R. Luckily he showed up, which I felt good about, and I thought maybe my phone call in Ibiza had worked. When we left the stage that night, Izzy just walked off, and that was the last we saw of him.

After we got back to the United States, Slash said, "We're getting a new guitar player. His name's Gilby Clarke." I had heard of him. He used to play with a band called Candy, which was basically like the Bay City Rollers or something—good-looking dudes with cool haircuts.

35

Madison Square Garden

Watch out for the wives, and I meet Donald Trump for the first time.

IN THE BREAK BETWEEN the European and North American/Japanese legs of our tour, I bought a condo in Shoreham Towers, becoming neighbors with Axl in the process. My place was on the sixth floor, number 607, I think, on the corner. From my bedroom window, I could see both Tower Records and Sunset Strip. I paid something like $175,000 for it, which is nothing looking back now.

During the tour, we had mostly been staying at Four Seasons and Ritz Carlton hotels, and I remember wanting my apartment to look like the inside of a Ritz Carlton suite, which was very art-deco inspired at the time. Before we left for Europe, I had also bought a Porsche, and people used to turn and look because they recognized me driving it, something that was very new to me. Maybe it was because the *Use Your Illusion* records had been released by that point—on September 17, to be precise—and I remember that Duff called me the next day to say, "You won't believe this, but we sold two million records in one day."

The tour started up again, and so did the debauchery. Now the Party Room had become a preshow warm-up to get the ambience and vibe up. We set aside a room in the venue where Slash, Duff, and I and sometimes Dizzy would go if we liked to see girls playing with dildos or eating each other out. Gilby didn't partake, as he was married to a beautiful girl named Daniella. He was very loyal and not much of a hard partier like the rest of us. A good guy in general—we all liked him.

The rest of us were different when the wives and girlfriends were around, though. You had to be careful when the wives were around… Once one wife knew something, she would tell the others. They were all just protecting their own sanctuary.

As luck would have it, the wives and girlfriends were only ever interested in coming to the "good" cities like New York, Chicago, LA, and Paris. None of them ever showed up in Iowa. As a result, we got up to all kinds of mischief in small towns like that. It's also why we organized things differently backstage when, after two gigs in Worcester, Massachusetts, we arrived at New York's Madison Square Garden on December 9.

We were due to play three nights in a row there, each of which had long since been sold out (we could have done ten gigs there if we wanted). It was a bit like the concert film *The Song Remains the Same* by Led Zeppelin.

After our first gig, Donald and Ivanka Trump came over to us. We had just finished our encore and were all sweaty, drinking beers. I remember Axl looked Trump from head to toe and said, "You know our music?"

He smiled and replied, "No, I saw you in *Forbes* magazine."

Before the second show, Billy Joel came over to our dressing room. We used to have these plastic bins full of ice, with all different kinds of chilled beer, wine, champagne, and vodka. We also had an icebox of Jack Daniel's and Jägermeister, and after Billy had circled around for a while, he said, "You've got almost everything, but you don't have any scotch."

Duff glanced at one of our guys and said, "Could you get Mr. Joel some scotch?"

Billy said, "I want Johnnie Walker Black, and can you make it a quart? You know, the big bottle."

Ten minutes later, Billy had the requested scotch in his hand, and he sat down with us to chat and drink. When it was time for us to head out onstage, I said, "Billy…see you after the show."

He gave me a thumbs up. But when we got back to the dressing room two or three hours later, Billy was passed out on the couch, and there wasn't a drop left in the Johnnie Walker bottle. We fetched his bodyguard, who was waiting outside, and he had to carry Billy away.

Around this time, Axl had started seeing the model Stephanie Seymour, who also played his wife in the "Don't Cry" video. She and the other supermodels of the day, like Naomi Campbell and Elle Macpherson, started showing up after our gigs. I was never with any of them, not that there weren't chances. I'll come back to that later, but first I need to talk about what happened a few weeks later, when we flew to Tokyo, Japan, to play three sold-out shows at the Tokyo Dome.

The other guys had been to the city before, and we had only just checked into the hotel when Slash and Duff announced, "Let's go to Roppongi!" Not long after, we were in an utterly epic rock club, called Lexington Queen—and if you were a rock star, you got all your drinks for free.

We went to the VIP section and were treated like royalty. They brought us champagne or whatever we wanted to drink, and the girls just flocked to us. I remember meeting a young girl named MILA, from the Netherlands, and she followed us back to the hotel. We didn't have any coke—it seemed impossible to get ahold of there, for some reason—but as we got to the lobby, Slash suddenly announced, "Ronnie's here. The Stones are here."

Soon after that, we were knocking on Ronnie's door. Ronnie Wood, who must have been around forty-five at the time, is the ultimate rock star. He's the funniest.

He let us into his room, and I said, "Ronnie, you don't have any cocaine, do you?"

Ronnie laughed and pulled out what looked like an eight ball, and it wasn't long before we were doing lines together. I swear, it was the best coke I ever snorted. Ronnie Wood had the best cocaine, he and Stephen Stills. They must have the same dealer.

Once we were done, Mila and I went back to my room, and I guess I must have fallen for her, because I kept ahold of her all weekend. Life on the road—you'd get lonely for real companionship and every once in a while there was this special girl.

The next night, it was time for our first gig. Ronnie was there, backstage, and one of us said, "Ronnie, you want to come up and play 'Knocking on Heaven's Door' with us?"

"Oh, yeah, I know that one, yeah, yeah!" he said.

"Cool," said Slash. "It's really easy, like three chords—G, D, C, and A minor."

"Oh, A minor," said Ronnie, "the saddest of all the chords."

Ronnie's appearance onstage was memorable to say the least. During the first eight bars, he just walked around the stage with his guitar hanging from his shoulder and a cigarette at one corner of his mouth. Then he went over to Slash and put an arm around him, nodding at the crowd. He moved on to Duff after that, and did the same there. When he finally played a chord, it was the wrong one. In fact, he didn't play a single chord right—three chords, and they were all wrong. But he looked cool as shit.

Later that night, we were in our dressing room as usual, when Duff suddenly turned to Gilby. "I really like that T-shirt. You wanna trade?"

Gilby grinned. "What you wanna trade it for?"

Duff burped loudly. "My Corvette."

"What?" Gilby said, laughing. But Duff was serious: he gave away a $60,000-car for a T-shirt.

I decided to ask whether I had anything he wanted to trade.

He looked me up and down and said, "Your jacket."

I laughed. "What do you wanna trade it for?"

"A trip to Hawaii."

36

Vacation with Duff

I renegotiate my contract,
and Duff finds an incredible body at a strip club in Hawaii.

AFTER JAPAN, WE HAD roughly a month off, and since I had swapped my jacket for a trip to Hawaii, Duff and I flew to Oahu for a few days' vacation.

It was around this time that Duff first started having panic attacks, and after checking in and boarding the plane at Narita Airport in Tokyo, he started to hyperventilate. Next thing I knew, he had run off the plane.

I got up, went after him, gave him a hug, and said, "It's gonna be okay."

Similar things had happened onstage. Duff would suddenly start to shake, and I would have to talk him out of it. In other contexts, like on the plane, it sometimes helped to give him a hug.

After standing there for a moment, he felt calm enough to board the plane and sit down. We were flying first class, and as soon as we were in the air a stewardess came over with a bottle of Dom Pérignon. I told her, "I'd like the bottle—and a bucket of ice."

A few minutes later, we had polished off the entire bottle of champagne, and when the stewardess came back, I explained that we needed another bottle and a second ice bucket. By the time we finished that bottle, it was time for dinner. The stewardess came over to pour us drinks from a bottle of Louis XIII—a Baccarat bottle, $750 a shot in a bar.

"Bottle?" I said.

She smiled. "Sir, no."

She poured us a tiny shot, and I said, "Could you at least make it a double?"

She was willing to do that.

When we landed, there was a white limo waiting for us, and the minute we sat down and popped a new bottle from the car's well-stocked bar, we told the driver to take us to a strip club called Centerfold. That was where Duff met his second wife, Linda Johnson.

Linda was a real *Penthouse* pet. She had been in the magazine, doing what they called a "special appearance."

Duff was on a mission to find the right girl at the time, but he fell for a stripper every time—and he definitely had a thing for tits. "I think she's the one," he would say, or, "What do you think of her tits?"

This particular evening, we hadn't even sat down at our table when Linda came out to do her performance, and Duff turned to me and said, "I'm gonna marry her."

He had previously been married to a girl named Mandy Brixx, and she was a real cool chick. But Linda had the most insane body, and we waited for her after the show. Duff and Linda exchanged a few words before she returned to her dressing room, and then the two of us headed back to the hotel.

We were really fucked up and instantly passed out in our adjoining suites.

The next day, we went down to the beach and lay chatting on the sun loungers. It was a private beach, and we had our own butler; not far away, Diana Ross and her gang were sunbathing.

It must have been sometime around noon, because the sun was high in the sky, but there was also a nice breeze. We had just taken a dip in the crystal-clear water when I saw a girl running along the beach. It was Linda, looking like Bo Derek in *10*. She threw herself at Duff, and within the space of ten minutes, they were up in his room, fucking.

I didn't see them again after that. They spent all their time fucking. When I went to bed in the evening, I could hear the pounding through the wall.

Still in Hawaii, I got a phone call from my friend Mike Fasano, who was staying in the guest room of the house I was still renting from Duff. My girlfriend Maura, whom I'd been with since high school, lived with me there too. I'd asked Mike to keep an eye on things, and now he said, "Matt, some guy's been sleeping in your room with Maura. I just gotta tell you."

It really pissed me off, even though I had been fucking around on her for years. This time we needed to call it quits. I remember calling her the minute Mike and I hung up. "You know what? You need to get all your shit and move out."

I don't remember what she said, but in retrospect it wasn't fair how I'd treated her for almost fourteen years. I was so one-sided with my jealousy, and I know she was hurt by me hundreds of times. When I got home a few days later everything I owned but the bed was gone. I had collected some amazing art deco furniture—a beautiful carved wood table, chairs, a matching bedroom set. It was really nice, like something from a Mae West film. I also had a coffee table made from blue glass. Maura took everything and disappeared from my life.

After arriving back in LA, I had a meeting with our manager, Doug. He lived in Coto de Caza, Orange County, and the first thing he said to me as he welcomed me into his home was, "Matt, how are you feeling about everything?"

I followed him into what looked like a dining room and sat down opposite him. "Well," I said, "it's been fucking hard, a whole lot harder than I thought it would be... I'd like to renegotiate my deal. I need double."

Doug looked up at me.

"I hear you," he said. "Let me talk to the band. I'll see what I can do."

37

The Freddie Mercury Tribute Concert

Axl might be a dick, but he's still the best,
and Duff gets into a fight with Extreme.

ON APRIL 20, 1992, we took part in the Freddie Mercury Tribute Concert for AIDS awareness at Wembley Stadium. Seventy-two thousand tickets had been sold, and the concert was being broadcast live in seventy-six countries.

Metallica, Def Leppard, Extreme, and GN'R were opening. Then the members of Queen were due to play with artists like Elton John, Robert Plant, Annie Lennox, George Michael, and David Bowie. Many of them were my heroes, so it felt particularly weird to be backstage. I could turn a corner and suddenly be face to face with Ian Hunter, Mick Ronson, or Elizabeth Taylor. Slash was also playing with Queen, and Axl was going to sing "Bohemian Rhapsody" with Elton John.

The day before the concert, we had a huge rehearsal. Everyone but Axl was there. And, like always, no one had any idea where he was or why he wasn't where he was meant to be.

All the bands had a kind of tent as a dressing room backstage, and Elton stuck his head around the door of ours and said, "Where's Axl?" We just glanced at one another and shrugged.

He didn't show up on the day of the concert, either, and I remember that we were all a little stressed about that.

Our tent was next to Extreme's, Metallica's after that, and then Def Leppard's. When I saw Rick Allen of Def Leppard walk by the entrance to our tent, I shouted, "You're amazing!" I really was impressed that he could manage to play the way he did with just one arm.

Right then, the guys from Extreme started singing and playing "More Than Words." Duff, who had dozed off, woke up and said, "What the fuck?" He grabbed a piece of fruit and threw it over the side of our tent, yelling as loudly as he could, "Shut up!"

Just a few seconds later, a piece of meat came flying our way in reply. Duff grabbed a banana, squashed it, and threw that over, and then we put some mustard onto some cheese and threw that too.

"Food fight!" someone on the other side yelled, throwing some ice cubes over. One hit me on the head, and suddenly people started getting seriously angry. We threw a cup full of water over, and they threw a glass at us. "Fuck those guys!" we yelled, storming through the curtain toward their tent. After that, we stood there yelling at one another for a while.

Eventually, once we all got tired of fighting, I went over to the side of the stage to watch Spinal Tap. From the corner of one eye, I noticed that Elizabeth Taylor had come over and was standing next to me.

The guys from Spinal Tap had thrown a cucumber wrapped in tinfoil onto the floor, and I thought, *Surely she can't be getting anything out of watching this.*

But clearly she was, because she stayed put. We started talking and quickly realized that we got along well. "I'm really honored to meet you," I said.

"Well," she said, "I'm honored to meet you."

I was just about to ask her something when she interrupted me. "Which hotel are you staying in?"

Right then, our tour manager came to fetch me. Axl had finally shown up, and it was time for us to perform. But on the walk back to our tent, all I could think was, *I could've had sex with Elizabeth Taylor.*

The short set we played that night went well, and once we were done, Duff, Gilby, and I were escorted to the royal box, where we watched the show from the front. Both Charles and Princess Di were there, and before long Queen was onstage, playing "Tie Your Mother Down" with Joe Elliot from Def Leppard on vocals. Slash started the song with a guitar tuned in a different key; GN'R always tuned half a step down, which meant that Slash was in E flat but the band was 440.

It sounded bad for a minute, but Queen's sound guy covered it once Brian May and the band kicked in. Slash's tech Adam Day got him another guitar, and the song rocked from that point.

Before long, it was time for Axl and Elton's rendition of "Bohemian Rhapsody." Like always, we had no idea whether he would even show up, but in the middle part of the song (the Mama Mia section) it went to massive screens of Freddie and Queen singing on video and tape with an amazing light show followed by a pyrotechnic explosion that set up the next section. Out strode Axl, wearing a black leather kilt, singing better than ever—he was totally awesome. He was unbelievable. He killed it.

All the stars had been there the day before to rehearse, but Axl didn't give a shit. People had been irritated, saying things like, "What a dick." But there he was, onstage, stealing the fucking show.

Suddenly, it was time for everyone to get up onstage and sing the final number: "We Are the Champions," with Liza Minelli as a lead singer.

Duff and I had been knocking back booze all evening, and we were so wasted that we could barely stand. Still, we managed to make it to the after-party, which was being held at a club called Browns. The first person we ran into was the bass player from Extreme, and when he saw how drunk we were, he just sighed and said, "What's the deal with you guys?"

Duff and I laughed and went upstairs. Everyone was there, and when I glanced over to the bar, I saw both George Michael and Liza Minelli standing there. I walked over and squeezed in between them. We chatted a little, and I immediately knew that I liked them both. I have no idea how the evening ended, but I do know that we flew out to LA the very next day, to prepare for our European tour.

38

If There's a Girl You Like, Grab Her Quick

I fall in love with Billy Idol's date.

I BEGAN MY TEMPORARY vacation in LA by buying a Harley-Davidson. I had recently gotten to know Billy Idol, and I'd known Steve Jones from the Pistols for a while, so we started riding around together. It must have been on one of these rides that Billy asked if I wanted to join him at a party some girl named Heidi Fleiss was arranging.

I had no idea who Heidi was or what kind of party it would be, but I liked Billy and I liked to party, so we headed out there later that night. I don't remember exactly where the house was, but I know that we had only just stepped into the living room when I saw Judd Nelson, Christian Slater, and Charlie Sheen—all those party-boy actors, and naturally a lot of chicks.

Billy winked at me and said, "If there's a girl you like, grab her quick, 'cause they'll be gone in a minute." So I grabbed a girl, and just as I did I saw a line of Rolls-Royces pull up outside. Some Arab sheiks and older businessmen spilled out of them.

I asked Billy about it, and he said, "Heidi's a *madam*, and these are all her girls."

"Do I have to pay?" I asked.

"No, we don't have to pay."

So I took this girl home, but unfortunately she turned out to be a complete loony tune. While I was fucking her, she was shrieking at the top of her voice, right up until she eventually came.

In any case, I kept going to Heidi Fleiss's parties, and I got to know Billy's assistant, Art. At some point, he invited me to a party at a hotel in Las Vegas. "It'll be you, me, and Billy," he said.

But when I got there a few days later, it was just him and two girls. One of them was Art's girlfriend, and the other had been set up to meet Billy. She was cute and blonde and introduced herself as BETTY.

"Billy's not coming," Art said, opening a small bottle of liquid as I stepped into the hallway. He poured a capful and handed it to me. I took it from him and gave him a questioning look. "GHB. It's a lot like ecstasy."

"Okay," I said, knocking it back. Art and the girls did the same, and next thing I knew I was making out with Betty.

Not long after that, we were both naked, having sex, and doing more GHB. There was something extra special about that night. It wasn't the GHB, it was something about Betty. She was really sexy, but she also had this quality that I thought I needed—a kind of hippie element to her.

The next day, she and I headed back to LA together, and she told me she was a model. I remembered seeing her in a Coke commercial, and over the weeks that followed, I really fell for her. I took her out to dinner several times, and after maybe the fourth time, I said to her, "I really like you. I think we should live together."

As I said it, she got a serious look on her face and said, "There's something I have to tell you first. Before I came down to LA, I was a stripper at Mitchell Brothers O'Farrell Theatre up in San Francisco. But we didn't call ourselves strippers, we called ourselves performance artists."

I felt a knot in my stomach. I didn't want a stripper girlfriend. Duff used to date strippers, and it always ended badly. But I also felt like I'd been bamboozled. I just got up and left without saying a word.

The problem was that I couldn't stop thinking about her, and a few days before I was due to head off on tour again, I realized

I missed her too much. So I called her up and said, "Fuck it. You don't do it anymore, right?"

"No," she said.

It was a lie, but I didn't know that then, so I continued, "Move in with me. I've got plenty of money, you don't need to work."

That seemed to be an offer she couldn't refuse, because she and her bags turned up at my door the very next day.

39

Pay-Per-View Special in Paris

Duff sweats cranberry vodka,
and I have group sex that spirals out of control.

WE STARTED THE SECOND leg of our European tour at Slane Castle in Ireland. By this point, Duff's drinking had gotten so bad that he had started to drool. He drank vodka all day long, until one evening he passed out onstage. I don't remember where we were, but I remember that we were just beginning "It's So Easy" when I saw him slump to the floor from the corner of my eye. The rest of us immediately stopped playing and worked together to carry him backstage.

The next day, I felt like I had to talk to him about what happened, so I went over to his hotel room. "Duff," I said, "How many drinks do you think you'll have before we go onstage tonight?"

"Uh...maybe ten?"

"Ten drinks?"

Duff, who still didn't seem entirely sober (if he ever was), nodded. "Ten vodka cranberries."

"Look, let's work out a deal," I said. "Either mix the vodka with more cranberry, or have five drinks—cut it in half."

Duff nodded, but I could tell he wasn't planning to do as I said. So when I spotted his bodyguard Butch a while later, I said, "Butch, count Duff's drinks. You make them, he drinks them."

The reason Duff was spiraling out of control in Europe, of all places, wasn't really surprising. It was more difficult to get ahold of coke there. With coke, you could keep your drinking in check—that's the reason we called it "the instant equalizer." But in the same way Duff was losing control over his alcohol intake, I had lost control over how much coke I was doing. Just a few weeks earlier, we had played a show in Mexico City, and that was where everything really started to go wrong.

I remember I stayed up all night before the show, doing line after line. I tried to get a few hours' sleep in the dressing room before we went onstage, but I couldn't do it. My heart was beating so hard that I quickly gave up and tracked down our manager instead. "Doug, I'm in really bad shape," I said. "I fucked up."

Doug was hardened to our behavior by that point, and he just shook his head and said, "Stop doing that shit. Have a few beers and relax. You're gonna be okay." A few hours later, I got up onstage and sat down behind the drums. It was pretty nerve-racking, because cocaine makes you think you're playing too fast or too slow. You lose all sense of time, or as we drummers say, BPM (beats per minute).

I glanced over to Duff and shouted his name.

He had a load of drool coming out of his mouth, and it didn't seem like he could focus when he turned to look at me.

"You help me and I'll help you!" I yelled.

Somehow, we must have managed it, because when I go back and listen to some of those shows where we were almost unconscious, I think, *Man, we were pretty good! We have this kind of ferocity to us.*

In early June, we were booked to play a pay-per-view special at the Hippodrome in Paris, which would be broadcast all over the world. We had invited a whole bunch of special guests—guys like Steven Tyler, Joe Perry, Jeff Beck, and Lenny Kravitz—and the stadium was already set up. So the day before the show, we went in early to do a sound check and to run through the songs with our guest artists. Like usual, Axl hadn't bothered showing up, and I remember how annoyed Steven Tyler was about that.

"What do you mean he's not coming? What do you mean?" he said, gesturing at our tour manager John.

"Well…he's not coming," John explained.

Steven clearly wasn't going to accept that answer, because he said, "I'm calling for another rehearsal. He's gotta come!"

So we booked a club for another rehearsal that evening, and we all headed down there. Tyler was there, Joe Perry was there, Lenny Kravitz was there. But no Axl. One hour passed, then another, and eventually Steven yelled, "I can't believe this guy!"

He didn't show up until the next evening, a few minutes before we went out onstage. Although Axl had started dating Stephanie Seymour, she was also dating Warren Beatty. Stephanie was currently in LA, and as we started the gig, I could tell Axl was irritated. Three songs into the set he went over to one of the TV cameras and said, "I'd like to dedicate this next song to a man who likes to play games…a man who's a parasite… I'd like to dedicate this song to a cheap punk named Warren Beatty…a man who has a family and a baby…but he's gotta spend his time fucking around with other people 'cause he don't know what to do with his own life… Well, listen, home fuck…this is a song called 'Double Talkin' Jive,' motherfucker!"

Next thing I knew, he had left the stage, and Lenny was sent on—even though he wasn't due to play until the end of the set.

Jeff Beck never joined us, due to a bad case of tinnitus, but Steven and Joe both came out. Axl also returned to the stage. Steven and Axl traded vocals, and you could tell that Steven was trying to outdo him. The thing is, Axl kind of crushed it, like always.

As our European tour continued, we eventually reached Milan, Italy. We were at our hotel when we bumped into Gianni Versace and his sister Donatella, plus some guy whom they introduced as her boyfriend. "Darlings," the boyfriend smiled, holding out his hands. "Come to the showroom, you can pick out whatever you like from Gianni Versace!"

My girlfriend Betty was on the road with us, so later that day she, Duff, and I headed over to the Versace showroom to pick out some free stuff. Sadly, I didn't find much I could wear; it was all yellow and green. I did grab a leather shirt with gold buttons, and

I found a leopard print suit that I later wore to the MTV Awards. I also found a few things for Betty.

Duff, on the other hand, grabbed a whole load of shit, all these gaudy dresses, and we took it all over to the counter.

Donatella smiled contentedly when she saw how much we had brought over, and said, "If you boys could just give me your credit cards?"

I remember thinking, *Didn't her so-called boyfriend say it was free?*

Donatella must have noticed my hesitation, because she said, "I just need the credit card information." We passed her our cards. "Duff, yours comes to thirty-five million lira, and Matt, yours is twenty-three million."

Shortly after that, we headed back to the hotel, where we asked our manager to work out the conversion for us. It turned out that Duff had spent $35,000, and I had spent $15,000.

I said, "John, Donatella's boyfriend said it was free! I don't wanna wear this shit! Can you call Donatella?"

But the store was closed. Duff gave everything he'd bought to his wife, Linda Johnson, and she hated all of it. As far as I was concerned, I just felt like I'd been screwed over.

That evening, the four of us decided to go out together—Betty, Duff, Linda, and me. I was wearing the leather Versace shirt with the gold buttons, and Duff came down to the hotel lobby in an all-white suit. The girls were dressed to the nines too.

Not long after, we were in a limo on the way to Club Hollywood. We had a VIP table in a roped-off section, and in the space of just a few seconds, it had filled up with bottles of liquor and mixers. I guess it wasn't long before we were all really drunk. Like always, Duff was the most wasted, and before long we noticed that his white suit was turning pink—he was sweating vodka cranberry, or most likely spilling on himself. Just a few minutes later, once he could no longer sit upright, the bouncers helped Linda take him out to a car.

One of the good things about Betty was that she had lesbian tendencies, and we often experimented with other girls together. That night, we saw two girls making out in front of us.

"What do you think?" I asked.

Betty smiled, and next thing I knew we started toying with the threesome idea.

It turned out Betty liked one of the girls in particular. She pointed to her, and said, "I wanna take her with us."

We got up and went over to them, but when Betty asked her favorite if she wanted to join us, she replied that she didn't go anywhere without her friend. Just like that, I was sitting next to two girls and my girlfriend Betty in a car heading back to the hotel.

Although I was really drunk, I still managed to take in what Betty was telling me as we took the elevator up to our room: "The one thing you can't do is fuck them. You can fuck me, and I'll fuck them, but you can't fuck them."

"Really?" I slurred, but she just gave me a stern glance in reply. So I nodded and said, "Okay."

We got to my room, and the girls started doing each other while I was fucking Betty. Next thing I knew, my dick was inside one of the other girls.

I remember fucking her while Betty was eating the other girl out, but suddenly Betty turned in my direction, leaped up, and yelled, "You asshole! I told you!"

I held out my arms and slurred, "Come on, she's great!"

Betty pointed to the girls, one after another. "I want both of you out, now!"

I didn't really want them to leave, so instead I said, "No, fuck you, Betty! *You* fucking get out!"

It was a bad move on my part, but done was done, and we began yelling at each other in front of the girls. Betty packed up her things and dragged her bags out through the door. I tossed everything she hadn't managed to grab into the corridor behind her and then closed the door. I had just bent down to pick up the last few things when she kicked the door open and the doorknob hit me right in the eye.

Before I knew what was happening, she was gone again. The girls were still there, however, so I continued fucking one of them until my phone started ringing. It was Duff.

"Dude, what the fuck? Betty's up here in my room, totally hysterical. What are you doing?"

I mumbled something in reply, but then I must have passed out, because when I woke up, I had no idea where I was. My eye was totally black and blue, my mouth was as dry as sandpaper, and right then—suddenly and relentlessly—the memories came rushing back to me. I felt like a real asshole, and that's how the others seemed to look at me when I went down to the lobby. No one spoke to me; they didn't even look in my direction, except Linda, who hissed, "Fuck you, Matt!"

The idea was that we would have a few days off in San Remo ahead of our next show, so later that day we checked into the Palace Hotel, down by the beach at the edge of town. Just as we were heading up to our rooms, Duff and I got into a fight.

"How could you treat her like that?" he yelled.

And I replied, "Fuck you, dude!"

Just like that, we started physically fighting in the corridor. "You can keep her!" I told him. "You can fuck her too, if you want."

Duff yelled back at me, "You're not coming on the boat!"

We were supposed to be heading out on a yacht later that afternoon, but now I clearly wasn't welcome. So while the others went off to do that, I hung back in my room, feeling like a loser. That self-hate followed me over the next few days, and by the time we reached Lisbon, Portugal, I took Betty out to dinner and apologized. "It won't happen again. Please forgive me," I begged, along with thousands of other things along the same lines. Somehow, we must have managed to talk our way through things, because we actually got back together.

40

The Enormous Heroin Cake

Supermodels galore, and Axl's psychic warns us not
to play in towns beginning with M.

After taking a few weeks off, it was time for the North American leg of our tour, with Metallica as support. It must have been after our gig in Washington, DC, that Axl decided to make our after-parties a big deal. The reason I remember is that I can still clearly picture him coming into the dressing room there with Stephanie Seymour, Naomi Campbell, and Elle Macpherson.

By that point, we always had certain things in our dressing room: food and enormous amounts of booze, of course. No one had ever thought anything was missing, but when Axl came in that day, he was upset. "Is this it?" he moaned. "The Rolling Stones wouldn't do it like this." And though I didn't say anything at the time, I did actually agree with him. We were playing stadiums, and we needed some kind of vibe.

So ahead of the next gig, Axl roped in his brother, Stuart Bailey, to take care of the parties. Each one would have a different theme, and I'll never forget Axl telling him, "I want ice sculptures, I want champagne fountains, I want a casino, and I want to give people money to play craps and poker. I also want a private Jacuzzi room with girls in it."

He went on: "Make it happen, Stuart. We're gonna do a casino, we're gonna have dealers, we're gonna have girls serving hors d'oeuvres. And when we go to Indianapolis, I want Formula 1 cars backstage, I want all the girls wearing checkered suits. I want a Greek theme when we get to Pittsburgh. I want them to bring in a pig—four guys dressed in Greek robes carrying it, and girls fanning the guys and feeding them grapes. Down in Orlando, I want a hippie party, with a sixties vibe."

Around this time, there was even an occasion when Naomi Campbell was into me. It happened in our dressing room, after a show. She was so coked up that it was coming out the sides of her mouth—foam, like drool. I remember her pushing me up against the wall and saying, "Let's go to my room." As I looked at her then, she did not seem hot to me. She was so coked up that it really didn't turn me on.

Someone I *was* interested in was Naomi and Stephanie's friend, Elle Macpherson. I always clammed up whenever she was around, and had no idea what to say or do. She was so beautiful it was like I turned into some shy, nerdy kid whenever she was nearby.

On one occasion I was in the dressing room and she was on the floor, because there was no room on the couch. I moved everything and said, "No, no, no, you sit here!"

I think it was probably the only I time I actually dared speak to her.

Back to the after-parties Axl's brother started organizing for us: After one show, I brought Lars Ulrich along to party. His eyes genuinely widened, and after a moment or two, he said, "Oh, my God, man. What do you think these parties cost?"

"I'm glad we're not paying for it."

Someone heard Lars saying that, and it got back to Axl, who then ejected him from the party.

Kicked him out, just like that, and refused to let him back in.

The after-parties weren't the only thing that cost a lot of money. There was also a vocal coach, Ron Anderson, who flew out to see us with his entourage every now and then. His wife always tagged along, as did a couple of other people—we never knew exactly what they did. They all stayed in suites, and they all flew first class.

"Why do we have to pay for that shit?" Slash asked John, our tour manager.

But he always gave us the same reply. "You know, it's a touring cost."

Ron was a little weird and he would sometimes turn up out of nowhere, grab my neck to feel my vocal chords, and say, "Have you slept at all? You'll need eight hours' sleep if you're going to sing."

Axl also had a psychic, and she told him we shouldn't play any shows in towns that began with the letter *M*, and that meant we ended up canceling—in Minneapolis, for example.

Despite that, we played a show in Montreal on August 8, 1992. Metallica's story about what happened there is pure bullshit, and I'll try to explain why.

During this leg of the tour, Metallica were constantly trying to outdo us with their pyrotechnics. Every night, they kept adding more and more fireworks to their set.

We used to sit in our dressing room and listen to the sound of the pyrotechnics going off up onstage. At first, they were only using them in three songs, but before long they'd added them to every single track. More and more pyrotechnics, more excitement—at some point I said to Duff, "Man, I think they're using more pyro than they should." It was something we had agreed upon in advance—who would do what, and how much. It was all there in black and white in the contract.

At that particular show in Montreal, James Hetfield managed to burn his arm—it was pretty much inevitable, given that Metallica's stage was starting to look more and more like a minefield. Pyro Pete, their pyrotechnician, was incredibly experienced and had previously worked for bands like AC/DC and Mötley Crüe. His thing was that everything was manual, so he had to push the buttons to make them go off.

As I understand it, he told James, "Don't go into that section, because I've got a new concussion thing that's gonna go off. I've got shit all over the stage."

He looked over at Lars, and James was over there, and he hit the button. *Boom!*

The minute we found out what had happened, Axl said, "Okay, guys, let's go up there and do this as quick as we can." Metallica's story was that we were *chilling* backstage, but that isn't true at all. Metallica had been clear from the outset that they wanted to do everything their own way; they wanted their own lighting, their own rig... That meant there was an entire production that had to be rearranged onstage before we could get out there—the whole process took around forty-five minutes. When we finally got up there that day, something was wrong with the PA. It didn't sound good at all, and Axl got pissed and yelled, "When the crew gets this together, we'll be back."

We walked off, and as we did, the crowd stormed the place and destroyed everything they could get ahold of.

That night, I got taken to the hospital because I was having trouble breathing properly. I was hyperventilating and severely dehydrated as a result of all the partying. Duff came with me; he always did.

Because I was so dehydrated, they had to pump me full of potassium.

Ordinarily, we would stay at the venue until around two in the morning, enjoying the band's after-parties. After that, we would head to the airplane and continue to party as we flew to the next city. But since everything had gone crazy that evening, the others were all waiting on the plane by the time Duff and I arrived.

Those flights we took were pretty out of the ordinary. No one would be wearing their seatbelts as we took off, and everyone had a drink in their hand. People would be dancing in the aisles, and there were always five stewardesses that we had picked out from photographs. On their nights off, we invited them to our shows, and they became like groupies. Actually, our tour manager John married one of them named Elanie, and they are still married to this day.

Around this time, I got ahold of a giant block of heroin from Baz. It was a huge lump, the size of an extra-large Hershey's bar, and it was pure opium.

As I tried it on the plane one day, Slash noticed the smell. He loved heroin, so he was already with me. Duff was too, though he was sticking to his coco puffs—cigarettes in which the tobacco had been mixed with coke. It was cool 'cause Axl came over to join us as well. He didn't usually partake in drugs based on the fact that he was taking care of his voice. I had a piece of tinfoil and held a lighter beneath it, using a straw to inhale the smoke. It made us feel kind of calm and happy, and we decided to meet up the next day to do more of the same. This time we were all in Axl's hotel room, sitting in a circle on the floor and basically passing the piece of tinfoil around. It's strange to say but it was the first time we were all in the same room together, laughing and having a good time as a band.

We were really chipping away at the block, but the thing about heroin is that it's really addictive.

A few days later, Axl called me. "Do you have any more of that shit? Would you come over?"

I went to his room, and we spent the whole night talking.

The bar of heroin lasted a few weeks, and since Axl was digging it, I managed to become really close with him. It didn't affect his voice or anything, and we were getting along great. Or we were until he called me up one day, and asked, "Are we out?"

"Yeah, I'm out."

He hung up on me without saying goodbye or anything. And that was it, the end of our band bonding session. But then, on my birthday a few months later, our manager Doug called up to my hotel room and said something along the lines of, "Hey, Axl's here; he's coming up."

"Okay."

The door opened, and Axl walked in with Stephanie Seymour. He was holding a huge package, and he grinned and said happy birthday to me. He knew I collected art-deco furniture, and when

I opened up the present, there was this amazing brass and marble sculpture of a famous French piece inside. It was probably a $5,000 statue, and I still have it.

Axl would make interesting gestures like that, as though he was trying to connect, but he was never able to actually say he was sorry, never able to have a conversation about everything we'd been through.

In retrospect, I think it was probably just his way of trying to ease the tension. I was blown away by the gesture, because it really was a beautiful piece. I remember Stephanie standing behind him, smiling. Axl had that kind of Elvis generosity about him—he once gave Doug a car, for example, and he bought people watches all the time. It was just his way of saying *thank you* or *I'm sorry* without actually saying it.

Back then, if I'd been the person I am now, I probably would have gone over to him and apologized for what happened between us. But I didn't. Back then, I thought it was a cool gesture, but it was still the other side of him. That was what you got with Axl; the very next day, you might turn up at a show, and he would completely ignore you. He wouldn't say hello, nothing. He would just walk straight by.

41

The Runaway

I ditch my bodyguards, try flying commercial, and report to Lars Ulrich.

AFTER TOURING FOR SIXTEEN months straight, I developed a kind of constant anxiety. It felt like I never got any peace, and by the time we played the Astrodome in Houston on September 4, 1992, I'd suddenly had enough.

The whole band had taken a bow, like usual, to thank the crowd from the stage when Axl, Duff, and Slash went back out for a second go.

I realized I was furious, but I didn't say anything until that evening, after we'd flown to Dallas and started the after-party with cocktails and blow in Duff's room at the Four Seasons.

"What the hell was that?" I said.

"What?" said Duff, pretending not to know what I meant.

"The three of you going out there alone."

Slash shrugged. "We started the band, so we get to take an extra bow."

"Fuck you guys," I said. "I'm your drummer now, since your last one took too much heroin."

"Yeah, but we started the band," Slash repeated.

"Fuck you," I shouted, storming out of the room.

Shortly after that, I was out on the street, where I hailed a cab. "Do you know who I am?" I asked the driver as I jumped, out of breath, into the backseat. I was still wearing my stage clothes.

The driver nodded happily at me in the rearview mirror.

"Nah, you don't," I said, handing him a hundred-dollar bill.

"Okay," the driver said uncertainly, taking it.

"Drive me to some airport hotel," I continued. "Doesn't matter which, as long as there's a minibar in the room."

A while later, he let me out by a tall, gray building. There had been a lot of press about GN'R in the local papers and reports on all the big TV channels ahead of our upcoming show in town.

When I got to reception and saw the two women's faces light up, I didn't ask them anything, just passed them a hundred-dollar bill and said, "You never saw me. Okay?"

Sure enough, there was a minibar in my room, and I managed to empty it within the space of a half hour. I crashed on my bed after that.

When I woke, I had to squint because of the morning sun flooding in through the windows. Despite that, I could make out the silhouettes of several people standing around me. One of them shook me roughly, and I realized it was our tour manager, John Reese. The band manager, Doug Goldstein, was standing behind him. I raised my head.

"Hey, guys," I mumbled, reliving the taste of old Baileys and Jägermeister. "I paid the cab driver and the girls downstairs not to say where I was." I cleared my throat. "How'd you find me?"

"Well...we paid them more," said John. Doug filled in: "You need to take a shower, then you've got to play at the Texas Stadium."

I sat up and shook my head firmly. "I'm quitting!"

Both John and Doug sighed. "You can't," said Doug. "It'd cost you a fortune."

I tried to moisten my lips with my tongue, but it didn't work. There was zero saliva in my mouth. "Then I want my own dressing room," I said. "And I'm not gonna go on the private jet; I wanna fly commercial. I want a van too. Fuck limos! And I don't want a bunch of guys with walkie-talkies around me all the time. I wanna live like a normal human being!"

They glanced at one another like they didn't know quite what to think, but by that evening I had my own dressing room.

As I sat there, on the only chair in the room, trying to feel like I'd won, there was a knock at the door. It was Lars Ulrich. He'd had to ask around to find me, and he seemed surprised. "Dude, what's going on? What are you doing here?"

There was always an air of competition the minute Lars stepped into a room. During our entire tour with Metallica, it was like he was competing with us. That's why he often swung by to see how things were going in the GN'R camp. I told him what had happened, and he listened intently, even if he looked a little skeptical when I reassured him it felt great. He looked even more skeptical the next day, when I told him I'd flown on a regular plane and been picked up in a van and loved it.

This was before the security checks at airports became a real pain in the ass. Still, it was tiring to fly that way when you had to keep to a tight touring schedule. Bags had to be checked in, and then you had to wait for ages to collect them. I only just made it to our shows in time.

I got sick of it after just a few days. So when I got to that evening's venue, I went over to the band's trailer and paused for a moment before going in.

Only Slash and Duff were inside. Duff was slumped on the couch with his obligatory vodka cranberry, and Slash was on a chair, playing one of his Les Pauls.

I didn't know quite how to bring it up, so I just cleared my throat and quietly said, "How're you guys doing?"

They looked up at me, and Slash said something along the lines of, "Yeah, it's cool."

That was that. I was back in the band dressing room.

42

South America

*I become friends with the cartel's head dealer and see Marilyn Monroe
talking about me and my life with a priest on TV.*

By the time we got to Venezuela, I was in really bad shape. My
alcohol and drug habits had long been out of control, but this was
when I first began to realize that they might even cost me my life.
They're also the reason there are huge gaps in my memories from
this part of the tour. What I do remember is that we had a girl
doing the interpreting for us and she and I hung out in the hotel
bar together. She was super hot, and after we'd been drinking for a
while, I said, "Let's go for a drive around the city."

Not long after, we jumped into a cab being driven by some guy
with a handlebar moustache. He had it kind of curled, and his jaw
was moving the way it does on people who've taken a line of blow
or two.

I said to him, "*Cocaína, amigo.*"

He replied, "*¡Sí! ¿Quanto?*"

"*¿La quinta?*" I said.

"*¡Cinquenta!*"

I told him, "I'll pay seventy bucks for ten grams."

He smiled and explained that we would have to drive to go get it.
I gave him a thumbs-up, and before long we were rolling along bumpy
roads flanked by dilapidated houses and kids running barefoot. The
interpreter girl was speaking to him in Spanish, and then she turned
to me and explained that this could be pretty dangerous. Since my

awareness of risk was pretty much nonexistent at the time, I just shrugged and smiled.

We soon pulled up outside what could only be described as a shack. The driver flashed his lights, and a guy came out and said, "*¡Buenos días!*" in a husky voice. He then threw a bag through the open window, and it landed on the front seat. The guy looked at me and asked if I wanted rum.

"Raw rum from the Caribbean," he hissed.

I said I'd happily take two bottles, and while he went to fetch them I saw the driver glance at the bag. He said, "*¡Amigo, para mí!*"

There were ten straws full of coke inside the bag, with both ends of each twisted. I fished out one of them, untwisted one end, and handed it to him. He deftly prepared himself a line, and as he snorted it, it was like his mustache was twirling.

Before I knew it, two days had passed, and I was sitting with the interpreter on my hotel balcony. We were completely wasted from all the snorting, drinking, and fucking we'd done since the cab driver dropped us off at the hotel, but that was when the call to attend sound check came in. The band was waiting for me when I turned up. There was a little staircase leading up to the stage, and I had trouble getting up it. Still, eventually I was sitting down behind my drum kit. I played a few beats on the toms and said, "Sounds great." Then I headed back down the stairs to my van and returned to the hotel.

After our show in Venezuela, we flew to Bogotá, Colombia. We had only just landed when we heard there had been an attempted military coup in Caracas, which meant all our equipment was still stuck in Venezuela. Before we got into our cars at the airport, our manager Doug announced that he had read in the paper that ten American citizens were kidnapped in Bogotá every week.

Doug said, "I want you guys to be careful. We're not going to leave the hotel."

We each had an SUV, and I got into mine. There was one guy on either side of me, each clutching a machine gun. Two guys sat up front, and one of them also had a gun. We even had cops with machine guns riding motorcycles in front, beside, and behind us.

When we pulled up outside our hotel, a tank and a load of armed guards were out front. I said to Doug, "What the fuck… What's the tank for?"

Doug gave me a serious look. "To protect you guys."

Like always, we had a whole floor to ourselves at the hotel, but the difference was that we had also been ordered not to go out. We immediately threw a party, with every door along the corridor open. There were people everywhere—our security guys, the horn players, and the female backing singers.

We soon found out that because our equipment was delayed, we would have to cancel one of our two scheduled shows in Bogotá. I turned to our tour manager John right after we heard the news, and said, "This is crazy; we have to be here for like two days with no show, and we can't even go out!"

John grinned. "We'll order in."

"What do you mean…girls?" I asked.

"Yeah!"

Only a short while later, the elevator doors opened and a guy—I think he introduced himself as Hector—stepped out into the corridor, accompanied by twenty or so beautiful Colombian women, all dressed up as schoolgirls. When they spotted us, they yelled, "*Yeeeah!*"

Hector shouted something in Spanish and clicked his fingers, and the girls gathered in a circle around him. Someone put on some music, and before I had time to work out what was happening, the girls had all undressed and were dancing naked.

Our next few days in Bogotá continued in much the same vein. The whole thing was one huge mess. During what should have been our first show, torrential rain caused the stage to collapse. It was rebuilt the next day, but we still had plenty of other problems. Back then, Colombia wasn't used to hosting big rock concerts, and when we arrived at the stadium we had to ride through a huge crowd.

We quickly realized that wasn't the only issue. There were just as many people *inside* the stadium, for example, because the organizer had said that all tickets were still valid. If you had a ticket for the canceled show, you could just come along to the next one—all because he didn't want to refund the money, of course.

Honestly, I felt pretty scared as we drove through all those people. It was similar to the feeling I'd had in St. Louis, but ten times worse. Before we headed out onstage that evening, I said to Doug, "Is this going to be okay? Is this safe?" And like a typical manager, he said, "You guys are gonna be fine! Just get out there!"

About an hour and fifteen minutes into our set, it was time to play "November Rain." Right that second, of course, the heavens opened and it started pouring rain. It was coming down so hard that my drums were all full of water.

Axl and the promoter (who spoke Spanish) explained to the crowd that we had to stop playing because the water could conduct electricity. But the crowd refused to accept that; they went crazy. They were rioting outside the stadium, too. People were throwing fireworks. And someone even got killed.

The minute we got back to the hotel, Doug said, "Pack your shit, we're getting the fuck out of this country."

The only problem was that something was going on between management and the promoters, and before we had time to leave, they stormed into the hotel lobby and started talking to Doug. I guess they wanted their money back or something.

Our accountant, Jerry Gendron, kept his briefcase full of cash handcuffed to him.

Maybe he took care of the whole thing; I don't actually know. All I know is that our problems continued. When we landed in Chile later that day, the government confiscated our plane to see if we had brought any drugs with us from Bogotá. Thankfully they didn't find anything. But it was probably a dumb idea to tell Axl about the stadium we were due to play at—the Éstadio Nácional. In 1973, a whole load of people had been tortured and killed there; Pinochet basically turned the stadium into a prison camp, complete with torture chambers.

After learning this, Axl announced, "I'm not playing this fucking place."

We were surrounded by local guards, and they heard what he said. Their chief security guy immediately stormed over to our manager and said, "If Axl doesn't go onstage, we'll have to arrest him. We might even have to shoot him."

Not long after, Doug took Axl to one side and said, "Look, man, you've gotta play. Do the show, because if there's a riot they're gonna shoot and kill people. They might even shoot and kill you. So get onstage now."

I don't think I'd ever seen Axl so compliant before. In an instant, he was transformed into some kind of schoolboy, and he started fawning over the crowd.

"How're you doing?" he shouted. "It's so great to be playing here in Chile!"

In Argentina, I was already drunk when we checked in to our hotel, and I went straight to the bar so I could keep drinking. I met a soccer team from Australia, plus a really hot Australian girl. I buddied up with her, and after we'd both had a couple of drinks, I took her to the bathroom at one side of reception. I just grabbed her by the hand and pulled her inside, locking the door behind us. I pushed her down on top of the toilet, yanked off her panties, and started eating her out. I hadn't been going for long when she suddenly started to squirt—not just a little bit, either. It felt like gallons of the stuff, so much that I was completely soaked. We both laughed about it, and then I went back to my room to wash and put on a dry shirt. When I got back to the bar, I saw that some guy had sat down beside her. I noticed that he was doing the cocaine thing—smacking his lips like he was chewing something, or like his mouth was super dry—so I turned to him and said, "How're you doing? Got any cocaine?"

"*Sí, amigo*...at *mi casa*."

"Cool," I said. "Where's that?"

"Follow me!"

The Australian girl and I followed him, and as we walked, he said, "My car is down in the garage." He glanced at me. "We'll put you in the back of the car and cover you with a blanket... You know, because of the fans."

Just a few minutes later, I found myself lying flat out on the backseat of the guy's car. There was a blanket over the top of me, but I could see through a tiny gap that we were driving through the nice part of Buenos Aires. There were fashionable houses with beautiful gardens on both sides, surrounded by high walls. Before long, we pulled up outside a huge mansion.

The house had these doors that opened automatically as you approached them. Soon, I was in what looked like the dining room. The man who had driven us over there disappeared and returned with a huge tray that had a bunch of coke on it. He put it down and opened a bottle of wine, and the room suddenly filled up with a whole load of other people. I stayed there for two days and probably would have stayed longer if I didn't have to head back for our show.

"Where have you been? Everyone's been looking for you!" John Reese yelled when he spotted me.

I shrugged in reply but hadn't gotten any farther than my room before the phone started ringing.

It was John again.

"Flush everything you have down the toilet. The *federales* are coming!"

I raced to get rid of everything I had left. Just a moment later, the door of my hotel room flew open, and the federales came marching in to search my stuff.

Once they were done, they told us all to come down to the banquet room—not just the band members but also the roadies, the backup singers, and the horn section. I remember us exchanging confused, worried glances.

The head federales said to Doug, "We've been following your drummer. He was with the head of the cartel." Doug flashed me an irritated glance. The guy continued, "He's been with the head dealer from the Argentinian cartel, and we want you to know that we're going to have to arrest him. We searched his room and couldn't find anything, but we want to interrogate him."

Doug seemed to have composed himself somewhat, because he said, "You realize that if you arrest Matt, you guys are going to have a riot on your hands, right? These kids will tear this fucking town apart. How about we do this instead: we play the two shows, then we get the fuck out of here. No one gets hurt, and I'll tell Matt to stay away from the cartel."

The head federales seemed to accept that solution, because he just nodded and grunted, and then he and his men left. Once he was out of earshot, Doug came over to me.

"You motherfucker…you were hanging out with the head of the fucking cartel?"

"I had no idea," I said, holding up my hands in innocence. "He seemed like such a nice guy!"

Though my life at that point surpassed any dreams I'd had as a kid, I was far from happy.

I always did a load of blow on the plane, and I had to do it before we landed—to avoid the risk of being arrested if anyone searched the plane. I didn't want to do it in front of the others, so I used to go to the back to do it. As we approached the end of the tour and flew to Cancún in Mexico, I took Duff back there with me. We did a whole bunch, and I was really jacked up when we left the plane that afternoon.

For some reason, we were picked up in vans rather than limos. Duff, Dizzy, Slash, and I ended up in the same van, and we had only just sat down when I asked the driver if he could find us some blow. He nodded and drove us to the Ritz Carlton, which was right on the beach. He dropped us off and then delivered the coke to my hotel room a few hours later. I did a few lines and then called Duff and Dizzy's rooms, but when no one answered, I kept going on my own. By this point, I couldn't leave my room while I was doing coke.

So I just holed up in there, snorting and drinking. I don't know what I was thinking, but we had three days off, so I guess I must have decided it was cool.

When I ran out of booze in the minibar, I only had to call down to reception, and in a few minutes someone would turn up to refill it. Honestly, it was one of the most horrible coke experiences I ever had. I was in there for like two days, and by the end I couldn't even stand upright. At some point, I must have crawled into the bathroom. When I finally emerged, I spent a couple of hours staring at the TV, convinced that Marilyn Monroe was talking to me. Suddenly, there was a green rabbit in the middle of my room. It had huge, razor sharp teeth and an evil, furious look in its eyes. It was climbing the walls and running across the ceiling, and every now and then, it hopped down toward me and laughed right in my face. I tried to ignore it and focused on the TV instead. Marilyn Monroe was there, with a priest, and the priest was smoking. Marilyn was talking about my life and how I felt, and it was so terrifying that I could hardly breathe. It was like I was paralyzed. I couldn't pick up the phone, couldn't talk to anyone. I only answered the door if it was the guy with the booze.

Eventually, I managed to call Betty and tell her how fucked up I was. "I can't do this anymore," I said. "I feel like shit."

Betty actually managed to talk me off the edge, and then on the third day I ran out of coke. I had finished an entire quarter ounce by myself. When I got home from Mexico, I decided for the first time that I had to get clean.

43

Cold Turkey

I help Betty become Shiva, and become close with Dracula.

GOING COLD TURKEY ALONE after doing coke and drinking alcohol pretty much every day for years is dangerous; it just isn't the kind of thing you're supposed to do on your own. But once I got home and made it through the first week of sweats, shakes, and regrets, I thought I'd managed to overcome the worst of it.

Betty had been nagging me to get my shit together for some time, and as far as I can remember, I did manage to stay away from coke—in the beginning, at least.

During the last leg of our tour, I hired a Swedish personal trainer named Hans who helped me get into shape. But I soon started drinking again, and I became a real asshole when I drank. If someone told me not to drink too much, I would tell that person to fuck off. I would break things, get angry, crap like that. And since Betty—who had changed her name to SHIVA by that point—was trying to make me stay sober, she took the brunt of it.

Aside from drinking more than ever once the tour finished, I also started sneaking around, hiding the coke from Shiva. One day, for example, I went into the bathroom to chop some lines using my credit card. Later that evening, we decided to get takeout and Shiva had the card between her teeth as she ordered. "Oh, my God, you fucker!" she yelled.

We got into a huge fight and ultimately broke up. I was a mess, and she was just fed up with me. She took off and moved into a little apartment. I had seriously bad abandonment issues at the time; I don't know where they came from—maybe that lonely, empty feeling I felt when my father left, or from my mom when she chose to sail off with my stepdad. Whatever the reason, whenever anyone left me, I always got completely fucked up.

Maybe that was why I went over to Shiva's place a few nights later. She wasn't home, so I just camped out on her front porch. Early the next morning, a car pulled up outside. I was still sitting there. Stalking her. A man I knew got out, followed by Shiva.

I walked over to the car. I didn't want to kick his ass; I knew it wasn't his fault. "Shiva," I said instead. "What are you doing? We love each other! I want to take you to a Grateful Dead show."

She loved the Grateful Dead, but she said, "I can't. We're not even together, and you're an asshole."

Somehow, I must have managed to convince her, because in June 1994, we headed down to Vegas for that show. "I have backstage passes," I told her once we checked into our hotel.

"I don't want to meet them!" she said, explaining that she couldn't handle meeting her heroes.

If you've ever been to a Grateful Dead show, you'll know that they're totally out there—very hippie, which was perfect for Shiva. She was pretty hippie herself, into yoga, meditating, and macrobiotic food. In any case, when we got to the venue that evening, she said, "I'm gonna go spinning now." Among the Grateful Dead fans (so-called Deadheads), that meant spinning around for hours on end with your hands in the air. A few minutes later, I saw her spinning like a madwoman in front of the stage with hundreds of others.

A few days later, when we returned to LA, I paid $2,000 to have her name legally changed from Betty to Shiva. She really hated her old name and wanted to be Shiva on her driver's license.

Not long after, Shiva and I began talking about where we were going to live, and Shiva said she wanted a ranch with goats and other animals. Once we started looking, we came across a place with palm trees and a pool, up in the hills above the ocean in Malibu. We had only seen the pictures, but Shiva said, "That's where I want to live."

"Okay," I said. "We'll take it."

We had never set foot on the property we'd eventually christen One Gun Ranch when we bought it for $850,000.

That's why I was a little shocked when we stepped through the front door and saw the floral paper on the walls. I turned to Shiva and said, "Well, looks like we're gonna have to do a little remodeling."

She nodded, but she didn't seem very enthusiastic about it. I just thought it felt good to have bought my first real home. I've always been interested in interiors and design and thought it was pretty cool once the renovation got underway.

There were five fireplaces in that house; it was killer. The first thing I did was to have one of the rooms transformed into a theater with velvet walls and surround sound. As for the furniture, it was all custom made. A Mexican guy from the construction company managed to make the wood look old, and I told him to do it to every cabinet, floorboard, and door. I ripped out all the old white banisters and replaced them with iron and bought myself a big gothic chandelier.

Shiva stayed in the Shoreham Towers apartment while I was working on the house, and when she came over one day, she had a tiny black puppy with her. It was Halloween, and she said, "They were giving them away at the grocery store, and I couldn't resist."

I squatted down and petted it. "We can't have a dog," I told her.

Right then, the puppy bit my hand so hard that it started to bleed.

"You little fucker! I know what your name's gonna be: Dracula!"

That dog became my buddy. I hated him at first, because he chewed *everything*. He ate all the books with pictures of dogs in them—like dog training books. But, as time passed, he actually became one of my closest friends.

A few days later, while I was in the house with the construction workers, I happened to glance up the mountain. I saw smoke, and

205

jumped into my little black Porsche and raced up there. I realized pretty quickly that there was a forest fire moving toward the ocean. I headed back down to the house and saw all the helicopters and fire trucks arriving. I told the construction crew to split, and then I grabbed little Drac.

As I stepped out into the garden, I spotted the old lady who lived in the house just down the hill from ours. "Have you seen my husband?" she asked.

I shook my head no. "Is he out there?

"Oh, my God, yes "

"Don't go out there," I said. But the old lady was already on her way.

Within fifteen or twenty minutes, the fire was only a few hundred yards from my house. The air outside was thick with black soot. I had never seen anything like it. Three houses not far from mine burned down in what felt like no time at all, and that was followed by what sounded like an explosion. I closed all the windows, turned on the sprinklers in the yard, and left.

I turned on the news the minute I got to our apartment in Shoreham Towers on Sunset Boulevard. The whole of Malibu was on fire; all the houses on the hill were lit up, right down to the pier. It was fucking awful—the worst fire Malibu had ever seen.

That was when I noticed the news ticker at the bottom of the screen: ELDERLY COUPLE DIES IN FIRE, followed by an image of the old lady and her husband. I felt my stomach turn. The whole thing was so awful. My thoughts turned to the house Shiva and I had bought. It was the biggest investment I had ever made, so once the fire department had managed to bring the fire under control a few days later, we decided to hike up there—all the canyon roads had been closed, and we had to get past the roadblocks.

The sight that greeted us was awful, something I'll never forget. Everything was black and burnt.

We reached the top of the canyon. Everything was gone—except for our house. I called my business manager and said, "We saved the house!"

"Oh, man," he said. "I had it covered for a million. You could've built a mansion with the insurance money."

Not long after, we moved back in. It was a nightmare. Every animal known to man had moved onto our property—or, more accurately, they'd fled the fire to our yard, where all the sprinklers were on. There were probably twenty dead animals in our pool, and we didn't have time to do much other than clean them out before Slash called and asked if I wanted to go over for a writing session. I'd barely heard from him since we finished the tour. But I wanted nothing more than to make music again, so I said, "Sure!"

By that time, Slash had a house way up on Mulholland Drive—practically on top of the mountain in Hollywood. I was sober, but I wasn't doing anything to take care of myself. After working for maybe the third evening in a row, Slash said, "You want a drink?"

Without thinking, I said, "Yeah, pour me one."

I had been clean and sober for six months, but just like that, I started drinking again. It didn't take long for the coke to follow—and the not going home. I started having super late nights with Slash. Once we finished a writing session, we would head out into Hollywood to party, and then I would crash on his couch.

We probably spent a good month up there on Mulholland Drive, just fucking around, and when I eventually drove home drunk one morning, Shiva was furious.

"Where the fuck have you been?" she yelled as I staggered into the hallway.

"Honestly, I don't know," I slurred, because I really wasn't sure.

"I know where you were," she continued. "You went to a house party. And then you..." All I could hear was *blah blah blah*.

"Please, Shiva," I groaned. "Let me sleep it off."

With that, I went and lay down on the floor beside my drums in the music room. I had only just fallen asleep when I woke up to her banging an enormous mallet on the bass drum right by my head.

"I fucking know where you were!" she shouted. We got into a real fight.

Shiva was shouting and hitting me, and I pushed her out of the way to get past. She followed me, and I pushed her again. Not long after, the cops showed up and arrested me.

It was over between me and Shiva. I gave her the apartment in West Hollywood and kept the house in Malibu for myself. She took our second dog, Anya (it had been trained by cops, so she'd feel safe while I was away), and I kept Drac.

44

Bone Daddy

I become a party planner and rate girls for Heidi Fleiss.

AROUND THIS TIME, I got to know an old Vietnam vet who looked like Billy Gibbons of ZZ Top. He was this really cool, wacky, eccentric dude who worked at a vintage jewelry store called Leathers and Treasures on North Stanley Avenue. His name was Bone Daddy.

I was still writing songs with Slash and thought it would be good to have someone to look after the house while I wasn't home. So one day while I was in his store, I said, "Hey, Bone Daddy, why don't you come live with me? You can be my groundskeeper." He seemed to think it was a good idea, because he moved into one of my guestrooms the very same day. He didn't want to sleep in the bed, though; he said he preferred a sleeping bag on the floor. We decided to start throwing parties at the house and to call these events Club Matt.

The next week, we headed down to a big market by the pier in Malibu, where we filled the car with steak and chicken, and then things really kicked off. Those parties, which often lasted three days, were actually pretty legendary. In fact, I still run into people today who say, "Hey, man, I used to go to your parties!"

Early on Friday evening, I would set up all the equipment by the pool—drums, PA, amps, guitars, and a grand piano, so we could jam.

The garage was full of booze, and we had a full bar, along with anything you could want to eat. Out in the orchard (I had, like, fifty trees—apples and oranges), we had futon beds so that people could go over there and do whatever the fuck they wanted. People would sleep in hammocks or on the couches inside, even on mattresses on the floor. By the second party Bone Daddy and I threw, we had all kinds of characters showing up—Stephen Stills, John Stamos, Jason Bonham, Tommy Lee, Carrot Top, Cher's kid Elijah Blue, and Billy Idol, to name just a few.

One of these days, when I was out shopping ahead of the party, I got a call from a girl who worked for Heidi Fleiss.

"Matt," she said, "we're going to break in some new girls, and, uh, Heidi wants to try them out."

"What do you mean?" I asked.

"Could I send them over to your place so you can rate them for us?"

I didn't know quite what to think, but the very next day, the girl I had spoken to came over with a couple young girls. I fucked each of them—together and individually—and afterward, I had to give them a rating and feedback. The same happened the next week, with a bunch of new girls. I remember one of them in particular, because she was super hot and brought a suitcase with a gigantic dildo inside.

We all took GHB, and the girl and I went into the theater room, where she started working herself with the dildo. The thing with GHB is that if you take too much, it can make you fall asleep, and that's exactly what happened to her—with this gigantic dildo still buzzing away inside her. I went over and yelled for her to wake up, but it was pointless. She was out of it for the rest of the evening.

Aside from those weekends and the days when Heidi's girls came over, I was mostly alone in the house—Bone Daddy was at his store during the day—and being alone was far from healthy for me.

The ranch was five acres total, but there were probably another four or five hundred acres around it, and they weren't owned by anyone in particular. It was all barren land, and since I always ended up doing the blow left over from the parties, it made me completely paranoid. It was so quiet that even the tiniest sounds made me think, *What the fuck was that?!*

Every little thing made me jump. I used to walk around in a robe—I never got fully dressed—and I'd also managed to get hold of a double-barreled shotgun. In other words, I would be walking around in my robe, coked out of my mind, peering out the window with a gun in my hand. On a few occasions, I actually let off a couple shots; I managed to ruin a couple of screen doors, thinking they were open as I shot through them. Maybe that was why I decided to sell the ranch and move back to the city.

45

Slash's Snakepit

I get steamrolled by the man in the hat—again.

NOT LONG AFTER OUR last gig on the tour, Gilby had gotten the boot. It was Duff who called to let me know. "Gilby's out of the band," he said.

I felt incredibly uneasy—maybe I was disposable, too. "Fuck, what happened?" I eventually managed to ask.

"Axl fired him. Slash called me."

"Why?" I asked.

"I don't know.

And I really didn't know what was going on either. Just three months earlier, Gilby and Axl had been the best of buds. Maybe the reason was that Gilby had signed a solo deal. Maybe Axl didn't think Gilby could write songs or something. I had no idea then, and I still don't know now.

Not long after, Slash and I were supposed to be playing some of our new songs for Axl. We had a bunch of demos—no lyrics or anything, just riffs—and I remember Axl coming over to Slash's house, where we were working. His face was completely blank as he listened to the tracks, giving nothing away.

Suddenly, he said, "It sounds like a cross between AC/DC and Lynyrd Skynyrd."

I stared at him. "Is that a bad thing?" I asked.

He didn't reply, but it was clear that he didn't like what he had heard, and without saying much else, he went out to his car and took off.

At about this time, Slash and I often went drinking at a bar called the Amazon, and after Axl left us that day, we drove down the hill toward Ventura Boulevard. Slash was really pissed off, which was unusual—he never usually got pissed off. He basically said something along the lines of, "Fuck Axl! Let's start our own band."

I agreed, "Yeah, fuck Axl! Let's do it."

Slash went on: "Yeah. I'm gonna call David Geffen myself. I'm gonna get us a deal."

"Yeah!" I said. "What are we gonna call the band?"

"Let's call it Snakepit."

Slash had already given the name Snakepit to his studio, because he had snakes all over the house, and whenever we weren't drinking at the Amazon Room, we headed in the other direction to a bar called Snake Pit on Melrose Avenue. I think the bar had the name first, but Slash clearly liked it so much that he wanted to use it for our band too.

Before long, we had a deal with Geffen. David Geffen had first dibs on releasing the album. Clearly he wanted to, because he offered us half a million dollars for the record.

Once the deal was signed, we recruited Mike Clink, who had produced Guns N' Roses, and then we started to talk about whom else we might want in the band. Or, more accurately, Slash asked me whom *I* wanted.

I liked Mike Inez, who was playing with Ozzy at the time, and who later started playing with Alice in Chains. I told him, "Mike's a good friend, a great bass player, and a cool guy. Let's get him."

"Okay, cool," Slash said, suggesting Gilby as our rhythm guitarist. With that, we had our band.

We did the same thing with Snakepit as we had with GN'R—we rehearsed all the music and recorded the whole album without a singer.

Aside from playing the drums, I also helped out with the arrangements, and once that was done I headed to New York so that I could avoid thinking about Shiva too much (it took me almost two years to really get over her).

I had booked a room at the Royalton Hotel for an unspecified amount of time. Back then, it was on Forty-Seventh Street, just off Broadway. I think it was one of Philippe Starck's first hotels, and it had all these weird rooms fitted out with equally weird furniture.

Mickey Rourke was a good friend of mine at the time and one of the first people I contacted when I arrived in NYC. After that, I called Nigel Mogg—nephew of Phil Mogg, the lead singer of UFO. Nigel was the bassist with the Quireboys (who were actually known as the London Quireboys in the United States). I also called Donovan Leitch, son of the folk singer Donovan. Still, I also went out quite a bit on my own, often to a club called the Tunnel—which is where I saw my first mixed bathroom. That place was fucking Caligula. There was a crazy mix of people inside, doing coke. There were transsexuals, drag queens, gays, rock 'n' rollers, models. It was like Studio 54, only in the mid-1990s. After spending a while there I would head to a place called the Scrap Bar in the East Village. That place was great for rock 'n' roll.

After-after hours, my New York friends and I would head to a club called Sway, which was run by a guy named Nur Khan. Nur still lives in New York, and he still runs nightclubs. We also went to an after-hours gambling club, and it was open until some time around noon. I was there with Nigel or some of my other buddies one day when it was raided by an NYPD SWAT team.

"Everybody, hands up!" the officers yelled as they stormed in.

The ceiling lights came on, the music stopped, and before I really had time to work out what was happening, they had us lined up against the wall. Everyone had to take out their drugs. They dumped everything on top of a big pool table. One of my buddies tossed away a bag of coke, and it went sliding across the floor. One of the cops yelled, "Make sure you don't pick that up on your way out!"

After that, they started taking pictures of each of us with a Polaroid camera. Before my turn came around, one of the officers came over to me and said, "I wanna talk to you outside."

He grabbed me, dragged me out onto the street, and, after assuring me that no one could see or hear us, said, "I came to one of your gigs here in town; it was one of the best shows I ever saw at Madison Square Garden. I'm gonna let you off the hook... Now get the fuck out of here."

I had been in New York for maybe two months when, out of the blue, I got a call from Gilby as I was lying in bed in my hotel room. "Matt," he said, "we've got a singer; the record's nearly done."

"What the fuck are you talking about?" I asked, quickly ending the call so that I could speak to Slash.

"Dude, who's the singer?" I asked Slash. "And how come this is the first I'm hearing about this?"

To me, it was crystal clear. Slash and I had started the band together, which meant we had to agree on who would be fronting it. Clearly he saw things differently.

"I'm coming home now," I said, immediately buying some plane tickets.

Unfortunately, I had to do the same thing three days in a row, because I didn't make it to the airport on either of the first two days. It was because I never got back to my hotel room before noon after my all-nighters, and once I did finally get to sleep, it was impossible for me to wake up in time.

Still, I eventually made it back to LA, and Gilby called me again. "You back yet?"

"Yeah," I said.

"Cool, come down to the Viper Room, 'cause I'm playing there."

Later that evening, I headed down there. For some reason, I walked in with Tommy Lee and the drummer from Skid Row, Rob Affuso. We all sat down in a booth at the very back, but during the gig, Gilby called each one of us up onto the stage. Rob got up first, followed by Tommy, and eventually it was my turn. Once I was up there, he said, "I wanna introduce everybody to the new singer from Slash's Snakepit."

I had already been drinking, and I lost it and said, "What did you say?"

Gilby was standing there with his guitar, and he gave me a kind of hesitant glance.

"*Slash's* Snakepit?!" I yelled.

Right then, some guy walked up onstage. I can't fucking remember his name, but he looked really glam. I just stared at him and said, "What the fuck is this?!" I threw down my sticks and stormed off, shouting something like, "Man, fuck Slash!"

People ran after me all upset as I headed toward the little black Porsche '88 Targa that I had at the time. I was so fucked up it was pure idiocy to get behind the wheel.

"Matt, don't go! You can't drive! Give us the keys!" they yelled.

But I had left the top down, so I jumped right into the car, did a burnout—to the extent that's possible in a Porsche—and tooled away.

Slash had moved to Sunset Plaza by that time because his house on Mulholland Drive had gotten all fucked up in the earthquake. He had this big gate out in front, and the minute I parked up outside, I rang the doorbell and yelled, "Slash, let me in."

Slash always tried to be super chill, so when he answered he said, "Come on, dude. Calm down."

"Let me in!" I yelled.

But he just said, "Go home and sleep it off."

That was the last thing I felt like doing—not until I'd told him what was on my mind, anyway. I started to climb the fence. It wasn't particularly high, but there were spikes on top, and I lost my footing and fell as I was about to climb down the other side. One of the spikes went through the arm of my leather jacket, meaning that I ended up hanging from the inside of the fence rather than hitting the ground.

Slash came out to see me. Like always when he wasn't playing the role of a rock star onstage, he was wearing shorts. He looked at me and said, "Come on, man. Relax. Come inside. I'll make you a drink and play you the record."

He helped me down, and the first thing I said once both feet were on solid ground was, "*Slash's* Snakepit…what the fuck?!"

216

"Well," he said, "the label was worried no one would know what a snakepit was."

I guess this was the moment when I stopped really trusting Slash. But at the same time, I also came to accept that side of him; I now know exactly who he is. Back then, though, I wasn't expecting it, and it really hurt me. I was really bummed out about the whole thing, because I genuinely thought we were going to form something new on our own. But instead, it just became his solo project.

We went into his house and he played me the record. I knew I didn't like the singer after just one song, and I told him so. "I think he sucks."

"Come on, man," Slash said. "Let's try another song."

"Here's what you can do, Slash," I told him. "You can replace my drums with some other drummer, and take my shit off that fucking record."

46

Neurotic Outsiders

My friend drives me to a support group meeting,
and I start a band with Steve Jones.

I KNEW A DRUMMER named Jack. He'd had a serious drug and alcohol problem, but he'd gotten himself straightened out. Though I was pretty fucked up myself, I was ready to get help, so I gave him a call and asked him to take me along to a men's support group he had mentioned.

I'll never forget the day he picked me up and drove me over to a big house in Brentwood. We stepped through the front door and into a dark hallway, and I followed him into a large room. There were a whole bunch of people inside, maybe thirty men, and after a moment or two, I realized that the guy sitting at the head of the table was a famous comedian. After that, I began to recognize even more familiar faces: actors, lawyers I knew, and other musicians and peers.

The idea at those meetings is that everyone shares, but as I sat down in an empty chair and my turn came around to talk about myself and why I was there, I suddenly started to cry. There were tears running down my face, the words caught in my throat, and my whole body started to shake.

It was like all the pain, from childhood to my success in Guns N' Roses, came to the surface in me. All the pain I had been numbing with alcohol and drugs. Honestly, I think that was the first time I felt any real emotion in about twenty years.

I saw a man get up and move over to me. "Let me give you a hug," he said.

I've been fortunate enough in my career to meet a lot of my childhood heroes, people who'd inspired me and motivated me as a musician. This voice sounded familiar. I was on my feet by then, still in floods of tears, when it dawned on me who he was. Right then, he took me in his arms and said, "I know how you feel."

I had hit rock bottom and was in the darkest place I had ever been, and there he was—like a sign from God, I was face to face with perhaps the biggest influence on me and one of the main reasons I ever became a drummer.

That moment really changed me. It was like I finally understood there was someone watching over me. A higher power, or whatever you want to call it. I knew I had a hard road ahead staying sober, but I finally had a place to go, and I was convinced that if one of my biggest musical influences could stay sober, I could too.

When the meeting ended, I was still crying. My journey of staying clean started that night.

Over the weeks that followed, I continued attending the support group meetings, and for the first time in a long while, everything felt great. The meetings were on a kind of carousel, meaning we were at different houses every time. On one occasion, the famous attorney who attended the meetings said we could use his office. The day after that meeting, I ran into John Taylor from Duran Duran for the first time. He and Steve Jones, whom I already knew, had agreed with Duff to play a benefit gig for a guy who had cancer. John asked whether I wanted to join them.

The show took place at the Viper Room, which was owned by Johnny Depp at the time. He was there with his girlfriend, and like lots of others, he got up onstage to play a couple songs with us.

The gig went so well that Steve suggested we do a residency at the club. Not long after, we took on the name Neurotic Outsiders.

We invited a famous singer every week—guys like Billy Idol, Iggy Pop, and Brian Setzer. I was sober, I was skinny, and I never had a shirt on; we all looked great. We were older, but we weren't completely wrecked. Before long, it was the coolest gig in town, and one evening as we sat in the dressing room, the door opened and a guy came in with his arms outstretched. It was Guy Oseary, a young A&R guy that had just signed Alanis Morissette and the Prodigy.

"I love this band," he said, "and I want to sign you to Maverick Records."

During the months that passed before we signed the contract, I began producing. The first artist I produced was a singer called Poe. We recorded some of her debut record at a famous studio called Ocean Way Recording on Sunset Boulevard—where artists like Frank Sinatra and the Beach Boys had recorded.

When I left the studio one day, tired after a long session, I bumped into Kato Kaelin in the corridor outside. He was a famous face across the US at the time. The O. J. Simpson trial was in full swing, and Kato had been staying in O. J.'s guesthouse; he was one of the key witnesses. I knew him from the gym, but I had no idea what he was doing in the recording studio. He said, "Hey, Matt. Phil Spector's over here, with Céline Dion. Wanna meet him?"

For as long as I could remember, Phil Spector had been a mystical figure to me. He was an incredible songwriter, a gifted producer, and the creator of the "wall of sound" concept. "Yeah," I said, "that would be cool."

So I followed Kato over to Studio A. The first person I bumped into was Jim Keltner (a famous drummer who had played with George Harrison, Bob Dylan, and many others), who was just leaving. When he caught sight of me he just shook his head and said, "It's weird in there."

I walked into the studio and stopped dead when I spotted Ike Turner, Brian Wilson, and Rodney Bingenheimer, the famous radio DJ, chatting right in front of me. Kato paused by my side and cheerily shouted, "Phil! Matt's here, from Guns N' Roses. The drummer!"

A well-dressed man with black hair and sunglasses got up from a brown leather armchair over by the mixer desk and came over.

"Nice to meet you," he said, his face perfectly blank. "I'm Phil Spector. I hear you're from Guns N' Roses."

"Yeah," I said, unnecessarily adding, "I'm the drummer."

Phil nodded and said, "I'd like you to play drums on this song."

I was so surprised that I didn't know what to say. Eventually, I managed to mumble, "Yeah, I can come back tomorrow."

Phil firmly shook his head no. "I want you now. How does five thousand dollars sound?"

Something about him made me realize that it would be best to go along with it. So I stepped to one side and called my drum tech, Mike. I said I needed my drums and his help.

"Now?!" Mike asked. "It's the middle of the night."

He arrived at the studio a few hours later and set up all my shit for me. While he was doing that, Phil played me the track a couple times. There was a full orchestra on it, all recorded in mono, and it sounded huge. As I stood there, trying to focus on how I was going to play, Céline Dion came into the room with her husband, René.

"Hi, Céline," I said.

She took my hand and said, "Oh, I'm so honored to have you play on my song."

In that moment, I could only agree with Jim Keltner that it was weird in there. I went out into the studio and sat down behind the drums. Through the large window, I could see Phil at the mixing desk, still wearing his sunglasses. Then I heard his slightly nasal voice: "I want you to give me some tom fills in this section. I love what you did on 'November Rain.' Do something like that."

The song started playing, and I did the tom fills. Once I was done, he shouted, "That's it! That's great! I love it!"

I assumed that meant I was done, but when I went into the mixing room, Phil told me to sit down.

He turned to the assistant engineer and said, "Roll it back!" Phil listened intently. "Hmm," he said, "I'm not sure I like it."

"I could do it again," I suggested.

Phil held up a hand. "Hold on…roll back the tape again."

The assistant engineer did as he was told.

Phil listened again, and then shouted, "I love it!"

Almost immediately, however, he got a serious look on his face and said, "Roll it back."

He kept that up for just over two hours, listening to the tom fill over and over again. By that point, Brian and Ike were long gone.

René went over to Phil, who was still sitting by the controls. "Phil, it's late," he said. "When can Céline sing?"

Phil looked up at him and said, "Céline can wait; she'll sing when I tell her to sing. I'll let you know once I'm done with the Guns N' Roses drummer."

With that, he calmly continued whatever it was he was doing.

After another hour or so, René returned. "Phil, Céline needs to sing now. We have a video shoot at nine a.m."

Phil calmly turned toward him and said, "You're not going anywhere."

But as the clock approached seven in the morning, René came over again. "Good night, Phil," he said, turning to leave.

That was when Phil leaped up and yelled after René, "Tell her she's not leaving until I say goodbye!"

Phil cast a glance in the mirror hanging on one of the walls. He smoothed his hair and told the rest of us to follow him out. A moment or so later, we were tailing him down the corridor.

The sun had risen as we stepped out onto Sunset Boulevard, and with Phil at the head, we walked over to Céline's Mercedes. Phil knocked on the side window, and Céline rolled it down, deliberately avoiding Phil's eye.

"Goodbye, Céline," Phil said, turning around and heading back into the studio with the rest of us in a line behind him.

The minute we got back inside, Phil started to yell like a madman. "I'm gonna ruin her! She's done in this business! No one walks out on Phil Spector!" He grabbed the phone and called Tommy Mottola, the CEO at Sony Music. "Céline calls herself an artist! Matt, you tell him!"

Phil passed the phone to me. I had worked with Tommy before, and he said, "Hey, Matt. What's going on over there?"

"Well, you know—"

"Matt, tell him what she did!" Phil yelled.

"She walked out of the session," I said.

"What time was that?" Tommy asked.

"Seven thirty a.m."

Phil grabbed the phone from me and shouted, "I'm not putting this record out. I own this material!" With that, he hung up on Tommy.

A few minutes passed. No one said or did anything until Phil suddenly shouted, "I'm hungry!"

There was a twenty-four-hour restaurant called Roscoe's House of Chicken & Waffles just across the street, so I said, "Have you ever had Roscoe's Chicken & Waffles?"

"What's that?" Phil asked.

"They do great soul food, chicken and waffles."

"Sounds cool."

Before long, one of us had called to order a whole load of food, and Phil sat down next to me and immediately started asking about Axl. "I can make the greatest record you ever made," he said. "Just get me on the phone with Axl."

"Well, I guess we could arrange it," I said, slightly hesitant.

Right then, the food arrived, and Phil said, "Okay, let's eat!"

Phil really was hungry, and he wolfed down his food. Suddenly, he stopped and grabbed his throat with both hands as if he were choking. He was making a load of really weird sounds.

"Mike!" I yelled, waving to my drum tech. "Heimlich maneuver!"

Mike leaped up and took hold of Phil from behind, firmly pressing his fists into his stomach. A piece of chicken came flying out of Phil's mouth, and he supported himself against the table and took a shaky breath. He turned to Mike and said, "You saved my life! You saved my life!" He then turned to the assistant engineer, pointed to Mike, and said, "Send him something! Give him a gift!"

He turned to me. "Let's go to a bar," he said.

"Okay."

"Let's get some girls too," said Phil.

"Okay," I repeated.

At that point, Mike announced he was going home, and I found myself alone with Phil in the backseat of a 1965 Rolls-Royce Silver Cloud.

Back then, you still used to see hookers on the street, and I heard Phil shout to his driver, "Pull over!"

"No, no, no!" I said. "I'll get some girls to come down. No street girls. I got it, Phil."

I told the driver to head over to a Mexican place called El Compadre, and I called a few girls to meet us there. Thirty or so minutes later, Phil and I were sitting at a table with them, and Phil immediately began to boast.

"I'm a secret partner of *Rolling Stone* magazine. I also own the LAPD. They're all on my payroll."

"Wow," I said, rolling my eyes at one of the girls. "That's heavy."

Phil then began to talk about the O. J. trial, and I quickly realized that he was completely obsessed with it. Suddenly it made sense why Kato had been at the studio that evening.

Before long, I realized from the girls' expressions that Phil's droning was boring them, and I actually felt like I'd had enough of him myself. I told him I had to go to the restroom, but I actually just snuck out of the restaurant. It was two in the afternoon.

The next day, my phone rang, and I heard a voice I didn't recognize on the other end of the line.

"Hello, Matt Sorum? This is Phil Spector's office calling. Mr. Spector would like you to come out to his residency in Pasadena."

"Oh, well, the thing is," I said, "I'm actually going out of town."

"Would you please call us when you return?"

"Yeah, definitely."

Not long after, Neurotic Outsiders began recording what would be our first and only record. I had been sober for almost a year, but after I added drums to all the tracks and went for sushi one evening, I suddenly realized that I wanted a beer with my dinner. I decided to order some sake, too. Somewhere, deep down, I knew it was a bad idea, but after I knocked back the beer it felt like the only way I could deal with my guilty conscience was by drinking more.

Just like that, I fell off the wagon, and once I got back into drinking, the drugs came rushing back. Within hours, I had a craving for coke, and on that particular evening I managed to get hold of some heroin (a drug I've always been scared of because it feels so good). In any case, I holed up in my house and smoked heroin on my own for hours. Heroin is like coke in that you're left always wanting another hit. The only problem was that the band had a photo shoot the next day, and I knew as I sat there that I'd never manage it. So I called management and asked them to call it off.

"We can't cancel. That'd cost thirty-five thousand dollars. You'd have to pay it."

I was so high I found myself saying, "Okay, I'll pay."

The rest of the band were really pissed about it because they immediately worked out exactly what had happened. John Reese, who had become the band's manager by that point, came over to my house and said, "Give me all your dope."

I was lying in bed at the time. "No can do," I mumbled. "I'll be sick as a dog."

He must have managed to find the heroin, because it was in his hand as he ran out. Shortly after that, Duff called to yell at me. Aside from the fact that the entire band was built on being clean, we had a tour booked, and we were all super nervous about how it was going to go. Looking back now, I can understand those worries.

When we arrived in New York a few weeks later, I ran into Jerry Cantrell (from Alice in Chains), who was a complete junkie at the time. After the gig, we met up and did a bunch of blow before heading to a strip club, and at four or five in the morning, someone said, "I know where we can get coke down on Wall Street."

We headed out onto the street, hailed a cab, and soon were walking into one of the huge corporate skyscrapers down there. After taking the elevator up a few floors, we bumped into a guard who asked us for a password. Someone from our group said, "Doberman," and the guard opened a door onto a full-on club.

The first thing I saw as we stepped inside were a bunch of stockbrokers and a load of strippers. The whole thing was a bit like *The Wolf of Wall Street*—suits smoking crack, hookers getting fucked, that kind of thing.

I got back to my hotel room at noon, at roughly the same time as the others were checking out.

"Great," Duff muttered when he spotted me and the guy I'd dragged back from the club.

"Go to your room, sleep it off, and meet us in Boston," said Steve.

Then he turned to the guy I had with me and told him to go to hell. He did as he was told, but only temporarily. Once the others had gone, he came back—with a couple of girls. We continued doing coke in my room, and I remember lying flat out on my back as some chick tried to blow what was left of my dick. The other guy was busy fucking his girl in the bathroom.

I didn't get any sleep at all, and drank to keep going. The show was at nine, so at some point that afternoon I called for a limo, lay down on the back seat, and bounced my way through Manhattan. Somehow, I actually managed to get on a plane to Boston, and the minute I landed, I got into a car that took me straight to the venue. I was still completely out of it, but I sobered up pretty quickly at the sight of Steven Tyler, Jimmy Page, Robert Plant, and Billy Idol in the dressing room.

Duff turned to me and said, "Are you still fucked up?"

"I'm fine, man!" I said, quickly adding, "This is gonna be the best rock 'n' roll show ever!"

Right after that, we headed out onstage, and I thought, *I'm gonna prove to these guys that I'm a total badass!* Somehow, I actually managed it.

47

Slash Leaves GN'R

We jam for several hours a night but get nowhere.

THROUGHOUT THIS ENTIRE PERIOD, Guns was renting a place called the Complex. The idea was that we would all hang out there and write songs for a new GN'R record, but since Slash was on a world tour with Snakepit, Axl decided that he was going to play guitar. He bought so many electric guitars—not to mention racks, amps, and pedals. He also hired himself a guitar tech named Jimbo.

Like always, he wanted to work at weird times of day. I used to turn up at the Complex sometime around six in the evening, and he would never arrive before nine or ten.

As a result, I had plenty of time for other things, such as producing—I had my first hit with Poe's "Angry Johnny," and got quite a bit of that type of work done. Whenever I wasn't in the studio, I would hang out at a strip club called Fantasy Island opposite the Complex, to watch girls and drink. Axl was often annoyed that the rest of us were always drunk. It was like he couldn't understand why. Axl had never been a big drinker—at least he wasn't during the years I played with him. He liked champagne, but that was all. Of everyone in GN'R, he was the one with the most normal relationship to alcohol. He was far from the bad boy of the band—the rest of us took care of that.

Axl found out about my producing when he heard the single I'd produced for Poe on KROQ-FM, a cool local radio station. When he arrived at the studio that day, he said, "I was driving from

227

Malibu and heard your name mentioned after a song by someone called Poe."

"Yeah," I said. "I produced that single and played on a few tracks on her record."

Axl nodded thoughtfully. "When did you do that?"

"Pretty recently," I said.

"It sounded really good!"

Axl and I did sometimes have moments like that, and once he realized that I knew how to produce, he started asking me all kinds of questions about production, especially when he heard another Poe track I'd produced, plus one by Sen Dog of Cypress Hill.

"What's that?" he asked, meaning the drums.

"It's a drum loop," I said.

"What's that?"

"Well...I cut a loop."

Axl had a habit of never really looking straight at you; it was more like he was glancing at you while thinking God knows what. In any case, it was crystal clear I had to explain what I was talking about. So I said, "You take a piece of music and cut the drum loop in one bar. If you imagine cutting the following from a song—*one, two, three, four, two, two, three, four*—you've got a two-bar loop."

He raised an eyebrow and said, "Okay, we're gonna do that! So how do we do it?"

"Well, I use a system called Pro Tools."

"What's that?"

"It's a computer program; you record using it."

At the time, Pro Tools was relatively new. The first time I ever came in contact with it was during the recording of Metallica's *Black Album*. Before that, everything had been recorded on tape. The new technology meant you could insert a take on the computer. I'd seen Metallica do it, and I learned how to use the program myself. Going forward, it was something everyone would use, but at the Complex where we were rehearsing, we had ADAT players for recording. They were cassettes that looked a little like VHS tapes. Eventually you could buy slightly smaller ADAT tapes. An ADAT player had eight tracks, so we used to have three or four machines linked up together.

Izzy had previously been responsible for a large part of all the songwriting, but it was a long time since he had quit. Slash was now gone too, and Axl had begun playing guitar instead, occasionally showing us some riff he had come up with. Duff and I played along, and so did the new guy, Paul Tobias, who had replaced Gilby on rhythm guitar. Paul was Axl's friend, but Duff and I didn't like him—not so much because of his personality but because the guy really didn't know how to play.

I remember that after the very first rehearsal with him, Duff had asked, "Who is this clown?"

Paul was what Slash called a "bedroom guitar player"—in other words, the guy had never been onstage and had never been in a band before.

On top of that, Axl often made a real noise with his guitar, and would yell—right when whatever he was playing was at its worst—"Loop it!"

Before I told him about loops, he used to make us play the riffs he'd come up with over and over again, so in that regard the technology really did make our lives easier. But he also began spending hours messing about with his guitar pedals.

Duff was usually the first person to give up and head home—often around one in the morning. He didn't bother saying goodbye; he just got up and left at roughly the same time every night. For some reason, I felt like I had to be there. As a result, we were often still doing God knows what at two or three in the morning.

Everything we did was, at the very least, recorded by a proper sound technician, who marked all the ADAT tapes with the date. Each one might say something like NOVEMBER 3 TAKE 3. After a couple of years, we had several hundred tapes, and after four years we had thousands. By that point, no one could remember what was on any of them. It would've taken at least a year of full-time work just to listen back to each of them. This was the point when the whole band seemed to kind of crumple from the inside, a process that I guess began back before Slash left, when we had an audition with Zakk Wylde.

Axl was the one who brought up his name one day during a session. "I want Zakk Wylde in the band," he said.

I noticed Slash squirming before he replied, "But he's a lead guitarist."

Axl didn't bother to reply, and I'll never forget the day Zakk showed up a week or so later. I thought, *Dude, what happened to the skinny kid I used to know?* The guy who stepped through the door that day looked more like a mountain man, with chains and a huge beard. He had brought his own amps with him, four Marshall stacks, and played ridiculously loud. It only took a few minutes before he was trying to outdo Slash by playing as many notes as he could. Slash, however, didn't give a fuck. He just stood there watching with a bored look on his face.

When Axl showed up the next day, he said, "Okay, we need to negotiate with Zakk.

Slash snuck out of the studio not long after, and he soon began showing up less and less often.

Before long, we also started seeing less of Duff, and eventually even I stopped bothering to turn up. That was when Axl decided to form a B-band. In other words, he made himself an alternative Guns N' Roses made up of stand-in guys. Dizzy Reed was involved, but he might spend a month just hanging out at the rehearsal space, not achieving a thing; he even slept on the couch there. He took all the shit and was like, "What other rock 'n' roll bands are looking for a piano player?"

Then I guess he decided it was better to keep quiet and do as he was told. Or maybe it was just because he had to pay child support to the three different women he'd gotten pregnant during the *Use Your Illusion* tour. Axl also called over a few other guys who were willing to just show up and spend all day jamming, trying to help him come up with songs. Paul Tobias was one of them.

After a lot of back and forth, we eventually agreed to hold a band meeting—one with Duff, Slash, Axl, and me—and the idea was that we'd actually try to communicate for once. Of course, it went wrong almost immediately. Axl had a memory like an elephant and began talking about things in the past, way before I was in the band. After that, he moved onto the music and started saying things like, "I wanna make this band modern. I wanna bring in more synths."

At that point, Slash said, "Why can't we just make a rock 'n' roll record?"

They started going back and forth about it—though they didn't yell, because Slash wasn't really the yelling type. Once they were done, Slash got up and said, "I'm leaving."

That was when Axl started shouting, "You don't fucking leave—get back here!"

That's when Slash left and never came back, and after that things within the band got even weirder—if that's possible.

Duff and I talked a lot about how we could find a replacement for Paul Tobias. Neither of us really believed that Slash had quit for good, but we couldn't think of anyone to replace Paul. At least I couldn't until I went down to Cirque du Soleil in Santa Monica and saw a band with a great guitarist. His name was Robin Finck.

I called Axl right away. "Hey, Axl. I just saw this fucking cool guitar player."

For once, Axl sounded happy, and he said, "Okay, I'm gonna go check him out."

A couple days later, Axl went to see Robin play. He called me back afterward. "Yeah, he's gonna be great to replace Slash."

"No, no, no," I said. "I meant for him to replace Paul Tobias... Let's get rid of Paul. Slash will come back."

But Axl had already made up his mind, and he repeated, "Nah, he's gonna replace Slash."

So Slash went off on his Snakepit tour for something like eighteen months straight while the rest of us continued rehearsing and trying to jam new songs. One day, I got to rehearsal early and went straight up to Paul Tobias. "You know what, man? Duff and I don't like you being in the band. I think you should pack up your shit and disappear."

He stared at me in horror.

"Yeah," I continued. "Just go."

Shortly after I got a call from management.

"You show up to rehearsals drunk. You can't bring booze anymore; you can't even drink anymore. You hear that?"

The next day, I deliberately took a bottle of tequila and a six-pack of beer with me to the studio. I did a few shots in front of the others, and necked a couple beers, trying to work up some kind of energy. Being stuck in that studio day in and day out, without achieving a single thing, made my body itch. Even now, when I think back onto that period, I feel terrible. It felt like I was going to be in that rehearsal space for the rest of my life. I thought I'd go crazy, and I was just about to throw in the towel when producer Rick Rubin suddenly showed up. We had previously agreed that he would produce our next record, and he had been waiting a long time to hear what we had come up with.

"Okay, so let me hear what you guys got... Where's Slash?"

I glanced at the others and then quickly said, "Uh, he's not here right now."

We then played a couple of tracks. Axl had one track he wanted to use for a Jackie Chan movie, and Rick really seemed to like that one. He turned to Axl after listening to it, and said, "Do you have any lyrics or melody?"

Axl gave him a surprised look. "No."

Rick scratched his head. The atmosphere was weird. "Okay," he said. Then he left.

After the door swung shut behind him, Axl said, "I never wanna see that guy here again. He's fired, fuck that guy."

Two days later, Axl showed up at rehearsal in a really great mood. "I went through some of the recordings," he said, "and I think we've got a good verse and a chorus."

The rest of us squirmed and exchanged confused glances. I thought maybe I'd misunderstood him, or that I'd heard him wrong, so I said, "How many songs do we have a verse and chorus for?"

Axl still looked as pleased as before. "We have one verse for one song and one chorus for another."

By that point, we had been at that studio for four years—*four years!* Thousands of thoughts raced through my head. Among other things, I thought, *If I don't get out of here, I'm fucked. I'll never get onstage again. I need to leave. But what am I gonna do?*

We were back at the rehearsal space the very next day. I was on the couch, and Axl was standing by the piano. Paul Tobias came in and said, "Man, did you see Slash on David Letterman? He really sucked."

It was like something in my head just flipped. I leaped up and stared at Paul as I snapped, "Hey, Paul! Shut the fuck up! You don't talk about Slash in front of me. He's still my friend. Fuck you!"

Axl turned to me. "Why the fuck are you defending Slash?"

"He's my friend," I said.

"Fuck Slash...I'm Guns N' Roses, and we don't need him," Axl continued.

"Oh, really, so you're gonna let *him* play the intro to 'Sweet Child o' Mine'?" I pointed to Paul Tobias and smiled mockingly.

By that point, I'd had enough, so I walked right over to Axl, got right up in his face. We glared at each other for what felt like an eternity. Axl could be pretty unnerving when he wanted to be. There was something in his eyes, and though I couldn't tell you why, just looking into them gave me the cold sweats. He had this kind of demented power, an aura. I can still see that effect in Slash's body language today whenever they play together. I can tell that Slash and the others are on eggshells around him. He's all ham and jam now, on time and shit. But there's still something about him. The only other guy I met with a presence like that was Phil Spector. When you're with people like that, it's like something comes over you. You don't know what it is, but it makes you feel uneasy, and as we stood there that day. I said, "Look, without Slash, there is no Guns N' Roses."

He said, "We don't need Slash, and we don't need you... So are you gonna quit?"

"Nah, I'm not a quitter."

"Okay, then you're fired."

"So what're you gonna do? Call the cops to get me out of here?"

"Yeah, I'm gonna call the cops."

"In that case, you'd better call an ambulance too."

I turned to leave, and Paul Tobias came running after me. "Dude, I'm really sorry for saying that shit about Slash."

"Fuck you, Yoko," I snapped at him. Then I rounded off by adding, "How does it feel to be the guy who broke up the best rock 'n' roll band of the last decade?"

I jumped into my car and drove back to my house. I guess I should have been sad, but I felt more relieved than anything. I was relieved to escape all the bullshit, all the standing still. But I was also worried, because GN'R had been my job, my livelihood for the past seven years, and not long afterward, I got a more formal departure from the band.

Looking back on this very pivotal moment for me with GN'R, I had a different outlook than I do now. Axl and I were actually very much alike. Especially the loyalty part. Guns was a band, and I think he wanted the rest of us just as dedicated. I think about bands like Metallica or U2 who don't really stray from the group. The band is the focus, not outside solo projects that are self-serving. In all those years the band went quiet, you think about all the great music that might have come if we could have just stayed together.

48

Rehab

I hit Dave Coulier and learn all about sneaky behavior.

I SPENT THE WHOLE of 1997 partying like I was still on tour, and by the fall of the next year, I was probably in worse shape than I had been when I started going to the support group. I had a girlfriend at the time, but, as ever, I wasn't exactly faithful to her, and I still got aggressive when I drank—something that ended in catastrophe in September of that year.

I'd been invited to *Full House* star John Stamos's wedding at the Beverly Hills Hotel. My girlfriend came with me, and the whole thing was really pretty nice. We watched John and Rebecca say "I do" and enjoyed the meal, though I had started to get drunk pretty early on. When you're an alcoholic, you're used to being drunk, and it means that up to a certain level, you can still sharpen up. The evening passed without any real trouble. But then John's colleague from *Full House*, Dave Coulier, invited me, my girlfriend, and a whole group of others to an after-party at his place.

Dave Coulier's house wasn't particularly far from the Beverly Hills Hotel, so it didn't take us long to get there. There was a great atmosphere, and we started doing shots in Dave's kitchen almost as soon as we arrived. After that, we moved on to cocktails. By that point I noticed that I couldn't find my girlfriend, so I started looking for her. I found her naked in the Jacuzzi with three random guys—taking us right back to the story I told in the preface. It was Dave who tried to calm me down and got knocked out for his trouble, and that's when I ended up running naked through Westwood, breaking into my girlfriend's house, and getting thrown into the drunk tank.

"Hey, rock star," hissed the homeless guy in the corner of the cell, "how's it feel to be down here in the gutter with us crackheads?"

When I sobered up the next day, I made collect calls to everyone I knew, asking them to help me with the bail money. But everyone told me, "Just stay in there." Even my manager told me to stay. That's how far gone I was.

Eventually, I contacted CHERYL, a party girl I knew. "Hey, Cheryl," I said. I quickly explained my situation and then continued, "Could you grab my black Porsche and give it over as bail so I can get out of here?"

Cheryl managed to bail me out, and then she gave me a ride home. As far as I remember, we barely made it into the hallway before we did a bunch of blow and knocked back a load of booze. Within the space of a few minutes, I was wasted again.

Cheryl turned to me, suddenly looking worried. "You need to get sober," she said. "You need to go into rehab."

Somewhere deep down, I knew she was right. Obviously, I'd been to support group meetings before, and I'd gained at least some kind of understanding of my illness, so I called a friend that same evening. "Hey, man…where's that meeting on Monday night? I need to go."

He said, "We're meeting in Beverly Hills, at the lawyer's office. You've been there before; you know where it is."

The next Monday, I headed over there, a complete wreck in every respect. But, like always at the support group, I was welcomed with open arms. Before I even had time to sit down, a drummer friend came over and said, "Matt, meet me at the pizzeria down the street later. I need to talk to you."

So once the meeting was over, I went down there to meet him. A famous actor turned up too, as did a psychiatrist who was well known for taking care of a whole load of stars. All three had been at the meeting, and my drummer friend said to me, "I'll pick you up tomorrow, at nine thirty, and I'll take you to rehab."

I immediately felt anxiety well up in me and had to take a deep breath before I said, "For how long?"

"A month."

"Oh, no, I can't do that," I said. "I'm working on a movie and a record."

"No, you're working on getting fucked up every day, that's what you're doing," said the famous actor.

"Pack your shit," my drummer friend continued. "I'll be at your place at nine thirty."

Not long after, I headed home for one last bender. I drank whatever I could get my hands on, and I was pretty wasted when my drummer friend showed up the next morning. He drove me to the Impact Treatment Center in Pasadena.

The Impact Treatment Center was the cheapest type of rehab center in LA, funded by the government. A rehab stay costs something like forty, fifty—maybe even sixty—grand a month, but this place was only about $2,000. Still, the minute I got there, I knew I liked it. The downsides were that you had to share a room with three other guys, and you were only allowed to take two T-shirts, two pairs of pants, and a pair of shoes.

There were no phones, computers, radios, or TV allowed in the center. That said, you could leave whenever you wanted—though you would lose your two grand if you did. I was shown into my room, and I said hi to the guy I was sharing a bunk with. He was a meth head—young but already a complete wreck. My second roommate, who was staring at the wall before he turned around to say hey, was Scott Weiland from the Stone Temple Pilots.

Aside from Scott being there, nothing about the treatment center reminded me of the life I lived otherwise. We had to get up early every morning, some time around five, to clean the toilets or help out with some other chores. It was pretty much as far as I could get from my normal life, but somehow it felt good, and before long I actually *wanted* to be sober. That was largely down to the fantastic team I had around me, headed by Bob Timmins, who had previously worked with the guys from Aerosmith and Mötley Crüe, and my personal counselor Bob Raymar.

After a while, I became good friends with the chef—we were heading over to the kitchen three times a day to eat, after all. He knew who I was, and we began chatting. At some point, he gave me a copy of *Alcoholics Anonymous*, a.k.a. the Big Book (written primarily by Bill Wilson, with the help of a few other founder members of Alcoholics Anonymous), and we started reading it together.

At the treatment center, the guys stayed at one end of the building. The girls were at the other, and we were forbidden from having any kind of contact with them. Many of the girls were broken, and some were even scary. But there was a porno chick in there (I recognized her from films I'd seen), and when we bumped into one another in the hallway, she always moved closer to me. It happened on a number of occasions, and at some point she came over to me and whispered, "I wanna suck your dick!"

I had no idea how to react, and I didn't know how she thought it would work—there were security cameras everywhere. Still, it *had* been a while, and I was pretty horny. I guess you could say that I was faced with the classic dilemma where I had a devil on one shoulder, telling me to go for it, and an angel on the other, trying to talk sense into me. Suddenly, it struck me that there were no cameras in one of the hallways, so next time I bumped into her I whispered, "Meet me by the staircase behind the cafeteria!" Later that morning, when she and the other girls were done with their meetings for the day, I waited for her there.

She smiled when she saw me, and without saying a word she dropped to her knees and began unbuttoning my pants. Next thing I knew, I heard myself saying, "Stop! You can't do this!" The girl looked up at me in confusion, and I don't know what the fuck came over me, but I continued, "This is just another addiction; you're not being honest with yourself."

The girl leaped up, a blank look on her face. "Really? You think so?"

"Yeah. Especially if we're doing it here, in secret."

She nodded but still didn't seem to get what I was saying. So I continued: "We're here to get clean." All this time, I was thinking, *Who is this guy?* It was like hearing someone else speak, even though the words were coming from my lips. The minute we parted ways, I thought, *Goddamn it, what did I just do?!*

I felt like I needed to break my pattern of behavior—not just in terms of drugs and alcohol, but everything to do with my old self. That meant I had to make sacrifices like that.

Right before I went into rehab, I had begun producing Sen Dog from Cypress Hill, and I knew the track needed to be finished pretty quickly. So when I had only a week or so left at the treatment center, I asked for permission to head home to finish the track. "Okay," they said, "we'll let you go, but we'll have to send a counselor with you."

Since I was being given permission to work, I was allowed to work around the no-phones policy by using one of the coin-operated phones at the end of the hallway. Just before leaving, I called Cheryl and said, "Go over to my house. Go to my bedroom. Lock the door, and when I knock *one, two, three, one, two,* let me in. We're gonna have sex."

When we got to my house, I told Harold, the counselor accompanying me, to wait for me on the middle floor. I went down to the basement so I could work with the band but quickly excused myself and said I needed to use the bathroom. Instead, I took a back route up to the floor where Cheryl was waiting for me, and after we had sex, I snuck back down to the band.

A few days later, I tracked down Bob Raymar, my counselor, and told him exactly what had happened. I told him I'd had sex with a girl when Harold accompanied me home. But rather than getting angry, Bob's face cracked into a grin, and he said, "Really? Tell me more!"

I did as he asked, and after listening to my story, Bob said, "Wow, that *is* sneaky behavior. That's gonna get you high again."

I instantly understood what he meant. I mean, it was always *I just sneaked a drink* or *I just sneaked a line.* So I said, "You're right, Bob!"

"I know," Bob said, before continuing: "I want you to get up at five tomorrow morning and write about it. Write about your sneaky behavior. I want ten pages."

I did as he asked, and not long after, my time in rehab was over.

Before I checked into rehab, a guy named Bart Dorsa had been staying with me. He came from a wealthy family and always had plenty of money, but he was also someone I could trust. When I got home to that house, he was gone. Another guy, who had been staying in my guesthouse, was also missing. I walked around that massive house, completely sober, not really knowing what to do; it felt so cold and empty. I just knew I had to get out of this place; I did so much partying there it just felt toxic and it was time for a fresh start. A few days later, as I drove down the hill with the Hollywood sign behind me, I wasn't just leaving that house behind; I was also leaving behind the ego I'd had when I moved in.

49

Reunion with The Cult

We get our biggest advance to date, but Billy is pissed, and Ian eats too many muffins.

AFTER MOVING INTO A cool pad in Nichols Canyon, I was lying on the couch one evening, flicking between channels on the TV, when I saw the band Buckcherry playing one of the songs from their debut record. Almost immediately after it ended, I called Billy Duffy in England.

"Billy!" I said. "I just saw a band on TV, and they're like a watered-down poor man's version of The Cult. I think rock 'n' roll could be coming back."

We talked through a lot of shit after that: what had been going on since I left GN'R, what he was up to (which wasn't much). Eventually, I said, "Let's get the band back together; let's book a tour and go to the press and say, 'The Cult is back!'"

Billy seemed to think it was a good idea, because just a few weeks later he flew over to LA and moved in with me.

That was the beginning of The Cult's reunion, and before long we had organized a sold-out theater tour. At roughly the same time, the record labels began snooping around, with A&R guys from Atlantic and Warner Brothers showing up at our gigs. The Cult had never been offered a million-dollar record deal before. The most they'd ever gotten was a hundred thousand or something like that, but things suddenly felt very different. I said, "Billy, we could get a million bucks!"

He turned to me. "Do you really think so, man?"

Before long, the offers started rolling in. We got $750,000 from Clive Davis and $900,000 from the Island Def Jam Music Group. Eventually, we signed with Jason Flom at Atlantic, who offered us just over $1 million.

When I played with The Cult in the past, I'd been a hired drummer, but this time around I was a full member. That meant I was making decent money again, and after kicking off a number of performances—among them eight sold-out shows in a row at the House of Blues in LA—it was time to try to make a record.

Billy had come up with a bunch of riffs, and we began rehearsing. But then one day, when our bassist Martyn Lenoble said something like, "What do you think about trying this?" Billy just stared at him. Without batting an eyelid, he said, "Ian and I write the songs for The Cult. You just play your bass, and I'll give you the ideas."

Each time we wrote songs, it was the same story. No one but Ian or Billy was allowed a say, and I remember Martyn coming over to me one day and whispering, "Why are we even here?"

"I don't know," I said with a shrug.

Around this time, Billy and Ian decided to start working with Bob Rock again. He came down and started working with me on the drums, and when he went over to Martyn, Billy quickly yelled, "Yeah, you do what he tells you, Martyn!"

This time, Martyn pushed back. He said, "No, I don't like that," which made Billy furious. Martyn grabbed his bass, smashed it on the ground, and stormed over to Duffy. He said, "You motherfucker!" and then yelled all kinds of other stuff at him.

Ian and I glanced at one another and kind of scooted out of the room. I remember Ian actually said, "A lot of what Martyn is saying is true." Not long after, Martyn came storming out. Without turning around, he shouted, "Fuck you guys, I quit!"

As a result, we had to finish the recording with a bassist named Chris Wyse. The only problem was that we didn't actually manage to finish it, and then Bob said, "Why don't you guys come to Hawaii and finish the record there?" Bob lived on Maui and had an amazing studio perched on the hill overlooking the ocean—probably built with the millions he made producing Metallica's *Black Album*.

We must have thought it sounded like a decent idea, because we flew out there the very next week and all checked into houses on the beach. In the end, we spent almost the entire advance making the record, which didn't leave much left to split between the three of us. Looking back it was crazy in those days with record deals. These days you could make ten records for that kind of money. But that was what we did. Big studios, big producers, big budgets, and it was all so over the top.

When the record—*Beyond Good and Evil*—was released, we headed out on tour. We took two buses, just like we had in the 1980s. Billy and I were in one, and Ian and Chris were in the other. We actually had a pretty good time and did what we could to promote the record. Or, more accurately, I did what I could. Ian and Billy quickly got bored, and then Jason Flom—from the record label—got in touch with me. I was the only person he could talk to. "What's going on out there?" he asked.

"The guys aren't doing the meet and greets," I said. "They ain't kissing any babies. They just don't want to do the work."

"That's not good," said Jason.

"I know," I said. "I've tried talking to them."

As a direct consequence, the record dropped off the charts. Despite that, the tour still went pretty well ticket-wise, and by the time we got to our final show, we decided to continue touring—as Aerosmith's support.

The first show was in Canada, and it went to shit almost immediately. Aerosmith had a huge ramp going from the stage out into the audience, with this enormous hand at the end of it. Before we headed out to play that day, Aerosmith's tour manager, Jimmy Ayers, said, "Listen, gentlemen, no going on the ramps."

We opened with "Wildflower," and Ian deliberately ran straight out onto the ramp and started jumping up and down on the huge hand. We had only just made it back to our dressing room after our set when Jimmy came storming in.

"You guys are off the tour. Pack up your shit and head home! Tyler's pissed!"

I glared at Ian and then turned to Jimmy. "Hold on," I said.

I ran over to Aerosmith's dressing room, where I found Steven sitting at the table, eating. I sat down next to him.

"What's up with that singer of yours?" he asked.

I cleared my throat to give myself a few seconds to think, then I said, "First of all, they're from England. We're speaking different languages, you know? *Tomato, tomahto*. So the whole ramp thing... they don't understand *ramp*. It doesn't mean anything to them. *Runway*, that's what they would call it."

"Okay..." Steven muttered. "But what about the side ramps?"

"Well, you know, I don't think they even have a word for that in England. *Ramp* isn't in their vocabulary."

Steven stared at me and didn't seem to know what to think. "You're fucking kidding me, right?" he asked.

"Steven, we're really sorry. I'll go talk to them."

"Okay," he muttered. "Just don't fuck up again."

When I got back to the dressing room, I said, "Ian, you fucking asshole. I just saved this tour for you."

I sat down on the first chair I could find and stared straight ahead. I was so sick of him. Every time we had an opportunity to go big, he completely fucked it up. He was such a dark cloud, always hanging over us, and with every gig he just got more and more sulky.

Billy and I went out to watch Aerosmith play that evening, and before we headed back to our bus, I said, "Wouldn't it be amazing to have a singer like that?"

Steven Tyler was the kind of front man that gave his all every night. An A personality for sure but a true showman and the reason that band is still on top today.

The thing was, Ian could have been so great too if only he'd stopped destroying himself.

With both him and another singer I would soon work with, that was the main issue. These guys could sing and were incredible front men at times, but they were their own downfall. They always sabotaged their potential. It was super frustrating. I could see their true potential and wanted to just shake them and say you're great and to just let all the other bullshit go.

When we played Madison Square Garden, Jason Flom showed up with his entourage, which looked a lot like a death march. There were no smiles, and I could tell the end was near. Sure enough, shortly after the tour was over, we were dropped by our label and decided to split up the band.

In those days you signed a deal covering several records, and if your label dropped you, they had to buy you out of that contract. I was owed my share of the money—somewhere around $140,000— but it seemed like Billy and Ian didn't want to give me anything despite the fact that my name was on the contract. I had to hire a lawyer, but they still didn't pay up—not until their manager's path crossed mine again, though I'll come back to that later.

50

Velvet Revolver

I lose a friend but gain a new band.

EVERYTHING THAT HAPPENED NEXT began with Randy Castillo's death.

Randy was a really good friend of mine. He was actually one of my heroes before I even became his friend. When I first moved to Hollywood, he was a premier drummer and the coolest guy. He spent a long time playing with Ozzy Osbourne, and we ran into each other on the road and became really close. Drummers are like that; we have a bit of a community.

That was why I immediately thought of Randy when Nikki Sixx called me up and asked if I wanted to be Tommy Lee's replacement in Mötley Crüe. I was reconnecting with The Cult at the time, so I turned him down and suggested Randy instead. He got the job, but just after the first tour with them, he got sick and collapsed on the sidewalk outside of the Cat Club on Sunset. He had a bleeding stomach ulcer that needed emergency surgery, and nearly died. While he was recovering, he found out that Mötley had replaced him with another drummer. That was often the way: *You're out— we'll just get another guy.* I was really pissed off and thought it was a fucked-up way to treat someone.

After a few weeks, Randy discovered a lump in his jaw. It turned out to be cancer. He got the right treatment, and the cancer disappeared, but only temporarily. Before long, Randy was in far worse shape, and when I found out how serious it was, I immediately went over to see him with my other drummer friend Paul Blazek.

246

Unfortunately, we were too late. Randy was already dead by the time I arrived, surrounded by friends in his tiny apartment.

He died at home because he—like many other musicians—didn't have health insurance. All he had were his gold discs, which were still hanging on the wall. *Fuck!* I thought. I couldn't help but feel bitter at the cruel fate this fantastic person had faced, though I knew he himself had never complained.

After a while, Ozzy showed up and sat down with the rest of us. No one said much—there was nothing to say. As I left, I felt more anger than anything because I had realized that Randy's death would largely go unnoticed. *He's not going to get a big headline. It's not gonna say LEGENDARY DRUMMER RANDY CASTILLO, etc. It's not going to be like when a singer or guitar player passes away,* I thought, deciding there and then to throw the most badass benefit ever. I wanted to celebrate Randy for the huge personality and great drummer he was, so I called Phil Soussan, one of his closest friends, who had played with him in Ozzy's band.

"Phil, we need to organize a tribute concert for Randy," I said. "We're gonna throw the biggest rock show of the century; we need to give him a great send-off—bring up his drum kit and put it under the spotlights."

Phil wondered whom we should contact, and I suggested Ozzy.

It turned out Ozzy couldn't do it, so I called Nikki Sixx instead. He claimed that Mötley Crüe couldn't manage it either.

Fuck it, I thought, *I'll put a band together myself.* So I called Slash. By this point, Axl had begun calling himself Guns N' Roses, so Slash and Duff were both free agents, just like me, and could do whatever they wanted.

Slash knew Randy, but he had never been as close to him as I was. Still, he did at least know that Randy had passed. "I was really sad," he said.

"Dude," I told him. "I need you on this gig. Let's do it: you, me, and Duff."

"Who are we gonna get to sing?"

"Let's get that guy from Buckcherry."

"Oh, he's okay," Slash said. "That'll work."

The singer in Buckcherry was Josh Todd, and he was happy to join us. He even brought along the band's guitarist, Keith Nelson. Slash, Duff, and I spent an entire day rehearsing with them—playing, among other things, a weird, mocked-up version of "Paradise City." We then announced the gig with only me, Slash, and Duff named on the bill. The tickets sold out in what felt like two seconds flat.

The day before the show, I got a call from Steven Tyler. "I heard you're doing something for Randy?"

"Yeah, would you come?" I asked.

"I'm in," said Steven. "Can we play 'Mama Kin'?"

"Of course."

That evening at the Key Club on Sunset Strip really was unforgettable, and a fitting tribute to Randy. The place was already buzzing as Phil Soussan, Steve Lukather, and Ronnie Montrose played, but that was nothing compared to the reaction when Steven stepped out onstage and began singing "Mama Kin" with me, Duff, and Slash.

The next day, I was at one of my regular breakfast joints—Swingers Diner on Beverly Boulevard.

I had just been talking to my old party buddy, Mickey Rourke, who had shown up with his little dog, when Slash called.

"Last night was awesome," he said. "I think it's time."

"Time for what?"

"For a band."

"Okay, cool. What are you thinking?"

"Let's get that guy from Buckcherry—the singer," he said.

"Okay," I told him.

Twenty or so minutes later, Duff called. "Dude, that was awesome. You ready? We're gonna form a band. It's time," he said. "Let's get the guy from Buckcherry, and the guitar player too."

I cleared my throat and said, hesitantly, "We gotta find out if they want to do it first. They've already got a band."

But Josh and Keith immediately jumped at the chance, and we started rehearsing with them at their place in the Valley. It took me at least an hour to drive over there every day, but I didn't care. I just wanted to get back in the game.

We had been rehearsing for almost two months when Slash came over to me during a rehearsal.

"I'm leaving the band," he said.

"What the fuck are you talking about?"

But rather than reply, he just grabbed his two guitars and left the studio.

I followed him out into the parking lot. He was already in his car, and he wound down the side window when I knocked on it. "Where do you think you're going?" I asked.

"I'm out of here," he said. "I'm out."

"What do you mean, you're out?"

"I can't take that singer."

"You're the one who wanted him in the band!" I said. He began to say something, but I interrupted him. "No, no, hold on a second. We'll get rid of *him*. *You*'ve gotta stay."

He looked at me and said, "Yeah, you're right. We'll find a better fucking singer!"

So we headed back inside. Slash could never tell anyone *you're fired*; he always got someone else to do his dirty work for him. That day, he said to me, "Can you get rid of him? Can you tell him he's out?"

I sighed and said, "Okay."

A while later, I'd managed to gather my strength. I took Josh Todd to one side and said, "Slash is out. He split. So me and Duff have decided to go with him. But we're taking Keith with us."

Josh looked at me like he thought it was all a bad joke. Once he realized it wasn't, he was really pissed. We had been in rehearsals for two months, and he had split from his other band.

Keith, the guitarist, was completely floored when I explained what was going on. But he was a cool guy and decided to follow me, Slash, and Duff when we returned to our old rehearsal space at

Mates Studios. Everything was fine and dandy after that—or it was until Slash decided he didn't want Keith either.

Oh fuck, here we go again, I thought. I stifled a sigh and said, "Okay, I'll tell him."

"Thanks," Slash told me, hurrying out to his car.

I cursed him under my breath before I turned around and went over to Keith. He was sitting on the couch. "Keith," I said. "You're out, man."

I couldn't help but feel sorry for him. Not only had he turned his back on his first band, he'd also abandoned Josh. He looked completely crushed, and in an attempt to comfort him, I said, "I feel like Josh wants to get the band back together again; they'll take you back. Bands are like old girlfriends. You might have to beg a little, but it'll be okay."

I was right. Buckcherry got back together again—with both Josh and Keith—and our own trio suddenly became a quartet when Izzy began showing up at the studio to rehearse with us. Back when GN'R split up, that was exactly what I had been hoping for. The four of us were back together again, and we were working every day.

This is gonna be good; this is gonna be cool, I thought. Izzy had a really cool style that gave us that special *something*, and he wrote so many songs. But one day, he just went off and disappeared, in typical Izzy fashion. By then, he had been rehearsing with us for maybe a month.

"What the fuck just happened?" Duff said to me once we realized Izzy wasn't coming back.

"You tell me," I said with a shrug. I didn't really see much point in trying to understand why Izzy had done what he had.

The next day, as we took a break on the couch, Slash said, "We're gonna meet with some manager, Carl Stubner."

"No fucking way," I said. "Carl Stubner managed me in The Cult. He owes me a hundred and forty grand. No way I'm meeting with him."

"Come on, dude," said Slash.

"Absolutely not."

Slash sat quietly for a while, then he said, "How about if we tell him to put some money into your bank account?"

I sighed. "If he does it by nine o'clock tomorrow morning, I'll go to the meeting."

Lo and behold, $80,000 appeared by wire transfer the very next morning. *Well, okay*, I thought then. *I'll go to the meeting.*

So we met with him but chose not to work with him anyway. Instead, we decided to come up with the plans for the band ourselves, and as we were leaving Carl's office that day, Duff said, "I know a guitarist. His name's Dave Kushner, and he's gonna come down."

"You mean the guy from that Japanese band Zilch?" I asked.

"Yeah."

Two days later, Dave came down to the studio. We knew we had found the right guy after just a couple songs.

51

Scott

We bring in cops to make sure our new singer
doesn't escape from the studio.

WE PROBABLY ALL HAD an ambition to make a modern rock album, but finding the right singer proved harder than any of us could have imagined. We had no idea where to turn and eventually put out an ad in one of the world's biggest music magazines, encouraging singers to send in demos.

Once they came in, we sat down in the studio for weeks listening to that shit. The whole process made me really grumpy, and over and over again I found myself saying, "This guy sucks!"

"Give him a chance!" Slash said.

"No! He sucks!" I insisted. "I can tell by the first note."

My bad mood wasn't made any better by the fact that we were spending day after day rehearsing and getting nowhere.

All the same, I was hungry again. I felt like I had something to prove, and I think that was infectious. We all started going to the gym and eating egg whites, and before long we were all in great shape. We were also playing better than ever before.

Around that time, we started to hear rumors that Scott Weiland had left the Stone Temple Pilots, and since we all thought he was a great singer, we decided to try and track him down.

Duff knew Scott from before, so he and his wife went out to dinner with Scott and his wife. The next day, when Duff turned up at the rehearsal space, he said, "Scott said he got fired from STP, so I think he'd be interested in coming over."

A warning bell immediately began ringing in my mind, and I asked, "Why'd he get fired?"

Duff must have known what I was thinking, because he quickly said, "No, man, he's getting it together."

To me, it made no real difference whether it was true or not, because when he eventually came down to the rehearsal space to sing with us, we sent him away with a CD featuring a tune I'd written. He added vocals to it, and it sounded really good. When our manager David Codikow heard the result, he said, "Let's tie this song to a movie. It'll give us a real jump start for the band."

Not long after, the track—"Set Me Free"—ended up in Ang Lee's *Hulk*. Ang loved the song and asked David, "Did they write that especially for *Hulk*?"

David was a smart guy, so without a moment's hesitation, he said, "Yeah, they wrote it for you."

A few days later, David had invited people from the film studio over to our rehearsal space at Mates. When they arrived, with a Chanel-clad Kathy Nelson from Universal Pictures leading the way, we had just finished warming up. Scott still hadn't made an appearance, and after another fifteen minutes, Duff gave him a call.

"Dude, what the fuck?" I heard him whisper.

"Oh, man, I'm right around the corner," Scott told him.

It was clearly a lie, because we had to wait another hour or so before he finally showed up. By that point, the movie people were all pretty annoyed, but I was actually less worried about that than I was about Scott.

He strode into the room wearing a hat and sunglasses, high as fuck, and headed straight over to the mic. Without batting an eyelid, Slash went over to him and said—so calmly and quietly that only Duff and I could hear—"I don't give a fuck where you've been and what you're on, but you need to sing better right now than you ever have before."

Slash's ability not to show his feelings had finally found a use. I remember looking at him with a reluctant sense of admiration.

Scott didn't speak, he just grabbed the mic and eventually we started the song. Once the movie people left a short while later, David followed them out. He came straight back with a grin across his face and gave us the offer—Scott had fucking crushed it.

A few months later, we were invited to a preview screening of the movie, and as the credits rolled and we heard our track, each of our names came up individually, reminding us that we needed to decide on a name for the band.

"How about Dead Velvet Revolver?" Scott suggested.

"You mean like Stone Temple Pilots?" I said sarcastically.

Right then, Slash said, "How about we just cut the 'Dead' part?"

And that was that.

"Set Me Free" quickly became a hit, which meant that the record labels started sniffing around. Before long, we had offers from RCA, Electra, and Warner Brothers. Tom Whalley from Warner was actually late to our meeting, and I got bored and said to the others, "Guys, I'm leaving. Fuck this guy!"

Instead, we flew to New York to meet the others—first Electra, then Clive Davis at RCA, a living legend who had signed superstars like Janis Joplin, Bruce Springsteen, and Billy Joel. We knew he hadn't signed any big rock bands lately; he was more involved with pop acts like Whitney Houston and Kelly Clarkson, which meant he probably wanted to add a rock band to his list. As it happened, we were right, and the first thing he said to us as we arrived at his huge office was, "They say I don't have an ear for rock 'n' roll; they say I only have an ear for pop music, but I'm gonna prove them wrong. I'm going to make you the biggest rock 'n' roll band in the world. We'll do that for you here at RCA."

Clive was old school, but in a good way. He was the real deal, and he talked our language.

"You're not gonna make us work with other songwriters, right?" Slash asked.

"I love your songs," Clive told him. "That's why you're here. Now, do you want to step into the bunker?"

We stared at him in confusion and then followed him into an adjoining room, which turned out to be soundproofed. There was a pair of enormous speakers at the other end.

"What would you gentlemen like to play first?" Clive asked.

So we put on our demos. We even played him "Slither," which we recorded right before we flew to New York.

"Oh, that's rock 'n' roll!" Clive yelled, sounding impressed.

After that, we played him "Fall to Pieces."

"Hmm," he said. "This one could cross over."

When we then played him the other ballad from the record, he got all emotional and said, "I want this band."

We flew back to LA the next day, but it wasn't long before we got two new contract offers: one from Electra and one from Clive, both of them for three records. They didn't include any merchandise or touring; they were just for the records. In their minds, they needed to pay more up front to secure us because that would mean we could put money in our pockets and make the record.

Duff, Slash, and I headed over to Scott's studio in Burbank to go through the contract with him. I'd never been over there before and was amazed when I saw the place. It was very funky, all purple and tapestries—very hippie. The only problem was that Scott wasn't there. We waited outside for an hour or so until a cab pulled up and Scott climbed out. He was barefoot wearing a pinstripe suit, and as he sat down on the floor in the studio, we realized he was bleeding from a gash on his head. It was clear he was on heroin. *Oh, fuck*, I thought.

"Scott, you're bleeding!" Duff told him.

Scott reached up to his head and looked down at the blood on his hand. "I was playing racquetball, and I got hit by the racquet."

"You played racquetball in a suit?" I asked.

"Yeah."

"Where are your shoes?" Duff asked.

He looked down at his feet like he had only just realized he was barefoot. I hugged him and told him about the offers. I'm sure he didn't understand a thing, but he did at least seem happy.

A few days later, we signed the deal with RCA and got started in the studio almost right away. Unfortunately, we didn't get very far before Scott was arrested for shooting up with some girl in his car outside the studio. He was shipped straight off to rehab after that.

"When can he get out to sing?" Slash asked as we sat in the studio.

"He'll need a police escort," our manager said. "It's gonna cost a lot."

"Scott should pay for that," Slash muttered.

Our manager sighed and said, "It's just the price for doing business with Scott Weiland."

So we started paying for all these cops; it cost something like $500 per guy per day. They sat inside with us while Scott was singing, and then they accompanied him right back to rehab.

To my surprise, Clive seemed cool with the whole thing. "Boys," he said, "let's just get the record done."

Though that proved easier said than done. After his stint in rehab, Scott continued to disappear without warning, and once, after going missing for two days, I got a call from a friend who said that he was in a crack house downtown. I headed down there to get him, and he looked just like a homeless guy. His clothes were all disheveled, and he was totally strung out.

His first words to me were, "You got any coke?"

"Scott, I'm sober!"

By some miracle, he managed to finish his vocals, and he even beat the odds to take part in the shoot for the "Slither" video. The plan after that was to release the album—called *Contraband*—in March 2004. But Clive said, "No, we can't put it out yet." We had no idea why, and the months passed. Eventually, I called him up to ask what he was doing.

"I'm holding it until the first week of June," he said. The first week in June was the only week no other big bands or artists had releases scheduled—and the band headed down to Vegas one evening to play a show.

That week, management took us to a conference room, where Clive called us on the speakerphone. "I've got great news for you," Clive said. "You're gonna enter the charts at number one on *Billboard*'s Top 200. Now you know why we waited, right?"

"Clive, you're a genius!" I told him.

In the first week alone, we sold 250,000 copies of the album, and whenever I turned on the radio, "Slither" seemed to be playing. Everything took off, just like that. The video was everywhere; the single was huge. We were on fire.

We headed over to New York to do some promo work, and one day, when Duff and I took the subway to a gym downtown, a young guy came over to us. "Hey, you're Duff and Matt from Velvet Revolver, right?" he said.

"Yeah!" Duff yelled.

We both felt fantastic. We had a new identity.

52

A Journey into the Abyss

Drac dies, and I fall off the wagon.

"YOU WANNA FIGHT, MOTHERFUCKER?" Slash shoved me and raised his right fist.

We were face to face in the lobby of the Grand Hôtel in Stockholm, Sweden. It was August 12, 2004, and Velvet Revolver was on its first big world tour. We had already played twenty-four shows in North America and had just arrived in Europe. Our debut album was topping charts around the world, and we really were on fire.

All the same, I'd recently found out that Slash had gone behind my back and tried to get rid of Happy Walters, one of our managers. He wanted to bring in Howard Kaufman, my old manager from The Cult, instead.

"Why the fuck have you arranged a meeting with Howard without consulting me?" I asked. "In this band, we all get an equal say." I really was pissed, so when Slash began to mumble something in his defense, I knocked the cigarette from between his lips.

When I did that, he actually looked me in the eye for once. He lowered his hand and said, "I'm going over to Howard." He did, too. I liked Happy, but the rest of the band also wanted to drop him, so Duff, Dave, Scott, and I left him but stayed with David Codikow.

A few days after our stare down, we were in Cologne, Germany. I was standing next to our tour bus in the parking lot after the show when Duff came over to me. I could tell from his face that something had happened and automatically assumed it was something to do with the band.

"Matt, there's something I need to tell you," he said, looking down. "Your dog died."

I had both the dogs by that point—I had gotten Anya back after the breakup with Shiva—and at first I thought he must mean the older of the two. "Anya died?" I asked.

Duff squirmed a little and said, "No, Drac."

It was like the ground disappeared from beneath my feet, and I dropped to my knees on the asphalt and started to shake. I'd had Drac ever since I lived in Malibu; the little guy had been with me through everything that had happened over the past ten years, and I loved him more than I loved practically any other living creature.

Maybe that was why I sneaked into the room where my girlfriend Ace was sleeping (I'll talk more about her later—she deserves a chapter of her own), grabbed a small bottle of Jack Daniel's from the minibar, and knocked it back. It was like the booze was calling to me, demons whispering, *You've got a great excuse, so why not?* Deep down, I knew it was dumb, but I couldn't resist. So I drank until my belly was full of booze and my head was full of guilt. Just like that, I had thrown away six years of sobriety.

The next evening, I went out to dinner with Ace.

We decided to share a bottle of wine—then another. In the days that followed, I continued to drink—every day.

Slash had also started drinking again around this time. I found out one afternoon when I headed into a bar near our hotel and saw him sitting alone with a glass of red wine in one hand. He didn't seem too happy to see me there; strictly speaking, he was supposed to be sober.

"It's just a little wine," he said, the subtext being that he wasn't *really* drinking again. But he was, and I was too, and Scott was constantly high. We actually had to get a couple of cops to help us stop him from escaping. It was like there was a huge sign reading

CATASTROPHE looming over the rest of the tour, which soon continued with a second American leg, a UK leg, and an Australia/Japan leg.

Between shows in Tokyo and Christchurch, New Zealand, Scott and I flew to Los Angeles to take part in the *47th Annual Grammy Awards*. We were nominated in a few different categories: Best Rock Album, Best Rock Song, and Best Hard Rock Performance.

I was wearing a really nice Gucci suit and was sitting next to Scott among all the other nominees when he suddenly leaned in to me and said, "I'm gonna go out for a cigarette."

"Don't be too long," I said. "This is going really fast."

It was true. Because there were so many categories, they were really racing through them up onstage.

In any case, Scott went off, and before long the presenter announced that we'd won Best Hard Rock Performance for "Slither." I looked around but couldn't see Scott anywhere, so I took a deep breath, got up, and headed onto the stage to collect the award. I even gave a brief, improvised speech. It was only once I left the stage that Scott came over to me.

"You went up to collect that yourself?" He nodded to the trophy I was holding.

"What was I supposed to do?" I asked. "You went out for a smoke."

He just stared at me. It was obvious he was furious with me rather than happy we won.

The tour lasted eighteen months, which was at least two months too long. It really burnt us out, and by the time we got home, we didn't even want to see one another. We actually didn't meet for six whole months, and by the time we next hung out, Slash had gotten hooked on heroin again, Duff had become a pill popper, and I was drinking as much as I had been before rehab. In other words, the guys who gathered in the studio I'd built out the back of my new house in West Hollywood were total wrecks. The plan was to record some new tracks. We had already decided we wanted Rick Rubin to produce our new record, and after working on it for a while, we invited him over to the studio to give it a listen.

Rick came, but on that same day, Scott showed up unexpectedly. None of us had seen him in six months.

After Rick listened to our ideas and said that none of them really held up, he gathered us together in the studio and asked how we were doing.

Slash, Duff, and I said we were fine—which was such a blatant lie it was actually pretty embarrassing. But when Scott's turn came around, he said, "I don't get along with Matt."

I stared at him. "What the fuck are you talking about? I haven't seen you in six months!"

"I can feel it," Scott went on.

"How can you feel it? I haven't talked to you."

Rick now gave me a stern look. "What's the problem, Matt?"

I knew I was about to lose my temper, and I raised my voice. "I just told you, there is no problem."

Rick squinted calmly at me. "Why don't you guys go out to lunch and work it out?"

"Work out *what*?"

Rick continued to come down to the studio every month or so, and each time, after listening to what we had written, he would say, "I don't think you have the songs yet, but keep writing."

We got pretty sick of hearing that, and Scott said, "Let's get Brendan O'Brien instead!"

Slash and Duff weren't convinced, because they thought it was a little too Stone Temple Pilots, but I was so frustrated by the lack of progress we were making, I thought it was worth a try. Brendan came down to the studio, listened to our tracks, picked out a couple he liked, and made some good suggestions as to how we could make them even better. He was quick and sure of himself, and he got us organized. We decided to move forward with him, and, oddly enough, everything seemed to flow smoothly from that point on— even though I had really started to suffer from my drinking. I was often so dehydrated that my whole body went stiff, and I couldn't move properly. I also kind of lost focus on my instrument. My party life had taken over again.

Despite that, and despite all the other problems we had, our record—*Libertad*—actually ended up being pretty good.

53

Ace

I experience a Sid and Nancy story.

NO ONE CAN EXPLAIN what draws one person to another. All I knew was that I was immediately interested in the blonde girl I saw at a Super Bowl party in 2004. I was there with Jerry Cantrell from Alice in Chains, and as yet I had only seen her from behind. If I'm being perfectly honest, more than anything I was just hoping she had a face that matched that ass. As luck would have it, she did, and I heard myself saying, "Hi, I'm Matt. What's your name?"

"Ace," she said, holding out her hand.

We talked for a while, and I noticed that she had a slight Oklahoma twang. She told me that she was at the Super Bowl to dance for Duran Duran and that she had been doing ballet since she was three. Before I knew it, she had slipped away, and I saw her again a while later, chatting to Jerry. *Typical*, I thought, because I knew Jerry had the same taste in girls as I did. I couldn't stop staring at her and was determined to get her phone number. I got it, but not until later that evening, when we headed to another party with a big group of others.

I was sober at the time, though Ace wasn't, and when I asked for her phone number, she swayed and stared into space. She gave me the number, and a week or so later, I called her.

"Hey, this is Matt."

"Who?"

She had no idea who I was and didn't remember a single thing from that evening, even when I tried to remind her. I realized it was going to be tough to get her to agree to a date, but I also couldn't stop myself from trying. So I continued to call her, and eventually— after maybe a month—she agreed to go out with me.

Ace was only nineteen at the time, and I tried to work out what she might think was cool. Eventually, I decided to take her to a Strokes show. I knew the guys in the band, and I thought it might impress her. It didn't, but she did at least let me take her out again. She let me buy her gifts too. I was chasing her that entire spring, and we didn't even sleep together.

Velvet Revolver was booked to play two shows at the Wiltern in LA, and I invited her along to the first one. She turned up with two friends, and I was a little nervous about what she would think. When I told her I had been in GN'R, she gave me a blank look and said, *What?*

I was in good enough shape to take off my shirt onstage every night, and as I stood there that evening, bowing to the crowd with the other guys, I could tell that Ace's friends liked what they saw. Ace clearly did too, because she came home with me afterward, and I quickly got her clothes off. She was a professional dancer with a dancer's body (Ace had been a backing dancer for all kinds of stars—Lenny Kravitz, Britney Spears, Jennifer Lopez, Pink), and I remember thinking *Holy shit!* as I touched her.

I had been waiting for that moment for so long that I had to try to calm myself down. At the same time, I felt like my patient wooing hadn't just produced a dividend; it had also been the only way to really win her over.

During this time, Ace lived in an apartment in the San Fernando Valley with a couple of her girlfriends. When we woke up together the next morning, I said to her, "We're gonna go pick up your shit, and you'll never have to go back to the San Fernando Valley again."

She moved in with me later that same day, and when our world tour moved on to Europe, she came with me. I had been sober ever since I met her, which meant she had no idea about my addiction problems. Ace herself was a party girl, and way too young to understand where I was heading as we drank wine together after I learned that Drac had died.

Ace and I began partying our way across Europe, deciding that in each of the countries we visited, we'd only drink local booze. That meant schnapps in Germany, scotch in Scotland, and so on. It was fun to begin with, but as we started drinking more and more, we began fighting more and more often. After one of our shows, in London, we even managed to destroy our hotel room; we screamed and shouted and threw things at one another. On a different occasion, we got so crazy that even Slash felt compelled to step in as the voice of reason.

We obviously had better times, too—moments that could be totally magical. Ace was just so fun to be around, and maybe that was why the other guys' wives hated me so much. They even called me "Creep." In Ace's defense, I used to say, "At least she's fun, not a jaded old Yoko Ono like you."

By that point, Slash, Duff, Scott, and Dave were all married, and they used to clear out right after the show—Duff to read and Slash to practice on his guitar. To me, at the time, it felt like the death of rock 'n' roll.

That might also be why Ace decided that we should set up our very own bar backstage, and that we should call it the Velvet Lounge. The next day, we set up a really nice lounge with all kinds of booze, and Ace suggested heading out into the crowd to give out backstage passes. I thought it sounded like a great idea, and after our show, she turned up in our lounge with four pretty girls. She smiled and told them to line up with their backs to us. The girls did as they were told.

"Now take off your pants and bend over," Ace continued.

Next thing I knew, I was staring at four bare asses.

I smiled at Ace, who began slapping the girls on their butts, one by one. The girls whimpered a little, but they didn't seem to have anything against it; more than anything, it seemed like everyone was having fun.

Right then, Scott came into the lounge. He stopped dead and stared in horror at the girls, me, and Ace. Without a single word, he turned and rushed back out.

When we got to the arena the next day, Ace and I couldn't find the Velvet Lounge. I asked our tour manager, Graham Cooper, what was going on, but he just squirmed and said, "Man, we got real problems. The Velvet Lounge has to go."

It turned out Scott had called his wife to tell her all about what was going on, and she had immediately called Duff's wife. So the wives got together, and once that happened, we were fucked.

I went over to Scott's bus, were he was watching cartoons in his pajamas in the back lounge.

"Dude!" I said. "What the fuck? You're gonna throw me under the bus? When it was you coming into my lounge?"

He looked at me and said, "You're disgusting—you and your eighties Mötley Crüe shit.'"

"Really?" I said. "Let's talk about your nineties grunge shit. What I'm doing is totally consensual. Those girls wanted to be there. They wanted to have fun. It's part of the experience."

Despite that, Scott gave me a disgusted look. "You need to grow up. You're a forty-year-old man."

I just shook my head, turned around, and left him there, in his pajamas.

Though Ace and I weren't allowed to continue the Velvet Lounge, we still had plenty of fun. It felt like my last hurrah. Somewhere, deep down, I knew that if I didn't stop drinking, I'd die—literally.

When we arrived in Dublin one freezing day in January, I said to Ace, "I know a really cool bar called Lillie's Bordello. I went there with Joe Elliott and Ronnie Wood a few years ago." Before long, we were heading over there in a taxi.

"Are there many flights to Glasgow from here?" I asked the driver.

"Yeah, several a day… Why d'you ask?"

"We want to party all night, but we need to be there by eight tomorrow evening at the very latest."

266

"No problem."

My memory of what happened next is a little hazy, but I do know that Slash joined us at Lillie's and that Ace and I were in the bar until five in the morning and managed to find some blow to take back to the hotel with us. We did all the coke and emptied the minibar, and when the phone began to ring some time the next day, I still hadn't managed to get any more than an hour's sleep. I was totally fucked up and felt like my head was about to shatter into a thousand pieces.

"We're leaving now," I heard Graham say down the line.

"Oh, okay," I said. "Listen, I'm gonna catch a later flight. Don't worry."

Graham was silent for a few seconds, but when he next spoke his voice was serious: "Matt, there's only one flight that'll get us there in time, and that's the one we're about to get."

"Oh, fuck," I said. "I guess Ace and I will have to sort out our own plane then."

"What do you mean?" he asked.

"Call the concierge and tell them to get us a plane."

"Okay," he said, hanging up. Before long, he called me back: "They have a plane you can charter, but it'll cost you six thousand euros."

"Holy shit!" I said. "What else have they got?"

"I'll check," he said. A short while later, he got back to me: "They have a prop plane for twenty-five hundred euros."

"I'll take it!"

I heard Graham sigh, and then he said, "Okay, I'll stay with you and let the band go."

Just before six that evening, Ace, Graham, and I got to the airport. The flight over the Irish Sea was supposed to take around an hour and a half, and our show in Glasgow was due to start at nine.

As a result, we all felt pretty relaxed—until we saw the plane. "Oh, no," I heard Ace say. I understood why, because the propeller plane parked on the asphalt in front of us really did look like it belonged in some kind of museum. The captain also looked like Benny Hill.

It was really scary, but I realized we didn't have any other choice; this was the price we would have to pay for our night out in Dublin.

We sat down on the rock-hard seats and were each handed a tray with a couple of sad cheese sandwiches wrapped in plastic. As the propellers began whirring in the fog outside, Ace and I glanced nervously at one another. Graham pulled out his phone and called his wife. "Babe," I heard him half whisper. "Don't worry, but I might not be coming home."

The plane got into position on the runway, bouncing roughly several times before eventually taking off. I glanced at Ace, who was gripping the armrests. Her face was white as a sheet. She looked back at me and said, "I hate you."

On the other side of me, Graham looked just as uncomfortable. "I hate you, too," he said.

The crappy little plane shook and rattled as we flew over the Irish Sea in the darkness, and I repeatedly thought, *We're all gonna die.*

Eventually, we landed in Glasgow. It was around eight in the evening, and there was a car waiting for us at the airport. Just half an hour later, we arrived at the arena. Slash was the first person we saw.

"You made it," he said.

"Yeah," I replied, trying not to let him see that I was still shaking.

"Cool, man," he said.

Going forward, Ace and I continued to party, and by the time we got back to LA, our arguments were worse than ever. Eventually, I reached a point where I was so far back into my old patterns of behavior that Ace and I broke up. We were definitely in love with each other, but we were having a hard time actually *liking* one another. I decided to rent out my place in West Hollywood to friends who had gotten divorced or kicked out by their significant others, and bought myself a new place up in the hills, on Doheny Drive, where I started throwing parties that lasted several days.

By then, Ace had moved into a small apartment of her own. The only problem was that being apart felt just as bad as being together, and before I knew what had happened, we were back together again.

She either came over to sleep with me and then headed home, or I went over to her place and then went back to my own house. We couldn't quite disconnect. Finally, I told her, "Fuck it, why don't you just move in again?"

So Ace moved into the house on the hill. The parties continued, but so did the fighting and the drama.

Out on tour, the only problem was Scott. He was in worse shape than ever, and began arriving late to shows almost right away. Sometimes he didn't show up at all, and during our second-to-last gig he and I got into a fight. Like always, Scott turned up when he felt like it. He was just like Axl in that respect, with the major difference that Axl usually sounded incredible when he finally got up onstage. Scott was drunk and high when he grabbed the mic that evening, and he sounded terrible.

He also began arguing with me in front of the crowd, and started a fight with my drum tech before rushing offstage. I leaped up, ran after him, and found him in his dressing room.

"Listen, you skinny little fuck!" I yelled. "Get back onstage now or I'll snap you like a twig."

Rather than replying, Scott threw himself at me, and we started to brawl. I went back out to the others and ended the show.

We had all had enough of him, and before we got into the van following our last show in Amsterdam on April 1, 2008, we handed an envelope to our tour manager, who passed it on to Scott. Inside was a note: YOU'RE FIRED.

During the whole second half of that year-long tour, I missed Ace so much that it hurt. On several occasions, I'd tried to reach her by phone, but she had changed her number. When I eventually got back to LA, I found out from friends that she had checked into rehab and gotten herself clean. I also heard that she would be performing at a club, so I went over there and immediately spotted her. She looked amazing, and I walked right up to the stage and yelled, "I love you!"

She just gave me a brief glance and then ignored me completely, which I can understand now—I was a total wreck and looked like utter shit. But that didn't stop me from feeling hurt, broken, and lost.

A few days later, I went to see my mom in Orange County for Thanksgiving, and she took me to a party her friends were throwing—probably because she hoped a little normal interaction would do me good. But being sober made my body ache, and I tried to score coke from someone there, all while my mom was just a few feet away.

On the way home from the party, I asked her to drop me off at a bar where I knew one of my old pals was hanging out. My memory of the rest of the evening is a bit of a haze. All I know is that I got really fucked up, got into a fight, and got thrown out. I also know that I took a cab back to Mom's place, where everyone was already in bed. I immediately began looking for more to drink and found an almost full bottle of vodka in the kitchen. Next thing I knew, I was on the floor with my back against the fridge, knocking back the vodka.

I woke the next morning to Mom shaking me. I was lying on the kitchen floor, and I remember being surprised that she looked so concerned—scared, even. "Matt," she said. "You need to get it together. I can take you to rehab."

"Don't worry about me," I mumbled. "I'll be okay."

A sad look appeared on her face, and she said, "I've been worrying about you ever since you left home at seventeen."

Later that day, I called my dad and said, "Dad...I'm gonna go to rehab."

"Matt, could you call me back?" he asked, as a shrill loudspeaker voice rang out in the background. "I have a horse in the third race." Just like that, he hung up.

In that moment, I gained some kind of understanding of what Mom had gone through being married to a gambler. I realized why she had kicked him out and also why she hadn't always been able to give me the attention and love I needed as a child.

The next day, she gave me a ride to a large, secluded house where I was shown into what was jokingly called "the rock star suite." It was a nice room, and the staff there were incredible.

Since I was in such a bad state, they had no choice but to medicate me. You can die if you go cold turkey. I spent my first week there heavily medicated, shuffling around in slippers and a robe the way I'd seen mentally ill patients do in movies like *One Flew over the Cuckoo's Nest*. By the next week, I began to feel a little better, and by the time I had just a few days left, I got a phone call. It was Ace, and she said, "I heard you're in rehab. I'm glad you're there."

I had been at the treatment center for almost a month by that point, and when I got back to the house on Doheny Drive, I called her.

Just an hour or so later, she was there with me. It was clear she had missed me too, because we made love almost immediately, and then we talked about being sober. She looked great, and I was doing much better.

I looked at her as we lay in bed and said, "Maybe if we stay sober, we could stay together."

That was the reason we both needed to keep on the straight and narrow. It might sound banal, but I really do think the love we shared helped us. I guess that's probably why I decided to propose to her on New Year's Eve 2011, in Cabo San Lucas, Mexico. We had only just arrived there, on what Ace thought was an ordinary vacation, when Sammy Hagar called. "I heard you're here, man," he said. "Could you come down to the club? I need you to play drums tonight."

Sammy was the proud owner of Cabo Wabo, a renowned rock club, and we had been friends for a long time. "I was going to ask Ace to marry me tonight," I said.

"Do it here! I need you, man."

I thought for a moment and promised to help out. I then took Ace down to a beautiful beach called Lover's Beach, and down by the turquoise water I dropped to one knee and held out the ring I had been carrying around in the pocket of my swimming trunks. "Will you marry me, Ace?" I asked.

She nodded and began to cry.

In that moment I made a commitment to Ace that has been the most important thing I've ever done, dedicating myself completely to our relationship and to another human being. The change in me was really starting to happen. I finally had someone special that made me so happy, someone to live my life with—my soon-to-be wife, Ace.

54

Playing with My Heroes

I go a whole tour sober with the godfather of rock 'n' roll.

AFTER VELVET REVOLVER, I was once again left with no idea of what to do. I guess that's pretty much the story of my career; I never had any consistency lasting more than three or four years before it all went to shit. As a result, when I got a text message from Lemmy one evening, asking if I could jump in to replace Mikkey Dee during Motörhead's USA tour, it felt like a sign from God. I mean, Velvet Revolver was over, so the message made me feel like everything might be alright after all. I also felt pretty flattered and quickly replied, "Why me?"

My phone beeped. "Dave Grohl's not available."

I laughed and wrote back, "When are we rehearsing?"

"We're not."

The first show was in Washington, DC, and as I walked into the club where we were due to play, Phil Campbell and Lemmy came out to meet me. I had known them both for some time and was happy to see them, though we didn't have much time to chat before sound check—which involved running through the entire set from start to finish.

"Sounds great," Lemmy said once we were done. "Let's go."

I remember being really nervous that evening. First, I was sober, and second, Mikkey was a different kind of drummer than me. I'd say he's more a heavy metal drummer, whereas I'm more rock. Besides, some of the songs were pretty challenging—"In the Name of Tragedy" and "Bomber," for example. Despite that, we rocked it, and I think everyone was happy once we left the stage.

There were just three of us in the tour bus—Lemmy, Phil, and I. Lemmy had the back lounge, and Phil and I shared the rest of the space. They both drank quite a bit, but Lemmy never seemed out of control. In fact, he actually spent most of his time watching war movies back there—aside from when he told the driver to stop the bus in the middle of the night. I sometimes woke to find us parked outside a casino. We often spent five or six hours parked like that.

The road was Lemmy's spiritual home; he was a real road dog, a vagabond. Phil was a little different—he had kids and missed his family. But Lemmy didn't have a family like that. He did actually have one son, Paul, but they didn't meet until the kid was already in his teens.

Before the shows, we all had our own dressing rooms, which I found pretty weird. Lemmy had a slot machine in his, and he liked to read books. He needed his quiet time before the show, but afterward he liked to meet people—particularly girls. As far as I was concerned, I was just glad to be sober, because I really had to fight my way through the shows. After just a couple days, both of my hands were completely blistered. I should've taped them, but I didn't, and before long I was in constant pain. It was brutal.

After we had played maybe ten shows, Lemmy came up to me in the bus and said, "I gotta go to Memphis." The reason was that a film crew was making a documentary about him, and the crew wanted to film while he guested with Metallica. So Lemmy and I took the bus down there, and Phil rode in the crew bus to our next gig in Orlando. Ace caught a plane down to Memphis and came out to meet us. In the movie, you can actually see me, Lemmy, and Ace walking into Metallica's tuning room. Lars looks up in surprise when he sees me and shouts, "What the fuck?!" He clearly had no idea I was playing with his idols.

One of the best shows I played with Motörhead was at Stubb's Bar-B-Q in Austin. That was also where Lemmy and I did an interview for *Classic Rock* magazine. The reason I remember it is that the guy asked Lemmy, "How would you describe your life in two words?"

Without even thinking, Lemmy said, "Fierce joy." I loved the sound of that, and when I recorded my solo album a few years later, I called Lemmy and said, "Do you remember the interview where you used those two words? I want to call the record *Matt Sorum's Fierce Joy.*"

I could practically hear him smiling as he said, "It's yours."

The thing I liked about Lemmy was that we were onstage every night, and we were on time at every show. That was what I told Duff when he asked me how life was on the road. "It's the best experience of my life," I said. "I can retire after this!"

My final show with Motörhead was in Denver, Colorado. After we finished, Lemmy called us all over to his dressing room. "We wanted to give you a little something," he said, handing me a framed certificate that read HONORARY MEMBER OF MOTÖRHEAD. It was signed by both Lemmy Kilmister and Phil Campbell.

During the months that followed, I began to think about starting a supergroup. I discussed it with a few people and before long, I got a call from this indie promoter guy named Gabe who said he'd heard about my plans. "I can get you really good money," he said, sounding confident. "We can do ten shows in South America."

I met Gabe through an old tour manager friend whom I'd done a lot of business with so I took it on his word that he was legit. And I said, "What were you thinking for the lineup?"

"James Hetfield!" he immediately replied.

"Okay…" I said. "But James Hetfield isn't gonna do it."

"Could you at least make him an offer?"

"Okay, I'll call James."

So that's what I did, but James replied, "Nah, I'm taking the kids scuba diving."

After speaking to him, I made a few more calls and eventually got a great gang together: Joe Elliott, Glenn Hughes, Sebastian Bach,

Duff, Gilby Clarke, Steve Stevens, Billy Duffy, and Mike Inez from Alice in Chains. But when I reeled off those names to Gabe, he said, "It's not enough. Could you get Gene Simmons too?"

I sighed to myself and said, "Okay."

I called Gene, and the first thing he asked was, "What's the name of the group?"

"I'm gonna call it the Rock 'n' Roll All Stars. Keep it simple. It's South America—easier for people to understand."

"Hmm," said Gene. "That sounds a lot like a baseball team."

"Nah, that's rock 'n' roll."

Either way, Gene wanted the money up front before he would agree to anything, so I got Gabe to arrange that with the bank. They wired the money across to him.

I then called Gene and asked, "Did you get the money?"

"Yeah," he said. "I'm in!"

Once we ended the call, I rang my friend Steve Strange, who is a big-time agent. "Beware of a Peruvian drug dealer in a white suit," he said.

"Okay, Steve. Thanks!"

"And make sure you get all the money up front!"

Shortly after that, I managed to gather my entire all-star gang for rehearsals. We sounded surprisingly good together. There was only one real problem: I couldn't trademark the band name, so I decided to call it Matt Sorum's Rock 'n' Roll All Stars instead. The ad for the tour went straight out on the internet, and at eight o'clock the next morning, I got a text message: "Matt, please come to my house. Gene."

I got into my car and drove over to Gene's mansion-like house in the hills. I parked on the driveway, walked up to the door, and rang the bell. After quite some time, Gene answered. He grinned and said, "Good morning, Matt! Come on in!"

I followed him inside, and my eyes widened; there was Kiss stuff everywhere. The whole place practically looked like a Kiss museum. Gene noticed my reaction and seemed even more satisfied as he said,

"You know, I have twenty-seven hundred licenses for Kiss products." He made a sweeping gesture with his arm.

There was no reason not to believe him, because no matter where you looked, the place was full of Kiss merchandise: surfboards, golf clubs, motorcycles—pretty much everything you could imagine. "Wow, Gene, that's impressive," I said.

"Thank you," Gene said proudly, and he beckoned to me. "Come this way. Step into my office!" In the room behind the door he opened was an enormous desk standing in front of the window. A black leather armchair was behind it, and he pointed to it and said, "Why don't you sit in my chair? Feel the power."

I thought, *Is he fucking serious?* I didn't say anything and simply sat down in the chair as Gene watched me.

"How does it feel?"

"It's a nice chair, Gene," I said, noticing as I did that there were a load of T-shirts on the wall behind him, which he had clearly designed himself. One of them read GENE SIMMONS'S TITANS OF ROCK.

"Let's talk about the name," he said, giving me a serious look. "There's a problem. Matt Sorum's Rock 'n' Roll All Stars—I can't do that. I wouldn't play in John Bonham's Rock 'n' Roll All Stars. I wouldn't play in Ringo Starr's Rock 'n' Roll All Stars. I wouldn't play in Tommy Lee's Elephant Balls. And I certainly won't play in Matt Sorum's Rock 'n' Roll All Stars."

"Wow," I said, turning gently from side to side in the armchair. "I couldn't trademark the name, Gene."

"In that case, I have a better suggestion," he said, pointing to the T-shirt I had noticed earlier.

"Gene Simmons's Titans of Rock."

"Gene…" I said, struggling to find the right words, because I realized we were in some kind of negotiation. "I called you. This is my band. I hired you to play in my band."

"Hmm," Gene said with a frown. "So how about we call it Gene Simmons's Titans of Rock Festival…featuring Matt Sorum's Rock 'n' Roll All Stars?"

"Festival?" I said, surprised.

"Yeah!" Gene grinned again. "A festival. You're gonna play at my festival."

I took a deep breath and said, "Gene, I know you think Rock 'n' Roll All Stars sounds like a baseball team, but *that* sounds like a wrestling team."

Gene laughed and then asked, "So what are you gonna do?"

"I'm gonna get rid of the 'Matt Sorum's' and just call it the Rock 'n' Roll All Stars. No festival. No Titans of Rock."

Gene looked me straight in the eye. I realized in that moment that he was a real hardcore businessman. "Hmm," he said. "Can I bring eight to ten basses backstage for the fans?"

"Of course you can!"

"And I'm gonna have my own VIP?"

"Let's go on tour."

The South America tour with the Rock 'n' Roll All Stars left me wanting more, and by the time I got back to LA, I realized that the idea of an all-star band felt right—partly because it was such fun to play with my friends, some of whom happened to be among the world's best musicians and singers, and partly because I had discovered that being a leader suited me more than I ever could've imagined.

So I called around and asked my friends whether they wanted to join me. After that, I began booking gigs all over the world. It became my fun project. In contrast to the stressful machine Velvet Revolver had been, forming an all-star band was pure enjoyment. I had also come up with a better name for the band—Kings of Chaos, a name that was thrown around for the Neurotic Outsiders lineup.

When I was offered the chance to play four gigs in South Africa, I thought it sounded amazing. I immediately said yes. Like before, the core of the band was Duff, Slash, Gilby, and me. I also called Joe Elliott, whom I knew had enjoyed the All Stars tour.

"Yeah, I'm in," he said, without a moment's hesitation.

I also brought in Ed Roland, from Collective Soul, and Myles Kennedy, because I needed more singers.

The whole band was surprised by the reaction when we played in Cape Town and Johannesburg. We sold out arena shows there, and I decided to put together a new South Africa tour the next year. I had to finance everything from flights (first class) to hotels and special requests from the musicians. It was a lot of work.

On that later tour, I convinced not only Billy Gibbons and Robin Zander to play with us but Steven Tyler too. He had been a friend of mine since my first tour with The Cult, but that didn't mean he was willing to play for no money. On top of his sky-high fee, he wanted a presidential suite at the hotel, a very specific rider, and his three personal assistants. I said yes to everything because I knew what a difference he would make to the tour.

One of our shows was in Sun City, and Steven flew in by helicopter. The suite I had booked for him was four thousand square feet, with an enormous Jacuzzi and a grand piano.

Once he was settled in his suite, I called his room, put on a fake voice, and said, "Mr. Tallarico" (Steven's real name), "this is the hotel concierge. Are you happy with your room? Did you find the baby elephant in the east wing?"

I heard him gasp down the line, but then he began roaring with laughter and said, "Oh, man, this is so great!"

55

Rock and Roll Hall of Fame

What should have been a fantastic moment
becomes something else entirely.

WHEN THE NEWS BROKE that Guns N' Roses were going to be inducted into the Rock and Roll Hall of Fame, all hell broke out between Slash and Axl. Axl said mean, disparaging things about Slash in public and refused to say whether he even wanted to be inducted.

That's why I decided to give Slash a call. "Man, what are we gonna do?" I asked.

"We don't do anything," he said, "but we should still go."

"Okay," I said. "But we're not gonna play?"

"No, we're not gonna play."

I asked Duff the same question—and got the same answer.

Time passed, and just a week or so before the induction was due to take place, we found out that Axl had written the Rock and Roll Hall of Fame a letter. There were rumors he wasn't going to show up and that Izzy and Dizzy weren't either.

When the day came to fly to Cleveland, Ace and I were in the boarding line when I spotted Gilby a little behind us. He was with his wife, and he also had his guitar. Since Gilby hadn't been inducted, I asked him what was going on. "Hey, man. What's happening? Are you coming?"

Gilby smiled and said, "Yeah, we're gonna play."

I froze and immediately felt my stomach turn. Next thing I knew, I spotted Slash and Steven Adler walking toward us with Myles Kennedy. Slash's wife Perla was with them too, and they all came over to us. Before any of them had time to speak, I turned to Slash: "What's going on?"

"Oh, we're gonna play," Slash said in his usual indifferent way.

"Who's we?"

He shrugged. "Me, Steven, Duff—and Gilby."

I had to make a real effort to keep my voice steady: "So what am I supposed to do?"

"I don't know," Slash replied. "Myles doesn't know any of *Use Your Illusion*, so we're just gonna play *Appetite* stuff."

In that moment, I felt like grabbing Ace and heading home. There was something so familiar about the whole situation. Somehow, I managed to stay calm enough to look Slash's manager straight in the eye and say, "Right, so this is a commercial for the Slash solo tour. Nice job," I added with a smirk.

The atmosphere was still terrible when we got together to rehearse in Cleveland the night before the show. I ended up doing some backing vocals and playing a little tambourine. We were supposed to play three songs—"Mr. Brownstone," "Sweet Child o' Mine," and "Paradise City"—and while we worked through those, Steven must have noticed how uncomfortable I was, because he came over to me during one of the breaks and said, "Listen, why don't you play 'Brownstone,' and I play 'Sweet Child' and 'Paradise'?"

"Well, thanks, Steven," I said. It was cool of him to offer that.

When we got to the gala the next evening, there was a band table ready for us. Ace and I barely had time to sit down with the others before some woman came over to me and said, "You and your guest will have to move from this table over to Green Day's."

I stared at her, not quite knowing what to say. Ace, on the other hand, knew exactly how to reply. "We're not going anywhere. We're staying right here," she said, without batting an eyelid.

Like so many times before, she was my rock. I honestly don't know what I would have done if she wasn't there that day. The woman left without a word, and I squeezed Ace's hand.

The whole thing was so humiliating that I wished I wasn't even there, and things didn't get any better when Axl's attorney called right before we were due to go out onstage. Apparently he wanted to stop us from using the band name, which he claimed he "owned." The attorney continued, in a pretty threatening tone, "You can't introduce yourself as Guns N' Roses, because you are not Guns N' Roses."

It was all so toxic and horrible, but then Slash said, "Fuck it. Let's go!"

Billy from Green Day had just finished his introductory speech, and Slash, Duff, Steven, and I went out onto the stage. Duff was the first to reach the microphone, where he gave a little speech, followed by Steven. Slash was up next, and he said more than I'd ever heard him say before. He finished up by saying, "Thank you all...let's go play." I guess he was trying to prevent any further speeches; I was the only one who hadn't said anything, but I also hadn't prepared a speech. Considering everything that had happened between us, and considering the mood, I should probably have left it like that, because what ultimately came out of my mouth was so steered by my feelings that it all sounded wrong. Rather than thanking my soon-to-be wife and the people I really cared about, I started talking about the day Slash called me up and said, "We had to kick out our drummer for doing too many drugs." I looked out at the audience of the who's who of the music business and said, "How the fuck is that possible in Guns N' Roses?" It was idiotic, I know that—especially considering Steven was the only one of the guys who had treated me well.

Anyway, as if I didn't feel bad enough already, the song I was to play on that evening ended up being cut on television. Everything that happened around the Hall of Fame brought up so many feelings for me and really turned me back into that old guy I didn't like. Even Ace said the color of my eyes changed. I had changed for the better over the years but obviously still needed to work on myself and some of the pain that was deep down inside. A few days later, when we got back to our house in West Hollywood, Ace came running into the room where I was sitting. "God, you're not going to believe what just happened," she said, her eyes wide and her hands raised in what looked like a pleading gesture.

"What is it, baby?" I asked.

"I broke your award."

I went into the next room and saw the trophy I had been given at the gala in pieces on the floor. Ace burst into tears behind me. As far as I was concerned, it felt like a metaphor for the time I was in the band, and I thought, *God, isn't that ironic.*

56

Reunion

Duff can't even look me in the eye and tell the truth,
and that's what breaks my heart.

IN EARLY SUMMER 2015, I heard a rumor that Alice Cooper was putting together a new band with Joe Perry and Johnny Depp. I thought it sounded exciting, so I called Alice's manager, Shep Gordon, at his house on Maui.

"Shep," I said, "Matt Sorum here. How are you? What's going on with this Hollywood Vampires band?"

"Well, you know," said Shep, "we're gonna try to do some shows."

"Who's your drummer?"

"Oh, we don't have a drummer—or a bass player."

"Well, I'll play drums," I said.

"You're in!" With that, we ended the call.

I went out into the garden. The air was still and hot, like it is in June in LA. I was so happy with how the call with Shep had gone and was thinking about who might be good on bass. The first guy who came to mind was Duff McKagan.

I went back inside, called Duff, and said, "Hey, man, you interested in doing this Vampires thing?"

"It sounds cool," said Duff.

Not long after that, I spoke to Shep again. "What do you think about having the rhythm section from Velvet Revolver and GN'R being the rhythm section for the Vampires?"

"I love it!" Shep shouted.

Later that summer, we—Alice, Johnny, Joe, Duff, and I, along with Tommy Henriksen on rhythm guitar and Bruce Witkin on keyboards—started rehearsing in LA. We played two nights at the Roxy on Sunset Strip in the middle of September, and then the real tour began, at Rock in Rio.

For some reason, I got to go in the private jet with people like Alice, Joe, Bruce, Tommy, Shep, and Bob Ezrin, the super producer. Since the band plane was full, Johnny took his own private jet, but Duff had to fly commercial. It didn't take long for him to call me up. "I can't fucking believe I'm like a second-class citizen."

"What do you mean?" I said. "Like on a flat bed in first class to Rio de Janeiro?"

"Yeah, I can't believe I'm not on the jet."

I held back a sigh and said, "Dude, I'll take the flat bed."

But I could tell that that kind of thing really affected Duff, because he'd never been second fiddle. In the Hollywood Vampires, it was Alice, Johnny, and Joe who were the front men; the rest of us kept to the background. We were really confused, because Shep had always talked about the Vampires as a kind of supergroup, not a band with three front men and musicians for hire. Duff and I weren't even in the promo shots, and I said to Duff, "You know what, this is the first time I haven't been in a band photo. Why would we be in this band if we're not in the photo?"

"Yeah, man, I don't like it," said Duff. "It's weird."

The whole thing seemed even weirder once we landed in Rio, where the fans were shouting for Duff and me almost as much as they were for Johnny—and definitely more than they were when they saw Alice. GN'R was clearly still a big deal in South America.

The gig itself was really fun, but the exhilaration I felt afterward disappeared in an instant when someone—I don't remember who—said to me, "They're gonna get back together, maybe play down here."

Oddly enough, it was like I immediately knew who "they" were, and my heart started racing in my chest.

On the flight home, I couldn't think about anything else, but I didn't say anything to Duff. Instead, I called him a week or so later. "Let's go have lunch."

"Uh…okay," said Duff. "So where are we gonna go?"

"How about Soho House?" I said.

Soho House is a members' club on Sunset Boulevard, so it's kinda fancy. Duff then said, "Oh, oh…" It was meant as a dig at my perceived snobbishness.

Anyway, a few hours later, while we were waiting for our food in the restaurant, I said, "Duff, look me in this eye or that eye or both eyes—whatever you want, but look at me—and tell me you guys aren't getting back together."

Duff immediately looked down at the table.

"Duff, no, no, stop looking down."

Reluctantly, he raised his eyes and said, "Well, there have been talks, but nothing's happened. It's just lawyers talking."

"Talks about what?"

"About the band getting back together."

"What band?"

"Well," he said, "right now it's just us three partners in talks—me, Slash, and Axl."

I looked Duff straight in the eye then, and said, "So you're gonna tell me, right? You're gonna call me before I read it online? You can do that for me, as my friend of thirty years, someone who was a groomsman at my wedding? Just let me know, bro. Just let me know first."

Around the same time Lemmy died, news that Guns N' Roses were reforming broke all around the world. There were reports that Slash, Duff, and Axl would, among other things, play Coachella that April. That was only the first of the letdowns. I just never saw it coming from Duff McKagan.

At Lemmy's funeral in LA on January 9, both Duff and Slash were sitting in front of me, in the front row at the chapel, when I got up to give my eulogy. It wasn't exactly easy to focus on what

I wanted to say about Lemmy. My thoughts were swirling around my head. So many of my friends had died in the space of just a few months (including my old bandmate Scott Weiland), and we were all sad about that, but it was clear that we couldn't manage to care about one another while we were still living.

I continued to call Duff, but he was constantly evading me, and I realized he wasn't telling the truth. "Duff, what's going on?" I said.

"Well, Axl wants to use his drummer," he said. "But the guy can't even play the drums. I've gotta talk to Axl and say I really can't play with this guy."

"Wait! Back up!" I said. "What do you mean you don't think he's very good? And you can't fucking tell Axl? That would be the first thing I'd say if I was the bass player and you were the drummer. Why do you think I asked you to play in the Vampires? Because you're my favorite bass player."

"Come on, man."

"No...go to Axl and tell him you want me on drums. Period. Now's the time."

"Oh, man," Duff said, his voice kind of shrinking. "I already signed the deal."

"What deal?"

But he didn't want to say any more.

A week or so later, I was due to play in my own all-star band, Kings of Chaos, in Cabo San Lucas. Duff was booked to play the gig, and he flew down on the day with his wife. As we were sitting in the van on the way to the show, I asked him again, "So what's going on?"

"We're just rehearsing with these guys. We're trying to wait till Axl makes his decision."

Next thing I knew, he had one of his panic attacks. I did what I usually did: I wrapped my arms around him and held him until we pulled over to the edge of the road. I glanced at his wife, but she just sat there not seeming to know what to do. He stopped shaking after a while, and we got out of the van to get some fresh air.

As we walked along the road together, I said, "What's going on with you?"

He didn't reply and just avoided looking at me.

"You can tell me, Duff. I'm a man; I can take it."

But he couldn't do it. He couldn't tell me the truth, and that broke my heart.

A few weeks later, the Hollywood Vampires were booked to perform a tribute to Lemmy at the Grammy Awards. I assumed we would arrive together, but during rehearsals I found out that we weren't going to be walking the red carpet as a band.

I called the Hollywood Vampires' comanager, Trudy Green—a British woman with a posh accent—and asked whether there had been some kind of misunderstanding.

"Oh, no, darling," she said—which, from a Brit, means *fuck you!*—"it's the three principal figures walking together; besides, Duff didn't want to walk with them."

"So...Duff doesn't wanna walk the red carpet with the band?"

I called him right away.

"Dude...we should walk with Alice, Joe, and Johnny as a band."

But, to my surprise, he said, "Oh, no, man. I'm cool, man. I'm gonna walk with my wife and daughter."

I still didn't understand, so I said, "Come on, dude...come on."

"Nah...it's okay."

He was giving me really bad vibes, but I said nothing, just like I said nothing when my wife, Ace, and I saw him at the Grammys.

Trudy and I had already argued about the way we were going to be introduced. She only wanted Alice, Joe, and Johnny to be mentioned by name before we went out onstage.

That's why, when I spotted Dave Grohl, I told him all about it. He frowned and said, "I got you, bro."

Not long after that, I heard him reading from the script, introducing me and Duff: "And now, for the first time on TV, joined by Matt Sorum and Duff McKagan, let's hear it for Alice Cooper, Joe Perry, and Johnny Depp—the Hollywood Vampires."

We played both "Ace of Spades," in tribute to Lemmy, and "As Bad as I Am," written by Johnny Depp.

After we finished, Johnny came over to me. "Duff's quit the band."

"What?!"

I didn't want to believe it. Above all, I couldn't believe that Duff had told Johnny instead of me, and then snuck out the back door without saying goodbye.

As if to throw salt in the wound, Trudy Green came over to me and told me something else Duff hadn't had the balls to say. "You understand," she said, smiling like she was actually enjoying the situation, "Duff told me a few days ago that the reason he didn't want to walk the red carpet with you is that he has another band now—his old one."

"Really?" I said, deploying my best poker face as a whole load of unpleasant feelings rushed through me.

A few months later, during the Hollywood Vampires' world tour, I joined Johnny Depp on a private tour of Alcatraz. Johnny had played the gangster Whitey Bulger in a film called *Black Mass* and wanted to see the cell where Whitey had spent the first part of his prison sentence. As we were being shown around the eerie prison block, I got a text message from Axl's manager, Fernando, whom I had first met (along with his mother, Beta) when he was a young kid from Brazil that Axl decided to take under his wing.

"Hey there, bud," he wrote. "How are you? Just reaching out to see how your schedule is looking. Wondering if you're interested in joining the band on a few shows and a few songs. Let me know."

I stared at my phone; I could hardly believe my eyes. I replied a little later, copying my manager, saying I would check my calendar.

Johnny and I hadn't even left the island before my manager called to say that Fernando had offered to pay all my travel expenses and hotel costs if I agreed to join the band. That was the only form of payment I would get. I asked my manager to get back to them with a polite "no thanks."

When my own tour with the Vampires came to an end, I got a message from Duff: "Hey, Matt. I just want to say that I miss you and I love you a TON. When things were taking off and the Frank stuff was going on… I retreated from basically everything, I hope you and I can sort things out, bro. Love, Duff."

His words stirred up all kinds of feelings in me, and one day in late September I sent him a message to suggest meeting for lunch at Le Pain Quotidien on Melrose Avenue.

The minute he arrived, Duff tried to hug me. It felt so uncomfortable that I backed up a little. Something seemed different about him. As he sat down at the table, he said, "I don't know why you didn't come play with us when we called to ask."

"We?" I said. "Why didn't you call me yourself instead of getting your manager to do it?"

"Well, I thought that management could handle it."

We sat in silence for a few minutes. Duff looked down at the table the way he always had when he felt uncomfortable or cornered. "There *would've* been money," he eventually said.

I stared at him, at a loss for what to say. After a while, I said, "One good thing about all this is that Izzy and I started speaking again."

As the words left my mouth, Duff got a dark look in his eye. "Fuck Izzy!" he snapped.

I knew his reaction was because of Izzy turning them down, so I calmly said, "Well…Izzy says fuck you too."

Duff didn't reply. Instead, he just poked at his food—he didn't really seem hungry—and then checked his watch and said, "I've gotta go."

"Where?" I asked.

"Rehearsal."

"Rehearsal? Didn't you guys just get off a three-month tour? Why are you rehearsing?"

"Because we don't have you on drums," Duff said.

We got up. As we were leaving the restaurant, two guys came over to us, wanting to take photos. I nicely explained that it wasn't the right moment.

Out on the street, Duff awkwardly tried to hug me again, then he walked over to his car and drove away. In that moment, he felt like a complete stranger to me, like someone I didn't know at all. But maybe I was the one who had changed, and he was the same as ever.

What I do know for sure is that our friendship would never be the same again.

I went through a wave of emotions during this time and really felt those old abandonment feelings coming up and rearing their ugly head; Duff was like a brother to me. We would fight and argue but it never seemed to change the way we felt about each other, and I really missed those almost daily calls and our musical partnership. I guess that was one of the hardest things to accept. Of course, a lot of people would ask me about the reunion every day and say the obvious things like, "Why aren't you in the band?" I tried to reply with a positive answer or just joke they must have lost my phone number.

As I started processing everything, I had to believe, as a guy who now bases his life in spirituality, that I wasn't supposed to be there. "God's rejection is God's protection" was an old expression, but it really rang true in this situation. Obviously the money part was the deciding factor, but what else was there? It wasn't going to be like the old days, of course. And who knows what might have happened to me out there? Would I have been happy? The rest of my life was going great with my wife and my career. I was completely in control of what I wanted to do. I was still making a good living playing music and was the happiest and healthiest I'd ever been. So I looked at it in a spiritual way; there's something else in store for me.

I really grew so much through the pain I was feeling. And I honestly have to say it was more about my relationship with Duff than anything. I was never as close with Slash after Velvet Revolver,

291

but I still consider him a friend, and he's done great things for me and my charity. You try to put yourself in their shoes, but it's always hard when I've never been that way. I've always considered myself loyal and maybe that's the Scorpio in me. I believe in people but when I feel scorned I've been known to sting back. Another thing I've worked very hard to change about myself.

The music business is called business for a reason. Unfortunately sometimes it's not pretty. I think I've had more than my share of hard knocks in this racket. But what a learning experience it's been! Now to try and grow from it is the gift. I don't want to end up bitter and resentful, so I work toward a positive outcome and hopefully, at some point, forgiveness.

When I look back at my career and especially my time in GN'R, it's like watching someone else's movie. It's almost surreal, and I wouldn't have it any other way.

57

This Side of the Grass
(A Long Road from Chaos to Redemption)

Ace and I move out into the desert.

I'VE BEEN IN HOLLYWOOD since the seventies and always felt I wanted to be around that city madness. I don't really know what happened, but something in me began to shift—organically.

Ace and I had gotten married in Palm Springs in 2013. It was the most beautiful, joy-filled day of our lives. So we fell in love with the energy of the desert. It is a very spiritual place for us, and we call it our Happy Place. Every time we went back to stay for a weekend we felt it like a calming effect.

In Hollywood, people always seem to want something from you. There's always an agenda. I was tired of walking out the door and hearing, "Hey, you're Matt Sorum! What have you been doing lately?" or, "What are you doing now?" Those are the Hollywood questions. Maybe there was a time I loved that attention, but my ego just didn't need it anymore. Now it's as though I feel completely at peace with who I am.

That's why we made a decision to get a place out in the desert, in Palm Springs, with our family unit that included our beloved French bulldogs, Lola and Bowie. We started to make new mutual friends—a lot of cool, interesting people that didn't necessarily work in music or entertainment.

We also felt like it was important to spend time with our families. Ace's sister started bringing her kids out to stay with us, and I got my brothers together for Thanksgiving for the first time in over twenty years. Ace's mom came to visit, and her dad turned up from time to time too. Even my dad came to see us—we spent some real quality time together, with no distractions.

Not long after Ace and I got our place in the desert, my mom moved into a house not too far away, meaning that the two of us were suddenly able to have lunch together on occasion. When you're a kid you expect your parents to be perfect. As you get older you understand your parents more and can give them a more human understanding of how difficult life's challenges can be. You realize your upbringing is what shapes you. Good or bad, it's all part of what makes you who you are.

I did a lot of reflecting and felt like I had really started to heal from my childhood. The bond between me and Ace had grown immensely over the past few years, and we were now in a place that represented the love we felt for one another every day when we woke up. We made a point to put God first.

I also started Adopt the Arts, a nonprofit organization that sponsors twenty-five schools across LA by, among other things, donating thousands of instruments. Why? Because that felt good too.

Writing this book with my coauthors, Leif Eriksson and Martin Svensson, has been a long and at times exhausting process that forced me to think back—not only to what happened but also to what I would do differently now. A recurring answer to that question is I wish that I'd understood the word *grateful*. I don't think it was even in my vocabulary back then. Yes, I was always nice to people and to my fans, but looking back now, I can see what a great adventure I had, what great people I met, what incredible opportunities I was given. As scary and confusing as things got at times, I'm really just happy to be alive and on this side of the grass.

I found writing this book important to speaking my truth. I think everyone has the opportunity to change, and through the trials and tribulations of my life, I have finally found happiness... Life is good.

Even with the charity work I'm doing now, I kind of have to give credit to Guns N' Roses. Going forward, that band is going to be at the forefront of my life and my legacy. I even want to go back to The Cult and thank them. If I hadn't been in The Cult, I wouldn't have been in Guns N' Roses. You have to look at the lineage—if I hadn't been in those bands I wouldn't have met Lemmy, and I wouldn't have been able to play with Motörhead. In the same way, I'm involved in a number of entrepreneurial ventures these days. It's also great I can call up a lot of guys and say, "Hey, this is Matt," and ask them to play in my band Kings of Chaos—which is all about the celebration of the music and friendships I've made throughout my career.

And being surrounded by people I respect.

In the spring of 2018, I got a phone call. When I answered, I heard Billy Gibbons's voice on the other end of the line. "Hey, Matt, do you want to come on tour with me? I have this new solo thing called the *Big Bad Blues,* and I want you to be my drummer."

That tour became one of my greatest experiences, musically speaking. It happened for all the right reasons, and it was all about the music. Playing with Billy every night, spending time with him, was a real blessing. He's like a twenty-year-old kid playing music for the sheer joy and love of it—he reminded me why I started playing music in the first place. Driving to Hollywood in my 1964 Rambler, I was so excited to just get onstage, to play some rock 'n' roll. I didn't care about how much I was getting paid; all I cared about was the energy I felt while I was doing it.

Once the tour was over, I realized that no matter what I do, no matter what happens going forward, I can never really escape music. I can't stop being a musician; it's in my blood. It's been a long road through the chaos, but now I feel I'm right where I'm supposed to be.

ACKNOWLEDGMENTS

Matt thanks:

My wife, Ace Harper, for your never-ending support and love.

Billy F Gibbons, for your friendship and the wonderful foreword.

Paul Ill for always listening.

My manager, Lil Gary, for believing in me.

Martin Svensson and Leif Eriksson, for traveling to the desert with over two years of dedication to writing this book.

Our French bulldog, Bowie; you are a wonderful, sensitive creature that warms our hearts.

My late French bulldog, Lola. You brought so much joy in our house for ten and a half years. We will miss you so much but will continue to honor the happiness you gave Ace, Bowie, and I.

Dean Serwin for the great advice and always having my back.

Pablo Lobo, you are mad…but I love the ride!!!

And all the fans who have stayed with me and supported me throughout my career. It has been an incredible honor to play music for you all around the world.

—Matt Sorum

The coauthors thank:

Matt Sorum, Ace Harper, Alice Menzies, and our families and friends. All our publishers around the globe and our great agents at Arena Scripts Literary & Film Agency.

—Martin Svensson & Leif Eriksson